Civic Environmentalism

Civic Environmentalism

Alternatives to Regulation in States and Communities

DeWitt John

Aspen Institute
and
National Academy of
Public Administration

PRESS

A Division of Congressional Quarterly Inc.
Washington, D.C.

Printed in the United States of America

Book design by Debra Naylor, Naylor Design, Inc., Bryantown, Maryland
Cover design by Ed Atkeson, Berg Design, Albany, New York

Library of Congress Cataloging-in-Publication Data

John, DeWitt, 1942-
    Civic environmentalism : alternatives to regulation in states and
communities / DeWitt John.
       p.   cm.
    Includes bibliographical references and index.
    ISBN 0-87187-954-9 :   ISBN 0-87187-948-4 (pbk.)
    1. Environmental policy--United States.   2. Environmentalism--
United States.   I. Title.
GE180.J64   1993
333.7'2'0973--dc20   93-27005
                                                                          CIP

To Jane, Seth, and Elizabeth

Contents

Tables and Figures

Tables

Figures

Preface

Two years ago *Sierra* magazine ran an advertisement that succinctly presented the traditional view of environmental politics. The ad featured the U.S. Capitol with the message: "Save the Environment. Start here." Below was a form to contribute money to the Sierra Club, including its lobbyists in Washington. The vast weight of power, money, and attention to environmental matters—in the media, in academia, and even in groups like the Sierra Club, which have strong local chapters—has long focused on federal-level statutes and regulations. But the focus of environmental policy and politics is changing.

One sign of change is the widespread discussion of alternatives to regulation—ideas like prevention of pollution and the use of market mechanisms and incentives instead of (or in addition to) regulatory requirements.

The steady growth in the number of experts in environmental management is a second sign of change. For example, the demand for environmental consulting engineers and for air pollution, resource recovery, and hazardous waste management is projected to grow by over 15 percent per year in the mid-1990s, increasing the cadre of professionals in state and local governments, private corporations, and nonprofit organizations who have built their careers around solving environmental problems.

A third sign of change is the public's awareness of environmental issues that require action outside Washington. Global environmental issues have commanded attention in recent years, and a network of international institutions and agreements are now emerging to address these issues. The 1992 Earth summit in Rio de Janeiro attracted more heads of state than any other meeting ever held, produced a detailed agenda for action, and built a worldwide network of nongovernmental advocates for environmental protection. The shape of environmental politics and policy is changing inside the United States as well as internationally. The Sierra Club recognized this shortly after the appearance of the advertisement mentioned above, when it announced that two of its three top priorities in the coming year would be state-level issues.

This book explores the potential for a new style of environmental politics and policy that would bring these disparate themes together. Instead of top-down regulation, "civic environmentalism" would focus on decentralized, bottom-up initiatives using new tools to address newly recognized environmental problems. The book explores the wide variety of proposals that have been advanced for reforming environmental policy, including the idea of "sustainable development," which was the central theme of the Rio meeting. It explains how states and localities stepped forward in the 1980s, when federal environmental policy was hampered by stagnant budgets and political gridlock. And it analyzes how three states are attempting to address the unfinished business of environmental policy, including prevention of pollution, management of ecosystems, and the reduction of nonpoint pollution (pollution that cannot be traced to a single smokestack or pipe). In Iowa, state legislation seeks to reduce the use of polluting chemicals by changing the practices of tens of thousands of farmers. In Florida, federal, state, and local leaders are enmeshed in a controversial effort to restore the Everglades. And Colorado has just joined other states in using market incentives to encourage energy conservation. State- and locally based civic environmentalism is not a substitute for federal regulation, but it can and should be a powerful complement to it.

The idea for the book was born six years ago during a dinner with Stan Johnson of Iowa State University. The Iowa legislature had just passed the Groundwater Act of 1987, and our conversation turned to new ideas about environmental politics that this legislation suggested.

Since then, many people have helped me explore state and local environmental politics, including Tom Curtis, Paul Guthrie, Richard Hayes, Doug Larsen, Ed Marston, Jeff Tryens, and others. Ray Scheppach and Joan Wills helped me to think about federalism. This is not to suggest that each of them will agree with all of the ideas in this book; indeed, I have learned much from their disagreement and debate.

Doing the field research for the book was a pleasure. I met dozens of intelligent, dedicated people who gave freely of their time and ideas. Several contributed insights that gave direction to the project. Indeed, some of the best conversations about the future direction of environmental policy were with people trying to solve specific problems every day while seeking to understand how their work fit into broad patterns. At the risk of leaving someone out and again mentioning people who may disagree with my ideas, I must thank Jay Brizie, Jerry DeWitt, Bruce Driver, George Hallberg, Paul Johnson, Steve Light, Gary Nakarado, David Osterberg, Paul Parks, Jim Spiers, Jim Webb, and Morey Wolfson.

Several people talked with me about the project and reviewed drafts of part or all of the book, including Amy Glasmeier, Bob Hahn, Mark Landy, Rick Minard, Beryl Radin, Kay Schlozman, Jeff Tryon, Jim Webb, Richard C. Kearney, two anonymous readers, and many of the participants in the case studies that are included in the book. I owe special thanks to Gary Orfield, Gerry Rosenberg, and Ken Wong of the University of Chicago Department of Political Science, who guided me toward a much more incisive and broad-based inquiry. John Moses helped gather the Renew America data that is discussed in Chapter 3. Diane Morton and Roylene Sims did an outstanding job of preparing the manuscript. Jeffery Thompson and Eric Walcott helped with the figures in Chapter 3. Amy Kays and Nola Lynch were excellent editors. Any errors of fact or judgment are mine.

I am grateful to the Ford Foundation, the Aspen Institute, and the National Academy of Public Administration for their support of this project. Walt Coward of the Ford Foundation supported the project as part of Aspen's State Policy Program. My colleagues at Aspen and NAPA provided a stimulating environment to work in.

It was a pleasure to work with the professionals at CQ Press. Brenda Carter helped to frame the book more clearly; Kathryn Suárez, Kate Quinlin, and Jackie Davey helped think through how the message could be presented more effectively; and Chris Karlsten provided a very helpful final edit while moving the text through the production process speedily.

When a person takes time out to write a book, the family naturally pays a high price. My children and wife managed without a father or husband on numerous weekends, early mornings, and late nights. My wife Jane used her professional skills to help compile an extensive bibliography and made many suggestions about how the drafts could be clearer and more interesting.

The book is dedicated to my family. I promise to spend more time with them enjoying the natural environment that God has given us, rather than sitting in an office writing about it.

CHAPTER ONE

New Directions for Environmental Policy and Politics

W e are entering a new era of environmental policy. We are addressing new issues, using new tools, and beginning to experience a
new kind of politics. This shift is part of a broader transformation in how
we do the public's business in an increasingly information-based society.

The new environmental issues transcend the current array of laws
and regulations. These regulations set limits on the emissions of hundreds of individual chemicals and other pollutants, or they protect specific environmental values, such as wilderness areas, endangered species, or the local quality of air and water. This one-by-one approach to
environmental protection does not always work. The future of individual species and special places depends on the health of broader ecosystems. For example, what happens to the rich variety of plants, animals,
and birds in the Everglades National Park depends on how water flows
through a vast area outside the park. The grizzlies, the wolves, and
perhaps even the spectacular geysers of Yellowstone National Park are
strongly influenced by what happens on lands outside the park. These
broad ecosystems, and others that are less spectacular, are threatened
by many kinds of pollution simultaneously, not to mention the stress of
human visitation and occupation. There is still much uncertainty about
exactly how ecosystems function, but we are learning that to protect
them, we must invest in public works, research, education, and public
participation. It is not enough to regulate individual pollutants or to
protect individual species and areas.

We are also learning how to address new forms of pollution. Most of
the laws of the 1970s and the 1980s related to large-scale "point

sources," including the smokestacks and pipes through which factories and water treatment plants send their wastes into the air or water. Now many firms are showing that by changing their production processes, they can prevent pollution before it reaches the smokestack; in the process, they can often reduce their costs and make themselves more competitive. We are also learning about the pollution caused by thousands of dispersed "nonpoint" polluters, such as farmers who spread chemicals on their fields, office buildings that waste energy with inefficient lighting and heating, and average Americans who drive farther each year on the trek from home to work or to the shopping center.

To take up this unfinished business—to restore and protect ecosystems, combat nonpoint pollution, and prevent pollution in the first place—we are beginning to use new tools. Regulation is still the backbone of environmental policy, but these new issues lend themselves to nonregulatory tools, which provide information and incentives rather than sanctions.

Debates about environmental regulation have often been battles between "black hat" polluters and "white hat" protectors of environmental values. As we address the unfinished business, we will still face tough choices. Although the debate may cool down as firms stop complaining that environmental regulation is too costly—instead accepting its inevitability and learning how to profit by preventing pollution—new cleavages may be emerging. For example, some local governments complain that they cannot afford to comply with all environmental regulations and that the regulations sometimes impose costly requirements of no measurable benefit. The new tools and the new environmental agenda may add to the cost burden, at least in the short run. It certainly will be expensive to restore ecosystems, although perhaps less costly than if we let them collapse.

The choices ahead will be difficult, but they may divide us less bitterly than past fights over regulation. The battle lines are less clear cut when the polluters are more numerous (including perhaps most of the citizenry), when governments use incentives as well as sanctions, and when the parties share information about how to solve problems.

These are the changes that are beginning to emerge around the edges of environmental politics, where federal law does not reach. At the state and local levels, there was a ferment of creativity in many areas of public policy, including environmental policy, in the 1980s and early 1990s. This book reviews practical evidence that has developed at the state and local levels about new approaches to environmental politics and policy. It asks:

- In states and localities, are governmental agencies tackling the unfinished business of environmental protection, including nonpoint pollution, the protection of ecosystems, and the prevention of pollution?
- Are states and localities using new tools like economic incentives?
- When states and localities tackle environmental problems in new ways, what happens to the process of making decisions in the political arena and inside the agencies?
- What role has the federal government played in state and local initiatives?
- Perhaps most important for the 1990s, what can the federal government do to provide top-down support for bottom-up environmental initiatives?

During the early 1990s, a consensus began to develop that a new approach to environmental policy was needed. Several national leaders spoke eloquently about the need for fresh ideas. For example, Gus Speth, then president of the World Resources Institute, told the winners of the 1992 presidential election, "I don't think we will succeed in bringing our economic and environmental objectives together with the current set of approaches. . . . We need to move to a new model of environmental governance." [1] The National Commission on the Environment, which included respected leaders of the U.S. Environmental Protection Agency (EPA) from both Republican and Democratic administrations, called for "radical reform." The commission's report stated that "the U.S. statutory and regulatory regime is woefully inadequate, cumbersome, and sometimes even perverse with respect to environmental issues." [2]

A second generation of environmental politics and policy seems to be emerging. There is no widely accepted label for the new tools, new policies, and new politics. Experts who focus on the tools often stress the importance of "market mechanisms" and "economic incentives," including fees, taxes, and tradable permits. But other tools—such as public education, technical assistance, and new ways of investing in and operating public works—are also important. Discussions of broad trends in policy often refer to "sustainable development." We will discuss this loose term in Chapter 2. The key seems to be the principle of ensuring that environmental considerations—including the benefits of a clean environment, the difficulty of predicting environmental impacts, and the risks of unexpected environmental collapse—be taken into account in the millions of decisions that are made about how to invest society's wealth.

The future of environmental policy will be shaped not only by the principle of sustainable development and the new tools of economic incentives, but also by the practicalities of political and administrative processes. The story of innovation at the state and local levels in the 1980s suggests what such a politics might be like. This book calls the emerging politics and policy "civic environmentalism" and suggests that civic environmentalism is the new paradigm that many have called for. It is the process by which sustainable development might become a reality.

COMMAND-AND-CONTROL REGULATION

Since the early 1970s, environmental policy has relied heavily on what insiders call command-and-control regulation. This regime is based on federal laws that set standards for air and water quality, for emissions of materials that might harm the environment, and for the handling of dangerous substances. To obtain permits from regulatory agencies, polluters must show that they will not violate these standards. With few exceptions, federal laws do not provide for balancing economic and environmental objectives. Rather, the Environmental Protection Agency is charged with setting standards that will protect public health and other environmental values; polluters are left to cope as well as they can.[3]

Three features of federal laws shape the patterns of traditional environmental policy and politics: federal preemption of state and local authority, fragmentation, and the combination of tough procedural requirements with ambitious goals.

Federal preemption began with a wave of federal legislation in the early 1970s. Before then, states and local governments regulated pollution as a nuisance that fell within their police powers. The federal government helped with research, technical assistance, and some funding for water treatment projects. But federal agencies did not tell states and local governments what to do.[4] As we will describe in more detail in Chapter 2, this division of responsibilities seemed clearly inadequate to deal with the pollution caused by modern industry. State and local officials were often reluctant to stand up to industries that belched smoke or fouled rivers. Faced with a choice between jobs and pollution on the one hand, or no jobs and no pollution on the other hand, pollution was accepted as the inevitable price of progress.

In the 1970s, this way of doing business was changed by the enactment of a series of tough federal statutes that set new standards and procedures for regulating pollution. Most federal environmental legislation does not prohibit regulation by states and localities, but it does set standards and procedural requirements to guide them. Federal laws also provide for the close supervision of state and local officials by federal environmental agencies.

In the words of former EPA administrator William Ruckelshaus, the federal role in command-and-control regulation is to be the "gorilla in the closet."[5] In other words, states and localities continue to regulate pollution, but only pursuant to detailed federal requirements. When industries resist state and local regulators, the regulators can threaten to let the federal gorilla out of the closet to force industry to comply with the law.

Although the command-and-control system is essentially top-down, driven from Washington, the idea was not to weaken states but to add to their power in dealing with polluters. In *The Politics of Pollution*, J. Clarence and Barbara Davies write that federal statutes increase state power by giving them the tools to regulate more effectively and the political backing to use those tools.[6] The federal gorilla is often kept in the closet, leaving states the task of applying federal requirements in diverse local situations. Furthermore, most federal environmental statutes set minimum standards and allow states to adopt tougher standards.

A second key feature of federal environmental laws is that they are fragmented. That is, they call for separate permits for different types of pollution, rather than a single, comprehensive permit. As early as 1970, it was clearly recognized that this was not the most rational approach to environmental regulation, because pollutants can move from one medium, like air, to another, like water. President Nixon told Congress in 1970, "Despite its complexity, for pollution control purposes the environment must be perceived as a single interrelated system.... A single source may pollute the air with smoke and chemicals, the land with solid wastes, and a river or lake with chemicals and other wastes. Control of the air pollution may produce more solid wastes, which then pollutes the land or water." [7]

Notwithstanding this fine argument, the political realities dictated a different way of organizing federal environmental programs. The EPA was created in 1970 by an executive order that brought together agencies that had been in different departments. There was no legislation to establish EPA or to provide it with a charter of cross-cutting, cross-medium authority. The separate programs in EPA for air, water, and waste have never been consolidated; and most subsequent legislation has focused on individual programs rather than overall management. In political terms, this means that the EPA is not a single gorilla, but a whole family of gorillas, one for each law and each program.

The third feature of federal regulation of the environment is that it is characterized by a combination of lofty goals, detailed procedural requirements, and tight timetables. When EPA was created and Congress passed the tough environmental legislation of the 1970s, both environmental advocates and members of Congress were familiar with the phenomenon of institutional capture—that regulatory agencies might come under the influence of the industries they regulated. To prevent this, each statute contained detailed procedural requirements as well as ambitious goals (for example, "fishable, swimmable" water). If EPA failed to act decisively, procedural requirements provided opportunities for congressional guidance through oversight hearings and for challenges by environmental groups in federal court.[8] In effect, each law created not just a family of EPA gorillas but whole hierarchies of gorillas.

Furthermore, the laws encouraged confrontational politics. The lofty goals and tight timetables encouraged an air of urgency and sometimes of desperation or cynicism within EPA, and they opened the door for vigilant congressional oversight, litigation, and protest.

Figures 1-1 (p. 8) and 1-2 (p. 9) show graphically how the command-and-control system works. At the top are advocates for the public's interest in a clean and safe environment. These advocates include environmental groups, congressional committees with jurisdiction over environmental matters, and sometimes the citizenry itself—for example, when citizens insist, "Not in my backyard" (NIMBY). These advocates exert pressure on EPA and other federal agencies through a variety of means. Often federal courts are involved. Sometimes the courts act almost as another independent voice for environmental values, because many environmental statutes contain clear statements of purpose and procedure while lacking guidelines about how EPA should allocate scarce personnel and political capital to accomplish its tasks. These statutes often encourage judges to issue detailed orders about how EPA should go about its business. Buffeted by these many voices for environmental values and pressured by industry, EPA watches over the states, which issue permits to polluters and monitor compliance.

CIVIC ENVIRONMENTALISM

This book describes another way of organizing environmental politics and policy, civic environmentalism. The central idea animating civic environmentalism is that in some cases, communities and states will organize on their own to protect the environment, without being forced to do so by the federal government. As we shall see, federal agencies can often play important roles in civic environmentalism, but not by forcing state or local action or by threatening to override decisions. Civic environmentalism is fundamentally a bottom-up approach to environmental protection.

Civic environmentalism emerged in the 1980s when, as we will describe in more detail in later chapters, federal environmental policy lost its momentum. There were many reasons, including cutbacks in the budget of the EPA; explicit efforts by Republican administrations to weaken environmental regulations and to turn authority over to states; and deadlocks, both within Congress and between Congress and the White House, on proposals for new environmental legislation. Stalemates and cutbacks in Washington created a vacuum into which stepped many state and local governments, as well as nonprofit organizations, citizens, and even some private businesses.

Figure 1-1 Command-and-Control Regulation

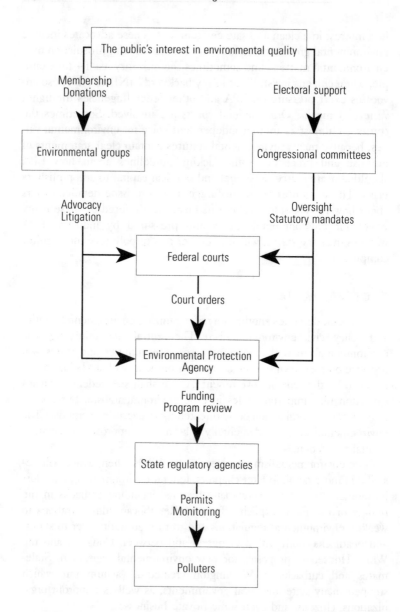

Figure 1-2   Fragmentation of the Command-and-Control
Approach to Regulation

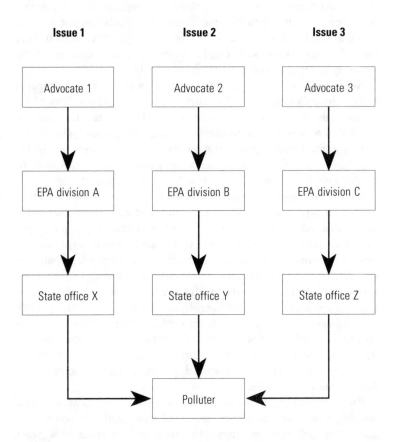

The style of policy and politics that emerged in these bottom-up initiatives is different from the command-and-control model in four ways: it tends to focus on a different set of environmental problems, uses different tools, seeks to overcome fragmentation, and searches for alternatives to confrontation.

As we shall see in Chapter 2, top-down regulation works best for large, clearly identifiable sources of pollution, like smokestacks, water treatment plants, and toxic waste dumps, rather than dispersed, small-scale sources like individual homes. The command-and-control model is more difficult to implement when there are large numbers of polluters and when it is difficult to monitor what each polluter contributes to an environmental problem. It is simply too difficult for regulators to keep track of so many sources. As one Iowan put it, "It may take an occupying army to regulate the 100,000 farmers in our state."

Nor is regulation usually adequate to protect ecosystems in danger or to prevent pollution before it occurs. The environmental laws of the 1970s focus on specific results—clean air and water, safe handling and disposal of wastes, and protection of endangered species—whereas the threats to most ecosystems in danger arise from a complex mix of factors. Also, most of the environmental laws now on the books focus on results, rather than on strategies to achieve the results.

To address these problems, civic environmentalism uses a variety of tools, such as technical assistance to farmers and small businesses, subsidies, public education, and new approaches to investing in public services and facilities. These tools are being used by many organizations, including economic and community development agencies, schools, universities, trade associations, and public-private partnerships.

Civic environmentalism also tends to involve a different style of politics than command-and-control regulation. There are still strong differences of opinion, but there are fewer confrontations between black hat polluters and white hat protectors of the public trust, and there is more bargaining among a diverse set of participants. Civic environmentalism is a more collaborative, integrative approach to environmental policy than traditional regulation.

For most readers, the most familiar example of civic environmentalism might be efforts to reduce household waste and to promote recycling. The polluters are numerous—in effect, everyone. For years, states and localities have been seeking to reduce household waste not by regulating how much trash we all send to the dump but with a much broader array of tools, including economic incentives, public education, and new ways of delivering public services, such as curbside recycling.

King County, Washington, and Seattle, its largest city, have been leaders in promoting recycling. The story of how they became leaders illustrates how civic environmentalism can emerge from traditional regulatory policies and politics.[9] For decades, King County dumped its trash into landfills with minimal environmental controls, until in the early 1980s, when landfills in western Washington either closed or had to spend millions for environmental controls. A landfill north of King County, which had received much of the trash from Seattle businesses, closed and became a Superfund site.* The city of Seattle also closed a landfill for residential trash.

These closures put more pressure on Cedar Hills, a large landfill operated by the county. As the volume of waste being trucked to Cedar Hills began to rise, increasing the number of trucks on nearby roads and exacerbating environmental problems, homeowners who lived nearby filed several suits to force the county to clean up. The state Department of Ecology also intervened, adopting regulations that forced the county to control drainage, vent gasses that were building up inside the landfill, and place plastic liners and two feet of clay under new parts of the landfill and on top of closed areas. King County eventually spent over $95 million to clean up Cedar Hills and another $29 million for remedial upgrades at four smaller rural landfills. (The state was far ahead of the federal EPA in adopting tough regulations for landfills.)

As it became more difficult and more expensive to operate landfills, and as it became clear that neighborhoods might organize to prevent construction of a new landfill when Cedar Hills filled up, both King County and Seattle began to rethink their solid waste policies. The classic environmental system of top-down, command-and-control regulation and bottom-up, NIMBY protests forced the city and the county to look for new ways to manage their trash.

Initially both Seattle and King County decided to build incinerators. Since the days of the energy crisis of the early 1970s, King County had been working on plans for "waste-to-energy" plants that would generate electricity by burning garbage. A new county executive was elected in 1986 and directed the King County Solid Waste Division to take these plans off the shelf and get to work. The county released a preliminary proposal to build as many as four incinerators in different parts of

---

*Superfund is a federal program for cleaning up hazardous waste sites. It was created by the Comprehensive Environmental Response, Compensation, and Liability Act of 1980.

the county, and Seattle proposed to build others.

Then all hell broke loose. By designating a half-dozen possible sites, solid waste officials had aroused a half-dozen NIMBY groups, who quickly organized a countywide federation of neighborhood groups and environmentalists who did not want incinerators or landfills anywhere. (This alliance still exists, as the Washington Citizens for Recycling, and has a small but busy office with a half-dozen paid staff members and volunteers.) Solid waste management became the central issue of local politics in 1986-1987, and an important state issue as well. The protesters attended hearings and picketed meetings of the county council.

Bowing to public will, Charles Royer (Seattle's new mayor) and Paul Barden (a law-and-order Republican on the county council) led the charge. The county organized citizen task forces on all aspects of solid waste management. By the end of 1987, both the city and the county had made formal decisions that waste reduction and recycling would henceforth be the preferred choices for managing trash, with incinerators put on hold. The state legislature also went to work, passing the Waste Not Washington Act in 1989, which endorsed the same hierarchy of preferred options for managing solid waste, and directed that counties work with cities and towns to prepare comprehensive solid waste management plans consistent with this hierarchy.

Five years later, King County had succeeded in doubling its recycling rate, from 18 percent to 35 percent of all trash. There were four reasons for this change. First, Seattle and most suburban cities adopted curbside recycling, consisting of a separate pickup for recyclables, which homeowners separate from the rest of their trash. Second, there were economic incentives for recycling and reducing waste. The cost of garbage service quadrupled, and a new structure of fees was adopted in most towns, charging less to pick up a smaller "minican" and more to pick up a second or third trash can. Third, there was an extensive public education campaign, including recycling weeks, programs in public schools, brochures for homeowners on how to recycle and how to reduce waste, and technical assistance for businesses that wanted to recycle or reduce waste. Finally, the political controversy over the incinerators was itself a stimulus for recycling and waste reduction. Western Washington prides itself on being a center of environmental consciousness, and citizens can demonstrate their support for environmentalism by recycling. Recycling has become as potent a political symbol in King County as motherhood and apple pie.

The story is not over. King County has set the goal of almost doubling its rate of recycling and waste reduction again, to 65 percent by the year 2000. Seattle aims for 60 percent by 1998. The state will require 50 percent by 1995. Meanwhile, as has happened in other cities where citizens are recycling enthusiastically, the markets for mixed waste paper, glass, and many other recyclables have become glutted. Seattle and King County are fortunate in having local customers for newsprint at local pulp mills. Also, because Seattle is a convenient port for Asia, over 90 percent of the mixed wastepaper is exported to mills in Taiwan, Indonesia, and other parts of Asia. But other cities on the Pacific coast are exploring the possibility of sending their trash overseas, and in the summer of 1992, one King County trash hauling firm had to pay an Indonesian paper mill over $10 a ton to take mixed wastepaper.

Some in King County want to return to command-and-control politics. The county and many towns are lobbying the state legislature for the authority to ban the sale of products that are difficult to recycle. The leader of Washington Citizens for Recycling is active in an effort to pass federal legislation to force manufacturers to assume responsibility for the waste they generate. At the same time, there are active efforts to use other tools to solve solid waste problems. The county and the state have established programs to expand the recycling industry, and these agencies are supporting technical studies, market tests, revisions of procurement policies, and other ways to build stronger markets for recyclables. What seems to be emerging is a mixture of regulatory and nonregulatory policies to manage solid wastes in King County.

As the city and county have emphasized alternatives to regulation, and as the debate turns away from hot spots like the Cedar Hills landfill, the politics of solid waste management has changed. Many of the leaders of the protests of 1985-1987 are now active members of county advisory committees and generally supportive of county policies and programs. As one neighbor of the Cedar Hills landfill said, "We have some quibbles with what some of the suburban cities are doing, like still charging a flat rate for trash collection, but basically we think King County is doing just fine."

In the search for more tools to influence the behavior of homeowners, businesses, and others, there are more efforts to bridge the gaps between different government programs and to bring environmental values directly into forums where the primary concern is not environmental protection but other matters, such as economic development. For example, the state's Clean Washington Center, which seeks to build a larger recycling industry, is part of the state Department of Trade and Economic Development. The King County Chamber of Commerce has established a solid waste task force, whose chair also serves as chair of the county's commission on recycling.

Figure 1-3 is a simplified picture of how civic environmentalism works. In contrast to the traditional command-and-control model shown in Figure 1-1, the relationships that characterize civic environmentalism are not primarily hierarchical—orders do not come down from EPA to states to polluters. Rather, these three key players relate to one another at almost the same level, as Figure 1-3 shows. Most of the links involve nonregulatory "carrots" like information, education, subsidies, and economic incentives. However, regulatory "sticks" are still important at times and do appear in the picture of civic environmentalism. The traditional model shown in Figure 1-2 includes separate hierarchies for separate pollutants. In contrast, civic environmentalism tends to address several related forms of pollution at the same time.

THE SIGNIFICANCE OF CIVIC ENVIRONMENTALISM

Civic environmentalism is not a replacement for traditional regulatory policies; it is rather a complement to those policies. Civic environmentalism is possible because the struggle to put regulatory laws in place has been at least partially successful. Polluters know that if they do not somehow reduce emissions, there may be political pressure for regulation. Also, the struggle to enact environmental legislation has helped to transform public attitudes about environmental values or, perhaps more precisely, to inform the public about the causes and nature of threats to the environment. This shift in values and knowledge is particularly important inside corporations and government agencies, which have hired large staffs of professionals whose careers are built on identifying and reducing environmental problems. As we shall see, these insiders play an important role in making civic environmentalism work.

Figure 1-3   Elements of Civic Environmentalism

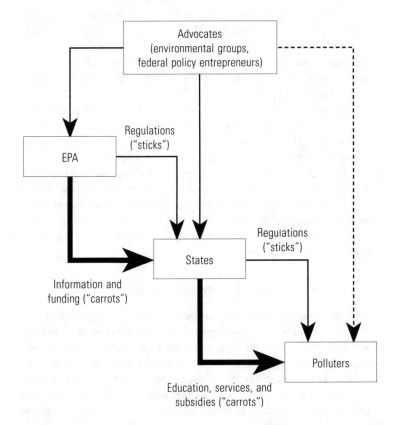

In short, civic environmentalism is possible because it is sheltered by a forest of environmental laws and nourished by new values and knowledge. But the fact that it is derived from the command-and-control regime does not make it less significant. It is like the second stage of succession in a forest. After a forest fire, some trees and bushes grow quickly under the direct light of the sun. Later, other kinds of trees grow in the shade—species that cannot survive in the direct light and drier soil. The second-stage vegetation, like second-stage environmental policy, adds vigor and diversity to the ecosystem.

During the 1980s, it became obvious that traditional regulatory programs do not provide no-risk protection for environmental values. Civic environmentalism is not without risk, either. For example, the traditional regulatory regime is much more effective in California and Minnesota than in Louisiana and Utah.[10] Civic environmentalism may also flourish more fully in "greener" states—those with stronger pro-environment policies.

Neither style of environmental policy and politics is a guarantee that environmentalists or their adversaries will always get what they want. However, there are examples of civic environmentalism in almost every state, and this approach does seem to be a more effective way to address certain kinds of environmental problems, including many of the problems that traditional regulation has not addressed adequately. Taken together, the two systems may provide an effective way of making decisions about how environmental values can be balanced with other values to increase the chances of achieving an economically and environmentally sustainable society.

THE FEDERAL ROLE IN CIVIC ENVIRONMENTALISM

Now that an environmentalist has been elected as vice president, and federal policy seems to be heading rapidly to the green side, should we expect federal government to assume the leadership in civic environmentalism? This might seem to be the natural next step. States are often seen as somewhat less than equal partners in the federal system, and certainly less than equal in environmental regulation. At their most assertive, they are usually seen as "laboratories of democracy," to use Justice Louis Brandeis's phrase. For example, during the 1980s, conservative presidents often sought to limit federal intervention, which left a vacuum that many governors and mayors rushed to fill with activist policies. States experimented with education reform, welfare reform, and new approaches to economic development, as well as with new styles of environmental policy. The image of states as laboratories suggests that when such experiments prove successful, the next step might be to move the innovation into full-scale production, presumably at the federal level so that the entire nation can benefit. This is what happened to many state innovations in Justice Brandeis's time; progressive ideas like workers' compensation were tested by states before the New Deal moved them into federal policy. Is this also the likely future for civic environmentalism?

Many political activists feel that the distribution of responsibilities between states and the federal government is not a particularly interesting topic because there are no principles other than short-term political advantage at work. When I told Joe Browder that I was writing a book that would reflect on federalism and the environment, he looked skeptical and said:

> I don't think there is much to say about that. We go through cycles; sometimes the federal government is more help in tackling environmental problems, and sometimes states are. People don't care about federalism; they just want to win, and they use whatever tools they have at hand. The real change in the last thirty years is greater participation in environmental issues. Nowadays, power is accessible for almost anyone.[11]

Browder should know what the players in environmental politics think about federalism. As a journalist in Miami in the early 1960s, he helped organize opposition to a jetport in the Everglades.[12] Since the defeat of the jetport, Browder has been assistant to the secretary of the interior in Washington and has consulted for environmental groups, native American tribes, electrical utilities, and mining companies on how to handle environmental issues. He still is an active lobbyist for protecting the Everglades.

Browder is right. The opportunities for people to speak up for environmental values have expanded. If there is something to say about federalism and environmental politics, it might be best to start with Browder's observation that people will use whatever tools they find handy. The question, then, is whether some tools are handier at the state and local levels, than in Washington, D.C. This question is a central theme of this book. The book will make the case that civic environmentalism is inherently a bottom-up way of doing the public's business because it uses a different set of tools than classic regulation. Certainly the federal government can play an important supporting role, but most decisions, and most often the leadership, must come from the state and local levels.

In the short run, the 1992 election provided environmentalists with an opportunity for much greater influence on federal policy, and their attention is likely to focus primarily on Congress, EPA, and other federal agencies for some time. But over the long run, environmental policy and politics will involve greater leadership by states, with the federal government acting not as a gorilla but as a partner who can bring specialized resources into decisions made at the state and local levels.

The case for continuing state and local leadership of civic environmentalism is made in Chapter 7. The intervening chapters lay a foundation. Chapter 2 tells the stories of how command-and-control regulation emerged, how a deadlock and policy vacuum developed in Washington in the 1980s, and what brought about the search for alternatives. Chapter 3 presents data from the fifty states about the kinds of policy initiatives that emerged at the state and local levels during the 1980s. Chapters 4, 5, and 6 present detailed case studies of how civic environmentalism works in the practical worlds of politics and administration. Each case study represents a different portion of the unfinished business of environmental policy. Chapter 4 focuses on nonpoint pollution in Iowa, Chapter 5 on managing an ecosystem in Florida, and Chapter 6 on conservation and prevention in Colorado.

The conclusion, in Chapter 7, summarizes the implications of civic environmentalism for our understanding of government, including how the federal system works, and for how citizens and communities can respond effectively to emerging problems in the environment and in other areas of public concern. It also presents ways in which the federal government and others can contribute to the growth of civic environmentalism.

NOTES

1. Gus Speth, "Statement," in *President Clinton's New Beginnings: The Complete Text, with Illustrations, of the Historic Clinton-Gore Economic Conference in Lit-*

tle Rock, Arkansas, December 14-15, 1992 (New York: Donald I. Fine, 1992), 340.

2. *Choosing a Sustainable Future: The Report of the National Commission on the Environment* (Washington, D.C.: Island Press, 1993), xi, xv. The commission was organized by the World Wildlife Fund and included respected environmentalists, former state and federal environmental officials from both Republican and Democratic administrations, and business leaders.

3. The Federal Insecticide, Rodenticide, and Fungicide Act, which regulates chemicals used in food and agriculture, is one of the few regulatory statutes that call for balancing environmental and economic objectives. Air and water regulation requires "best available" technologies. For a sample of the many critiques of this approach, see Paul R. Portney, "EPA and the Evolution of Federal Regulation," in *Public Policies for Environmental Protection*, ed. Paul R. Portney (Washington, D.C.: Resources for the Future, 1990), 7-25, and other articles in that book.

4. Advisory Commission on Intergovernmental Relations, *Protecting the Environment: Politics, Pollution, and Federal Policy* (Washington, D.C.: Advisory Commission on Intergovernmental Relations, 1981).

5. Rochelle Stanfield, "Ruckelshaus Casts EPA as 'Gorilla' in States' Enforcement Closet," *National Journal*, May 25, 1984, 1034-1038.

6. J. Clarence ("Terry") Davies and Barbara Davies, *The Politics of Pollution* (Indianapolis: Pegasus, 1975). Terry Davies later became the executive director of the National Commission on the Environment, whose report is cited in note 2.

7. "Message of the President Relative to Reorganization Plans No. 3 and 4 of 1970" (July 9, 1970), in *Environmental Quality: The First Annual Report of the Council on Environmental Quality* (Washington, D.C.: Government Printing Office, 1970), 295. Quoted in Alfred Marcus, "Environmental Protection Agency," in *The Politics of Regulation*, ed. James Q. Wilson (New York: Basic Books, 1980), 267-303.

8. See Marcus, "Environmental Protection Agency."

9. This account is based on DeWitt John, "A Case Study on Solid Waste Management in King County, Washington" (Draft report, National Academy of Public Administration, Washington, D.C., 1993).

10. There is an extensive literature comparing how "green" state policies and programs are. See James P. Lester, "A New Federalism: Environmental Policy in the States," in *Environmental Policy in the 1990s*, ed. Norman J. Vig and Michael E. Kraft (Washington, D.C.: CQ Press, 1990), 59-79. For a review of the literature, see James P. Lester and Emmett N. Lombard, "The Comparative Analysis of State Environmental Policy," *Natural Re-*

sources Journal 30 (1990): 301-319.

11. Joe Browder, interview with author, Washington, D.C., April 20, 1992.

12. A book for fourth graders, Judith Bauer-Stamper's *Save the Everglades* (Austin, Texas: Steck-Vaughn, 1993), portrays Browder as an early leader of the modern environmental movement. Another volume in the series tells the story of Rosa Parks, whose refusal to take a back seat on a bus in Montgomery, Alabama, sparked an early protest in the civil rights movement.

CHAPTER TWO

Beyond Regulation

The foundations of environmental politics today can be traced to decisions made shortly after Earth Day, May 1, 1970. On that day millions of Americans marched and rallied to protest that the environment was being polluted and that government was not responding adequately. Earth Day was a national teach-in, with lectures and demonstrations to educate the public about threats to the environment. Organizers were confident that they had tapped a deep reservoir of social and political energy and had created a large pool of political capital. In the following weeks, they debated vigorously about what to do next. The questions were who would continue the educational process and how it would lead to action.

One group of organizers, the romantics, thought the hope for the future was to educate the public at large about a new environmental ethic. The others, political operators, thought the best step would be to press the federal government to pass tough new laws that would force state and local authorities to be more vigilant in prosecuting polluters and to protect national parks, wildernesses, and other valuable federal lands.[1]

Two years before Earth Day, Garrett Hardin had published an article in *Science* magazine that was widely read and may well have influenced the debate. This article, "The Tragedy of the Commons," explained that if people were left to their own devices, they would often be driven by their short-term economic self-interest to pollute the environment, even if they preferred not to do so and even if pollution was contrary to their long-term economic interests. Hardin illustrated this assertion with the example of sheep grazing on common lands. All shepherds would prefer that common lands be verdant and productive, and all would gain if the total number of sheep grazing on the commons was restricted so that the grass could grow. But each shepherd could gain by adding to his flock, so the result would be chronic overgrazing.[2]

Soon after the appearance of Hardin's article, journalists and political scientists documented how Hardin's theories seemed to be working out in practice, as whole communities allowed their environment to be fouled. The logic was the same; just as shepherds allowed overgrazing for fear that other shepherds would do so if they did not, communities were afraid to stop pollution because if they cracked down, polluting businesses would relocate to other areas and jobs would be lost.

In 1969, James Fallows, then a disciple of Ralph Nader, told the story of the need for a federal gorilla in *The Water Lords*, a book about how a large timber company had fouled the waters and air in Savannah, Georgia. Fallows described Savannah as a company town. Although the air stank and the waters were poisonous, Union Camp, along with American Cyanamid and Continental Can, blithely disregarded weak state efforts to control pollution. Local leaders had offered Union Camp many incentives to open a timber mill in the 1930s, and they accepted what Fallows called the myth that the company had saved the city. "Together with the threat that 5,000 company jobs might disappear overnight, this feeling of indebtedness [had] done an extraordinarily effective job of blunting all criticism of Union Camp." [3]

Political scientist Matthew Crenson found the same story on the South Side of Chicago. Here steel mills were polluting the air, but no one complained. Local residents accepted dirty air as a necessary consequence of having a steel mill to work in. They even welcomed dirty air as a sign that the mill was operating and that people were earning money. In *The Un-Politics of Air Pollution*, Crenson, like many others, explained American politics in terms of a contest between organized interests. The struggle was not entirely fair, because some interests were more powerful than others. But at least it was a relatively open, democratic process, promising hope that all legitimate interests would gain some recognition. Crenson noted that no one on the South Side spoke against air pollution. Crenson felt that this silence raised disturbing questions. Was the lack of a voice for environmental values a failing of the interest group theory and of democratic politics?[4] Who would speak for environmental values? Who would represent the birds and grass and natural world? Who would force polluters to behave in a socially desirable manner?

Hardin's solution to the tragedy of the commons, or of Savannah, was to trust in administrative law, that is, in governmental regulations. Others, including the romantics among the organizers of Earth Day, responded that in the long run, polluters would organize politically and would be able to forestall effective regulation. If so, perhaps there was no hope; the political problem of protecting the environment was insoluble. Or perhaps the only hope of saving the commons was a fundamental shift in morality, so that people would refuse to acquiesce in the despoliation of the natural world.[5]

In the months after Earth Day 1970, a few federal politicians decided to seize the opportunity. When millions of Americans marched and rallied, these politicians decided that they would speak for environmental values. And they quickly settled on command-and-control regulation, guided by the federal gorilla, as the way to protect the public's interest in environmental quality.

Three individuals were particularly important in establishing the political settlement of the questions that were raised by Hardin, Fallows, Crenson, and others and were dramatized on Earth Day. In the four months following Earth Day, Sen. Edmund Muskie, President Richard Nixon, and EPA chief William Ruckelshaus took precedent-setting steps to force state and local authorities to stand up to polluters like Union Camp.[6]

Muskie, a Democrat senator from Maine, made the critical decision that ended the era of federal deference to state and local regulations. Muskie had made a national reputation in the 1960s by writing new federal laws to tackle air and water pollution. As a former governor, Muskie had been sensitive to governors' desire for control over environmental matters, so he had framed the Clean Air Act and the Clean Water Act to allow for substantial state discretion. However, not a single state air quality plan had been approved by the federal government.

In 1970, the Clean Air Act was scheduled for reauthorization by Congress, and Muskie was thinking of running for president. A Ralph Nader study group published a report, *Vanishing Air,* which explicitly attacked Muskie for selling out to industrial interests and which demanded tough federal air quality standards. President Nixon took advantage of the political opening to propose tougher federal controls than Muskie was proposing. So Muskie reversed his longstanding deference to state authority. The Clean Air Act of 1970 required state and local air pollution agencies to apply tough new federal air quality standards and meet specific goals and timetables. The law has been called an example of legal conscription. It "challenges the very essence of federalism as a non-centralized system of separate legal jurisdictions and instead relies upon a unitary vision involving hierarchically related central and peripheral units." [7]

Also in 1970, President Nixon made decisions that caused the Environmental Protection Agency to emphasize the role of advocate for environmental values rather than that of balancing environmental values with other values. Nixon was considering a complete reorganization of the executive branch, which would have included among other things the formation of a Department of Environmental and Natural Resources. That department would combine the air quality program of the Department of Health, Education, and Welfare (HEW) and water quality programs that had just moved from HEW to Interior, both of which were about to assume strong regulatory responsibilities, with programs of several development-oriented agencies, such as the Army Corps of Engineers, the Bureau of Land Management in the Department of the Interior, and the Forest Service. Thus the new department would have to balance environmental advocacy with other objectives, such as development.

But Nixon decided not to establish this new department. The secretary of the interior was the logical candidate for secretary of such a department, and Nixon did not want to give the job to Walter Hickel, who was the incumbent. Among his other objections, Nixon thought Hickel had been overenthusiastic in endorsing Earth Day. Also, Hickel had publicly criticized Nixon's response to the shooting of antiwar protesters at Kent State University. Furthermore, several agencies were reluctant to see their programs move over to Interior. HEW was especially reluctant to cede its air quality responsibilities to Interior but was willing to see both air and water quality programs move to a new independent agency.

So a few weeks after Earth Day, Nixon formed EPA by executive order. The agency would not include units that were involved in developing natural resources; the Army Corps of Engineers, the Forest Service, the Bureau of Land Management, and the Bureau of Reclamation would remain in other agencies. EPA would be an advocate and an enforcer—a voice for the environment and the driving force behind command-and-control regulation—rather than a balancer of environmental values with other values.

Since EPA was formed by executive order, there was no effort to ask Congress to write authorizing legislation for the agency. This meant that EPA was organized with no overall legislative mandate to pursue broad goals of environmental quality; its mandate is the sum of separate authorizations for individual programs.

EPA's orientation toward regulation was further strengthened by its first administrator, William Ruckelshaus. Ruckelshaus was a lawyer who had won his reputation as a tough prosecutor in Indiana and at the U.S. Department of Justice. He decided to take the same approach at EPA. Ruckelshaus made enforcement his top priority. He opened proceedings to force Detroit, Atlanta, and Cleveland to stop discharging sewage into local waters, and he took action against powerful, longtime polluters like Reserve Mining, Armco Steel, U.S. Plywood-Champion Paper, and ITT Rayonier.[8]

The two EPA administrators who succeeded Ruckelshaus, under Presidents Ford and Carter, maintained EPA's orientation toward regulation and its role as an advocate for environmental values. Under Carter's presidency, key positions in EPA were held by former congressional staffers who had helped draft federal legislation and by former environmental activists.[9]

When President Reagan took office in 1981, he appointed officials who had a very different view. In late 1981, James Watt, the new secretary of the interior, opened a speech to the American Mining Congress with the memorable words, "I am from the government, and I am here to help you." The delegates responded with laughter and thunderous applause. They knew he meant it.[10] Reagan appointed another Coloradan as EPA administrator, Anne Gorsuch Burford, who took Reagan's philosophy of deregulation very seriously. She put former lobbyists for industry in several key positions and proceeded to cut staff, weaken regulations, and give states more discretion.

The net effect of these efforts was to strengthen, not weaken, the idea that EPA should be a tough regulator and an independent advocate for environmental values. Burford's initiatives were widely unpopular. National environmental groups organized a counterattack; their memberships soared; and after a tumultuous term, Burford resigned. To replace her, Reagan brought back Ruckelshaus. Soon after his arrival, Ruckelshaus addressed EPA staff and made it clear that he would return to the enforcement-minded approach of EPA's earlier days. (This was the speech in which Ruckelshaus called EPA the "gorilla in the closet.")[11]

Although the return of Ruckelshaus reinforced the myth of EPA as the gorilla, it did not bring back the crusading spirit of EPA's early years. Indeed, the business community had already mounted an effective defense against new environmental legislation. As explained by Terry Moe, a political scientist at the Brookings Institution, the battle between environmentalists and the business community had already reached deadlock before Reagan and Burford took office.

> After the 1977 adjustments [to the Clean Air and Clean Water Acts], legislative politics surrounding the air and water acts remained just as intense and explosive, but for the next decade the contending forces were in total deadlock. The election of Ronald Reagan and the resurgence of business political interests did not shift the political balance sufficiently to shatter the status quo.[12]

The deadlock eased slightly in the 1984-1989 period and was broken partially in the Bush administration.[13] President Bush did announce that he would be the "environmental president"; he did appoint a career environmentalist as administrator of EPA; and he did cooperate with Democratic leaders in Congress to pass major amendments to the Clean Air Act, ending a standoff that had lasted for a decade.[14] The EPA budget also rose somewhat, although not to the levels of the late 1970s (in constant dollars). However, many EPA initiatives were opposed and watered down, or defeated, by the president's chief of staff or by the White House Council on Competitiveness, chaired by the vice president. Since at least 1977, the political fact is that, notwithstanding the image of EPA as a gorilla, the agency has limited ability to promulgate and enforce tough regulatory standards.[15]

Furthermore, as state and local budgets have become tighter in the late 1980s and early 1990s, states and localities have begun to complain about the cost of environmental mandates. For example, states have begun to complain about the Safe Drinking Water Act. Under this and most other federal environmental statutes, states must win the right to "primacy"; that is, they must demonstrate their ability and willingness to operate permit programs consistent with federal standards and regulations. If they fail to do so, EPA can step in and operate the program itself. Very few states have turned back primacy, but as the EPA's contribution to state agency budgets has shrunk, EPA's leverage has decreased. In the spring of 1992, Gov. Pete Wilson of California announced that his state would continue to administer the federal Safe Water Drinking Act, but would not enforce EPA's new standards for copper and lead because they were too expensive. According to Tom Curtis, who lobbies Congress on environmental issues on behalf of the states, it is quite possible that EPA can do nothing to force California to act on these standards, because it lacks the staff and management capabilities to take over operation of the program itself: "Governor Wilson opened the door to an EPA takeover, and we have found out it is just like the Wizard of Oz. There is no gorilla, just a skinny old man blowing smoke and pulling wires." [16]

Some local governments have also become recalcitrant, objecting that they could never afford to meet EPA standards. The cities of Columbus, Ohio, and Lewiston, Maine, have prepared studies of the total cost of meeting current federal environmental regulations. Columbus estimates the cost at over $1 billion, or $2,000 per resident. Lewiston's figures are comparable. A large portion of the costs involve construction of separate facilities for treating stormwater runoff so that the runoff does not overburden sewage treatment systems.[17] These estimates can be disputed, and no one has yet suggested exactly what should be done if cities are unable to meet the cumulative cost of EPA requirements. In late 1992, EPA organized a permanent advisory committee to provide for dialogue with local governments about the problem.

FEDERAL SUCCESSES AND FAILURES

As the limits of the command-and-control regime became apparent, there were numerous proposals to reform the system. Before turning to those proposals, however, it is useful to consider whether federal laws have done a good job of protecting the environment. There is little agreement about this point—which is not surprising, given the numerous opportunities and incentives for various parties to take issue with federal policies and regulations.

The conventional wisdom among experts is that there have been some successes and some disappointments. Specifically, air quality in most metropolitan areas has improved, and many bodies of water are cleaner. (For example, Lake Erie was once considered unable to support substantial populations of fish but is improving.) Some endangered species, such as the alligator and the peregrine falcon, now seem safe, and a few have been removed from the official list of endangered species. On the other hand, about 50 percent of all Americans live in areas where air pollution standards are still exceeded more than once a year; high-altitude air pollution, including depletion of the ozone layer, acid rain, and the greenhouse effect, has become more serious; and indoor air pollution has been discovered to be an important problem. Groundwater pollution, toxic waste dumps, loss of wetlands, damage to parks and wildlife refuges, soil erosion, and scattershot development of the countryside are continuing concerns. Of the seventy-eight species first listed as endangered by the federal government in 1967, most now have stable or increasing populations, but three have become extinct and another seventeen are declining.[18]

This mixed picture leaves plenty of room for differing assessments of how well the United States has done in protecting the environment. For example, when Barry Commoner, a biologist and active environmentalist, addressed EPA employees in 1988, his speech carried the title "The Failure of the Environmental Effort."[19] In contrast, the Conservation Foundation, a relatively conservative environmental organization, two of whose presidents have become EPA administrators for Republican presidents, said in its 1987 *State of the Environment* report:

> The United States does not now face an environmental crisis. Progress continues in abating some kinds of pollution in some places, and in the short

haul no impending disasters can be predicted from a failure to address any of the lengthy list of environmental issues. Looming ahead, however, is a set of complex, diffuse, long-term environmental problems portending immense difficulties for the economic well-being and security of nations throughout the world, including ours.[20]

The report also articulated the widely held view that "the easy problems have been taken, the obvious solutions applied." [21] Some intransigent environmental problems involve multiple causes or numerous polluters, whose wastes are not visible to the public or perhaps even to themselves. The Clean Air Act and Clean Water Act targeted obvious point sources like industrial smokestacks and the pipes that dump effluent from sewage treatment plants into rivers. The tougher problems include those that arise from nonpoint sources, including chemicals used on farms or runoff from urbanized areas. Another set of unresolved problems involves the protection and restoration of whole ecosystems, such as the Florida Everglades, the Great Lakes, or the Northwest's Columbia River.*

THE SEARCH FOR ALTERNATIVE
WAYS TO PROTECT THE ENVIRONMENT

The inconclusive evidence of improved environmental quality and the many opportunities for complaining about environmental quality have fueled a search for better ways to address environmental issues. Dozens, perhaps hundreds, of ideas and proposals have been advanced. These proposals fall into three broad categories. The first strategy of suggestions calls for giving greater weight to environmental values, for example, through tighter regimes of command-and-control regulation. The second category includes suggestions for reorganizing and refocusing environmental programs to strike a better balance between environmental values and other values. The third category is a collection of

---

*An ecologist would say that each of these three areas was actually a combination of ecosystems; the Everglades, for example, includes lakes, wet prairies, and saltwater marshes. We use the word *ecosystem* not in a technical sense but in the political sense of a fairly large geographic area knit by a web of environmental interactions.

ideas traveling under the banner of "sustainable development." Sustainable development is far from a coherent doctrine, but it does represent an effort at fundamental rethinking of environmental policy. The following sections offer critiques and proposals in each of these three categories.

A Stronger Voice for Environmental Values

There have been many efforts to strengthen the voice of environmental forces within the policy-making process. For example, to strengthen EPA's resolve, in 1984 Congress added "hammers" to the Resource Conservation and Recovery Act, which provide that if EPA misses deadlines for promulgating regulations, dangerous chemicals will simply be banned.[22] EPA employees who feel their bosses are too lenient on industry have been encouraged to become whistleblowers.[23] There are proposals to increase EPA's clout by elevating the agency to cabinet status and by creating an independent, politically neutral agency to gather statistics about environmental quality.

There are also proposals to expand EPA's authority so that it can tackle problems that the existing array of statutes do not address adequately. For example, Ken Cook, a leading environmental advocate on farm issues, has long worked for stronger federal laws to address the impact of farming on water quality. He says: "When we talk to the farm community, we say that if you open this door, there might be a gorilla in it, and meanwhile we are furiously trying to set one up." [24] Cook advocates adding tough regulatory requirements to the federal farm bill.

Other advocates of change have looked outside the current command-and-control hierarchy for new voices to support environmental values. Thousands of local groups have emerged to protest dumps, mining, clear cutting of trees, and similar activities. These "not-in-my-backyard" (NIMBY) protests have halted some pollution and have indirectly encouraged many firms and local governments to seek ways to clean up or to reduce their wastes. Some analysts feel that NIMBY protests in poor neighborhoods are an early sign of a new progressive alliance between environmentalists and broader forces for social reform.[25] In the early 1990s, several national environmental groups and foundations made a concerted effort to make "environmental equity" a major concern, suggesting that the poor bear more than their share of environmental risks.

The most radical proposals to strengthen the voice for environmental values come from individuals and groups loosely clustered around the concept of deep ecology. The roots of the deep ecology movement can be traced back to the romantics among the organizers of Earth Day 1970 and further back to environmentalists like Aldo Leopold and John Muir, who felt that the real answer to environmental problems was a change in values. Deep ecologists assert that environmental values are generally more important than the economic values that dominate American society. They want not only stronger environmental enforcement, but a rejection of the traditional vision of the United States as a land that provides opportunity through economic growth.[26]

Deep ecology is biocentric rather than anthropocentric; indeed, it is the polar opposite of the frontier economics view that human beings were placed on the earth to use nature for their own purposes. Advocates of deep ecology often oppose economic growth as a matter of principle and instead seek harmony with nature. Often deep ecologists celebrate native Americans and other indigenous peoples as exemplars of how humans should live. If industrialized societies do not rediscover these ways of life, deep ecologists say, then they should expect the collapse of ecosystems and of societies that depend on these ecosystems, including perhaps the global ecosystem itself. The depletion of the global ozone layer, the greenhouse effect, and the destruction of the Amazonian rain forest reinforce the idea that perhaps deep ecology, or something close to it, is in fact a realistic approach to environmental issues.

Translating the principles of deep ecology into political terms would require fundamental changes. Most deep ecologists call for radical decentralization of economic and political activity, and many environmental activists inspired by this vision seek ways to make their communities and regions economically self-sufficient.

Better Ways to Balance Environmental and Economic Values

A second group of proposals for changes in environmental policy and politics focuses on how environmental values are balanced with other values. As with proposals to strengthen regulation, some of these ideas are more radical than others. We will quickly sketch five different critiques, moving from the least to the most radical.

The first critique is that policy should use additional tools that would give incentives for reduced pollution. From the early 1970s, eminent economists have complained that a heavy reliance on regulation alone would be inefficient. They argue that if policy makers would use market incentives, decisions about how to achieve environmental goals would be made by private industry rather than by bureaucrats and goals would be achieved at lower cost.[27] For example, government might impose fees on the emission of pollutants and adjust the fees to achieve as much reduction of pollution as desired. Or statutes could employ "bubbles" or "tradable emission rights." These tools would permit firms that cannot reduce emissions from a particular source, except at great cost, to reduce emissions elsewhere. Bubbles allow trades within a facility, and tradable rights allow firms to pay other firms to reduce their emissions by the desired level. Room has been made in the federal Clean Air Act for using economic incentives. Bubble approaches were tried in the early 1980s, and the Clean Air Act Amendments of 1990 featured a scheme to allow utilities to trade the right to emit sulfur dioxide.

Some economic incentives operate within the context of regulation. Tradable emissions, emissions fees, and fees for permits are good examples. Others operate independently of regulations. Examples would include a hefty tax on carbon, higher fees for the use of public lands, deposit-return systems (such as the bottle bills that many states have passed), commitments by government to purchase recycled materials in preference to virgin materials, technical assistance, and public education.

A second critique is that EPA might turn its attention to the prevention of pollution rather than focusing simply on cleaning up. The environmental legislation of the 1970s focused on smokestacks and discharge pipes, and the discovery of toxic wastes at Love Canal in Niagara Falls, New York, led to creation of the massive Superfund cleanup program. To avoid costly cleanups, the focus of environmental policy could travel "up the pipe" and concern itself with minimizing waste, preventing pollution, and conserving energy. The federal government began experimenting with pollution prevention in earnest in the late 1980s, and in 1990, Congress passed the Pollution Prevention Act. The EPA pollution prevention effort includes a small grant program to help states provide technical assistance and information about pollution prevention, as well as a number of voluntary programs under which corporations can commit to reducing their emissions.

A third critique is that environmental statutes and agencies are too fragmented. The essence of the science of ecology is the effort to understand the interrelationships between all aspects of an environmental system. In contrast, political jurisdiction for environmental issues is divided among numerous congressional subcommittees—sixteen by one count[28]—among separate environmental statutes, and among air, water, waste, and toxic divisions within EPA. These divisions make it difficult to deal with broader environmental problems, to deal with problems of endangered ecosystems, or to set priorities for different programs on a rational basis. To rectify this problem, there are periodic proposals that Congress pass an organic act for EPA and that EPA or the states try to coordinate planning, budgeting, or permit programs.

A fourth critique is that EPA's priorities are misplaced. In 1986, the EPA Office of Policy, Planning, and Evaluation organized a cross-section of seventy-five high-level EPA administrators to consider whether EPA was investing its resources in the environmental problems that merited the most attention. They found a mismatch between EPA's current priorities and actual risks to human health and ecosystems. They concluded that EPA had made significant progress in "abat[ing] the most visible forms of pollution, but there is still much unfinished business." In particular, the report, entitled *Unfinished Business*, was critical of spending on the cleanup of toxic wastes. A large portion of the EPA is dedicated to Superfund, which has cleaned up only a handful of toxic waste sites. Meanwhile, EPA spending on indoor air pollution and stratospheric ozone was relatively low.[29]

Two years later, the EPA administrator asked the EPA Science Advisory Board, a group of distinguished outside experts, to review the *Unfinished Business* study, taking special care to consider the availability and quality of data used to assess risks. This group was much less willing to rank the risks of different problems but did affirm the thrust of the original report.[30] To address the mismatch between problems and resources, EPA has invested in studies of the comparative risk of various environmental problems. Also, EPA has encouraged states and localities to convene broad-based advisory groups to identify the most important local problems, essentially replicating the *Unfinished Business* study at the state or local level.[31]

A fifth critique is that EPA is making a fundamental mistake in defining the objectives of environmental policy. In *The Environmental Protection Agency: Asking the Wrong Questions*, Marc Landy, Marc Roberts, and Stephen Thomas say that since the Carter administration, EPA has placed too much stress on the risks to human health, has exaggerated these risks, and has given a spurious certainty to estimates of risk. Drawing on a detailed study of five important environmental issues, Landy, Roberts, and Thomas draw damning conclusions about EPA's performance:

> EPA repeatedly treated "safety" as if it were a scientific notion defined by experts, rather than a social construct necessarily based on values as well as science. In addition, the agency's efforts to muster public support contributed to an unwarranted level of public anxiety. The best studies suggest that environmental hazards account for only a small percentage of the total cancer burden. . . . EPA did not help citizens to understand that some "cancer clusters" will inevitably occur just due to bad luck. . . . Rather than clarify this point, EPA allowed toxic waste to become the functional equivalent of witchcraft in colonial Salem—the hidden evil force that accounts for all of our troubles.[32]

Whether or not one agrees with this appraisal, it is clear that managing risk and explaining to the public which environmental problems deserve the most attention are difficult tasks.[33] Landy, Roberts, and Thomas argue that the responsibility for educating the public about risks and priorities lies with the top officials of EPA. They condemn what they say is a pluralist notion that agency officials, like other players in the political game, should focus on the demands of narrow constituencies. Instead they urge that top EPA officials educate the public about the clashes of values and difficult choices to be made in setting environmental policy. Landy, Roberts, and Thomas want EPA to be not only a gorilla, but also an educator:

> Thomas Jefferson had hoped that political parties would serve to foster those important qualities like civic virtue, breadth of vision, and solidarity that the pluralism of the founders had tended to erode. . . . Our alternative is to focus on government itself. We look to the higher echelons of the bureaucracy to

provide the leadership required to nourish and sustain the values of education, responsiveness, and respect for the merits that we cherish. Specifically, we expect government to promote three critical processes that foster those values: deliberation, integration, and accountability.[34]

Others have suggested that the tasks of setting priorities and assessing risks can be better handled on a more decentralized basis. A subcommittee of the Science Advisory Board argued that state, local, and individual action is necessary to tackle the unfinished business.

> Most of the problems remaining now are neither conspicuous nor ubiquitous. Instead, they are site-specific, varying from area to area and requiring tailored controls at the regional, state, or local level for effective mitigation.... State and local governments and individuals will, in the future, frequently be making basic decisions about which environmental problems deserve governmental attention and what the nature of that attention should be.[35]

Some pollsters report that the public agrees with this assessment that the solutions to environmental problems will be found at the state, local, and private levels. In summarizing their findings, the pollsters note that respondents did not rank environmental issues as particularly important for the federal government.

> So why doesn't the environment rank higher as a problem facing the country or a priority for the federal government? Because, first, the environmental problems that most concern Americans are local—landfills and garbage, air pollution and water pollution. And, second, Americans are more likely to see actions by individuals and businesses as more important in solving environmental problems than federal regulation or federal spending.[36]

Sustainable Development: An Effort to Rethink Environmental Policy

Sustainable development is a more radical approach to environmental policy than any of the other alternatives. Actually, it is more a cluster of ideas than a coherent body of thought. One expert once commented that he started to collect definitions of "sustainable development" but quit when the count reached sixty.

Like deep ecologists, advocates of sustainable development demand that environmental values take a more central place in decisions. However, advocates of sustainable development do not dismiss economic objectives as unworthy or inherently in conflict with environmental values. Indeed, many advocates for sustainable development argue that sometimes both objectives can be met simultaneously. For example, pollution prevention can sometimes cut costs by encouraging the use of fewer or cheaper materials. Environmental consulting and cleanup may be growth industries for a community or nation. And firms that anticipate new environmental regulations and find technical alternatives to polluting may be able to win a market edge over firms that are slower to adapt to changing standards.[37]

Beyond simply asserting that environmental progress may be consistent with profit and prosperity, sustainable development asserts also that prosperity depends on environmental protection. This assertion is based on three ideas that have proven to be highly appealing in many parts of the world, if not yet in the United States. The ideas are the limits to growth, the link between poverty and environmental quality, and the uncertainty about environmental outcomes.

The limits to growth is an old idea, dating at least to Malthus, as well as a central theme in deep ecology.* One of the best-known exponents of sustainable development, economist Herman Daly of the World Bank, speaks of a global "Plimsoll line," like the line on the hull of seagoing cargo ships that shows how far they can be loaded safely. According to Daly, the greenhouse effect and other ecological threats are signs that the earth is close to its Plimsoll line. He points to rapidly rising population and economic activity as the reason, but he accepts economic development as a valid social goal as long as steps are taken to avoid crossing the Plimsoll line.[38]

Some writers trace the emergence of the idea of sustainable development to debates in the United Nations and other international organizations. In the 1970s, many Western environmentalists were persuaded by the Club of Rome's econometric study that there were "limits to growth"; that is, that a continuation of current patterns of economic growth would inevitably lead to ecological and economic collapse.[39] However, when they brought these concerns to representatives of the Third

---

*The notion of limits to growth is also inherent in Hardin's "tragedy of the commons."

World, they were accused of trying to place a lid on Third World growth. Indeed, it was said, the very poverty of the Third World leads to ecological disaster, as poor people must choose between eating their seed corn or dying. For example, poverty forces the poor to cut trees for firewood, to farm highly erodible soils, and to engage in other environmentally damaging practices just to avoid short-run economic disaster.[40]

In addition to limits to growth and a focus on poverty, especially in the Third World, advocates of sustainable development draw on a third powerful idea: the notion of deep uncertainty about the environment. Proponents of sustainable development argue that small environmental changes can sometimes result in catastrophic changes in ecosystems. They point to examples of past civilizations that have perished suddenly when climate changed, soils were exhausted, or volcanos erupted. They also point to the hole in the ozone layer, the extinction of many species of plants and animals, and the greenhouse effect as possible modern precursors of catastrophe.

Preoccupation with uncertainty, especially about major disruptions, divides advocates of sustainable development from conventional thinking about environmental policy. Conventional wisdom and sustainable development both assume that environmental quality must be balanced against economic prosperity. (In doing so, both diverge from deep ecology.) But advocates of sustainable development want to change how the balance is struck. They want change not only in environmental policies but also in a wide range of other social policies. As they see it, the United States is currently managing environmental issues on a fragmented basis, after the fact. That is, environmental regulations are constraints on decisions that are made fundamentally on economic grounds. A better approach might be to search for development strategies that are both productive and environmentally benign. As explained in *Our Common Future*, the report of the World Commission on Environment and Development chaired by former Prime Minister Gro Harlem Brundtland of Norway, sustainable development involves ending the fragmentation of policy by bringing environmental values directly into councils where economic development decisions are made.

[Sustainable development] requires major shifts in the way governments and individuals approach issues of environment, development, and international co-operation. . . . The standard agenda [traditional ways of managing environmental issues] reflects an approach to environmental policy, laws, and institutions that focuses on environmental effects. [Sustainable development] reflects an approach concentrating on the policies that are the sources of those effects.[41]

Advocates of sustainable development want environmental values brought into the center of economic decision making because they do not approve of how economic development decisions are being made. For example, economists teach that rational decisions about investments should adjust estimates of future benefits and costs by a discount rate, because money that is not invested today can be saved and will earn interest. This approach devalues long-term costs and benefits; if the rate is high enough and the costs or benefits are far enough in the future, discount rates reduce their value to close to nothing. Advocates of sustainable development feel that decisions must be made with an eye to the long-term welfare of humanity, and perhaps of ecosystems as well, and that environmental catastrophes could threaten the future.[42]

Another difficulty is that neoclassical economic theory, which explains how economic development decisions are made, does not handle discontinuities easily. Instead, it focuses on incremental change at the margin. For example, in neoclassical economics prices are set by how much it costs industry to produce one additional unit of product and how much one consumer will pay for this last unit. A similar idea is implicit in pluralism; pluralist democracy asserts that political forces are balanced incrementally, at the margin. If environmental forces gain strength, then governments will eventually bend and make adjustments in public policy to give greater weight to environmental values. Conventional thinking about environmental policy, which is shaped by pluralism and neoclassical economics, tends to deal with issues in the same incremental fashion. As new problems emerge, new laws are passed. If environmental conditions worsen, standards can be tightened and permits made more difficult to obtain.

However, sustainable development advocates feel that the incremental approach is not adequate when small changes in environmental conditions can lead to catastrophic changes. Instead of traditional incremental economic and political criteria, decisions should be determined by "what is necessary for the maintenance of ecosystem resilience." [43] In practical political terms, advocates for sustainable development do not want an incremental balancing of individual risks and costs, organized around the design of fragmented environmental programs. Instead, they want to put everything on the table—the economic and environmental future of the community or nation (and other values like equity and justice)—and they want a very cautious treatment of any possible step toward the collapse of whole ecosystems.

It is easy to find places where environmental values might be brought into decisions about economic development in the Third World. The World Bank and other regional development banks are obvious targets. It is also easy to fit the concept of sustainable development into plans for industries that are clearly dependent on natural resources, such as timber, farming, fishing, and even tourism—the viability of such industries clearly depends on not exhausting natural resources (timber, soil, stocks of fish, pretty views) on which they depend. But in the case of a highly decentralized economy like that of the United States, it is not easy to decide which decisions the advocates of sustainable development might want to influence. In the United States, many public policy decisions about economic development are made at the state and local levels. Perhaps this would be the level for dialogues that would blend the public interest in environmental values with the public interest in development.

The political agenda for applying the notion of sustainable development in the United States is not well developed. In Canada, on the recommendation of a national council of environmental ministers and corporate executives, several provinces have created roundtables to bring environmental organizations, government agencies, and corporations together to discuss how economic and environmental issues could be integrated.[44] In the aftermath of the Earth summit in Rio de Janeiro, in June 1992, Kentucky and some other states have organized similar forums. In addition, several firms have hired full-time environmental advocates and have entered into wide-ranging dialogues with environmental groups.[45] In the final chapter, we will speculate about how dialogues concerning sustainable development might emerge in the United States and what issues they might involve.

NEW APPROACHES TO ENVIRONMENTAL POLICY

Of the three broad critiques of environmental policy—the need for stronger advocates for the environment, better balancing of environmental and economic values, and sustainable development—which best explains how environmental policy is changing? Our answer is that each critique is persuasive in different circumstances and that the best way to understand the future of environmental policy is to focus on four themes that are common to all three critiques. The first theme—unfinished business—is the idea that the current regime of environmental management leaves some issues inadequately addressed. One category of unfinished business is control of nonpoint sources, such as the pollution caused by the use of chemicals on hundreds of thousands of farms or by the trash that millions of homeowners send to landfills. A second category is prevention, including energy conservation as well as measures to reduce the production of wastes of all kinds. A third category is the protection and restoration of endangered ecosystems.

The second theme common to critiques of environmental policy concerns the tools that government uses to address environmental problems. In particular, regulation does not seem to be a sufficient answer to problems of nonpoint pollution, endangered ecosystems, or pollution prevention. Since regulation alone does not work, we must find other devices to encourage the desired behavior, such as education, technical assistance, economic incentives, and a revised set of subsidies. In addition to regulating, governments must be catalysts for action and provide incentives for appropriate steps.

The third theme is fragmentation. The current structure of environmental laws and policies makes it difficult to set priorities, to assess cumulative impacts on the poor and other disadvantaged groups, or to manage whole ecosystems. In addition to operating current programs, government must create institutions to link independent programs and find ways to develop strategies that cut across organizational and professional lines.

The fourth theme concerns procedures for dealing with uncertainty, risk, and complexity. To make good decisions about priorities, or about how to address complex problems such as endangered ecosystems, we need to find new ways to bring together divergent sources of information as well as divergent values. In situations of uncertainty, we must be able to experiment and adjust policies as we learn more about the nature of the problem and the effectiveness of our responses.

The four themes are closely interrelated. Consider how they work together in the three major areas of unfinished business.

Nonpoint Sources and the Four Key Themes

Regulation is a rather straightforward administrative process when there are a few, easy to identify polluters. But for nonpoint pollution, it may be difficult to identify the polluters and monitor their behavior. For example, consider the difficulty of monitoring the emissions of individual automobiles. Current federal regulations do require that auto emissions be checked regularly, but there is a great potential for evasion because auto service stations have strong incentives not to be too strict with their customers. Also, so many cars and checkpoints are involved that it is not feasible to check each car more often than once every year or two, even though a car's emissions may change dramatically if the car gets out of tune.

In some cases, it is possible to convert a nonpoint problem into a point source. This is precisely what auto emissions standards do. Instead of regulating millions of drivers, these standards regulate a much smaller number of automobile manufacturers. Another way of turning emissions into a point source would be to impose a hefty gas tax. Then the administrative burden would fall on gas stations, or perhaps on wholesalers.

However, some nonpoint sources are not easily converted into a point source. For example, consider household solid waste, or the use of chemicals by farmers. Because of the administrative difficulties of monitoring so many polluters, methods like taxes and public education would seem to be preferable. At the least, regulatory programs might be more effective if allowed to work in tandem with other ways of influencing polluters. Using these other tools often is beyond the grasp of regulators. Using them requires crossing the boundaries that separate environmental policy from other kinds of policy, including taxation and investment in public infrastructure. In short, to solve nonpoint pollution problems, we must use nonregulatory tools and overcome fragmentation.

Prevention and the Four Themes

Regulation is an appropriate tool when an environmental agency focuses on the end of the pipe, where pollutants enter the environment. But regulation is a less useful strategy for preventing pollution. Certainly the prospect of facing harsh regulation may be an incentive for individuals or corporations to conserve energy or water or to reduce their emissions of wastes. But there may be many reasons why reducing wastes seems difficult.

For example, a small dry cleaner or manufacturer using toxic chemicals may not know of other ways to clean clothes or manufacture products. If the company can afford to hire researchers to find other ways to get the work done, and if the threatened costs of regulation are sufficiently large, the business may assume the burden of finding answers, or an entrepreneur may be able to find answers and sell them to the small firms. Otherwise, there may be a role for universities or government agencies to subsidize the development of the dissemination to greener processes and businesses of information about these processes.

The task of preventing pollution is even less amenable to regulation in situations of great diversity. For example, if production processes change rapidly because firms are constantly modernizing or adapting to changed markets, rather than engaging in large-scale mass production, regulators may have a hard time keeping up with the changing mix of pollutants. Every few months, the pattern of emissions may change and a new permit may be required. A better strategy than regulation might be working with the industry to subsidize research and the commercialization of technologies that are generally less dangerous to the environment. As in efforts to address nonpoint problems, designing effective prevention policies requires reaching beyond the boundaries of regulatory policy to influence other issue areas, such as public support for research and business assistance.

Ecosystems and the Four Themes

Of all environmental problems, perhaps the most refractory are those in which an entire ecosystem is affected. These problems often have one or two dramatic symptoms, but they are quite complex and characterized by a great deal of scientific uncertainty. Furthermore, the political authority to manage ecosystems is usually fragmented, and restoration can be costly to the taxpayer and to private interests. The practical consequence of these factors—complexity, uncertainty, fragmentation, and cost—is that regulation alone is an inadequate tool to manage an endangered ecosystem and is wholly inadequate to restore one. Regulation certainly has a place; it can be an entering wedge and an indispensable element, but several other kinds of governmental tools can also be useful, such as research and monitoring, public education, and investment of public dollars in new facilities and services.

In an ecosystem in danger, there are usually one or two dramatic symptoms, like a sharp decline in a well-known species, such as birds in the Everglades or grizzlies in the northern Rocky Mountains. Behind this red flag lies a long and complex chain of causation. The fundamental problem may have to do with a long-term accumulation of subtle changes in water, land, or air. For example, harvests of shad, oysters, and rockfish in the Chesapeake Bay have dropped sharply in recent years, even though the largest industries have reduced their emissions of pollutants. Environmentalists worry that the blue crab may be next.[46] As scientists trace the chain of causation, their attention has moved to fertilizer that flows into the bay from farms, lawns, and golf courses. Wetlands once filtered these nutrients from streams. But as development fills in wetlands, more nutrients are reaching the bay, where they cause a rapid growth of algae, which cuts off the light that subaqueous vegetation needs to grow. This reduces the food available for young crabs and fish, and the biological productivity of the bay drops sharply.[47]

Because they are so complex, endangered systems are often not well understood. Ecosystems are usually threatened in ways unimagined by those who originated the underlying problems. In many cases, scientists are still learning about how ecosystems function and are just beginning to explore strategies for restoration. The problem of toxins in the Great Lakes illustrates this point. Toxins have entered the Great Lakes from several sources, including rain that picks up chemicals from industrial smokestacks as far away as Mexico and rivers that dump wastes into sediments along the lake shore. Toxins in the rivers come from pesticides spread on farms and from the wastes of metal platers and other industries in large cities. Storms and harbor dredging stir up these sediments. Subaqueous plants absorb the toxins, small bugs eat the plants, and fish eat the bugs. The result is that toxins are concentrated in fish. As this process of transfer is repeated, toxic substances become more concentrated and hazardous.[48]

For several years, scientists were concerned about whether toxins would cause cancer in humans who drank water or ate fish from the lakes. But after years of study, a group of scientists recently concluded that the most serious problem may be the effects of toxins on human reproduction. Concentrations of toxins in fish are so great that pregnant women and young children who eat them are at significant risk.[49]

The complexity and uncertainty of problems that affect whole ecosystems are unsettling. They raise the question of whether we know as much as we think we do about the world in which we live. Scientific uncertainty also creates tremendous problems for politicians. Governmental responses to endangered ecosystems must challenge entrenched ways of doing business, but they may not be able to provide a clear alternative vision. Instead, restoration efforts should include opportunities to review operations and must allow for future modifications as scientific knowledge improves.[50]

Typically, power to address the problems of imperiled ecosystems is fragmented. Because the problems are complex, many different authorities may be responsible for different aspects of a solution. Two agencies may be responsible for wildlife, six for water, and a dozen others for promoting economic activity in the ecosystem. Furthermore, many ecosystems cross state lines or national boundaries, compounding the problem of fragmentation.[51] There are also problems of implementation in ecosystems. Some agencies may operate programs that exacerbate problems; for example, economic development agencies may be trying to attract more industry to an area rather than upgrading the competitiveness of firms already there, and local water systems may be charging fees so low that consumers are encouraged to be wasteful. In such a situation, protecting the ecosystem requires much more than simply imposing new regulations. Existing nonregulatory policies must be changed as well.

For example, efforts to clean up the Chesapeake Bay have included a wide array of efforts, including proposals for controls on residential and

industrial development in Maryland, new standards for highway construction in Virginia, and more careful handling of manure on Pennsylvania farms.[52] In the Great Lakes, the International Joint Commission
has been organized to support research, warnings to fishermen and consumers, and cleanups.[53] State governments and a private foundation
took the lead in exploring the problem of toxins in the Great Lakes and
have cooperated in forming networks of informed scientists and citizen
groups and a grant-making foundation to complement the efforts of the
commission. To deal with global warming, leaders must deal with fragmentation on a global scale. Global warming was the leading topic for
what was perhaps the largest meeting ever held on earth, the 1992
United Nations Conference on Development and the Environment in
Rio de Janeiro, Brazil.

Civic Environmentalism

Civic environmentalism ties these themes into a single concept. It
addresses the unfinished business of nonpoint pollution, prevention,
and ecosystems. It uses a variety of regulatory and nonregulatory tools.
It links the divergent worlds of economic development and environmental policy. And it engages citizens and experts in dialogues and learning
about the relationships between our environment and our economy. In
the following chapters, we will see how state and local officials have
responded to the search for new approaches to environmental policy by
creating civic environmentalism.

NOTES

1. Speech by Denis Hayes to the Washington Natural Resources Council,
   Washington, D.C., December 1989. See also Joanna Underwood, "Groping
   Our Way Toward an Environmental Ethic," in *Voices from the Environmental
   Movement: Perspectives for a New Era*, ed. Donald Snow (Washington, D.C.:
   Island Press, 1992), 54.
2. "The Tragedy of the Commons," *Science* 162 (1968): 1243-1248, re-
   printed in Garrett Hardin and John Baden, eds., *Managing the Commons*
   (New York: Freeman, 1977), 16-30.
3. James Fallows, *The Water Lords: Ralph Nader's Study Group Report on Indus-
   try and Environmental Crisis in Savannah, Georgia* (New York: Bantam
   Books, 1971), 154.

4. Matthew A. Crenson, *The Un-Politics of Air Pollution: A Study of Non-Decisionmaking in the Cities* (Baltimore: Johns Hopkins University Press, 1971).
5. See, for example, Beryl L. Crowe, "The Tragedy of the Commons Revisited," in *Managing the Commons*, ed. Garrett Hardin and John Baden (New York: Freeman, 1977), 53-65. Crowe's article is reprinted from *Science* 166 (1969): 1103-1107. For a more recent, pessimistic view, see Geoffrey Wandesforde-Smith, "Moral Outrage and the Progress of Environmental Policy: What Shall We Tell the Next Generation About How to Care for the Earth?" in *Environmental Policy in the 1990s*, ed. Norman J. Vig and Michael E. Kraft (Washington, D.C.: CQ Press, 1990), 325-347.
6. The following account is based on Marc K. Landy, Marc J. Roberts, and Stephen R. Thomas, *The Environmental Protection Agency: Asking the Wrong Questions* (New York: Oxford University Press, 1991), 26-33.
7. Mel Dubnick and Alan Gitelson, "Nationalizing State Policies," in *The Nationalization of State Government*, ed. Jerome J. Hanus (Lexington, Mass.: Lexington Books, 1981), 51-69.
8. Landy, Roberts, and Thomas, *The Environmental Protection Agency*, 35-36.
9. Ibid., 38-42.
10. James Watt, Speech at the Annual Convention of the American Mining Congress, Denver, 1981.
11. Rochelle Standfield, "Ruckelshaus Casts EPA as 'Gorilla' in States' Enforcement Closet," *National Journal*, May 25, 1984, 1034-1038.
12. Terry M. Moe, "The Politics of Bureaucracy," in *Can Government Govern?* ed. John E. Chubb and Paul E. Peterson (Washington, D.C.: Brookings Institution, 1989), 320.
13. For a discussion of deadlock before the Bush presidency, see Michael E. Kraft, "Environmental Gridlock: Searching for Consensus in Congress," in *Environmental Policy in the 1990s*, ed. Norman J. Vig and Michael E. Kraft (Washington, D.C.: CQ Press, 1990), 103-124.
14. See Gary C. Bryner, *Blue Skies, Green Politics: The Clean Air Act of 1990* (Washington, D.C.: CQ Press, 1993).
15. The Environmental Protection Agency (EPA) remained under tight presidential control. As well as having its regulations reviewed by the Council for Competitiveness under the Bush administration, EPA has long had its regulations reviewed in detail by the Office of Management and Budget (OMB). OMB has used these reviews to balance environmental and economic considerations, and often to weaken proposals advanced by EPA. Ibid., 267-329.

16. Tom Curtis, interview with author, Washington, D.C., May 25, 1992.

17. City of Columbus, Ohio, *Ohio Metropolitan Area Cost Report for Environmental Compliance*, prepared by Michael J. Pompili, September 15, 1992; and City of Lewiston, Maine, *Testimony on the Review of Existing Regulations, "The Regulatory Flexibility Act,"* prepared by Robert J. Mulready and Christopher C. Branch, May 15, 1992. Submitted to the Environmental Protection Agency.

18. Michael E. Kraft and Norman J. Vig, "Environmental Policy from the Seventies to the Nineties: Continuity and Change," in *Environmental Policy in the 1990s*, ed. Norman J. Vig and Michael E. Kraft (Washington, D.C.: CQ Press, 1990), 3-31; Conservation Foundation, *State of the Environment: A View Toward the Nineties* (Washington, D.C.: Conservation Foundation, 1987); and David Wilcove and Michael J. Bean, *Whatever Happened to the Class of 1967?* (New York: Environmental Defense Fund, 1993).

19. Barry Commoner, "The Failure of the Environmental Effort" (Paper delivered at the seminar series of the Air and Radiation Program and Office of Toxic Substances, EPA, Center for the Biology of Natural Systems, Queens College, City University of New York, January 12, 1988).

20. Conservation Foundation, *State of the Environment*, xxxix.

21. Ibid., xiv.

22. Landy, Roberts, and Thomas, *The Environmental Protection Agency*, 262.

23. See William Sanjour, "In Name Only," *Sierra*, September-October 1992, 75-77, 95-103. Sanjour, a twenty-year EPA employee and a whistleblower himself, says, "The EPA is a wimpish regulator" (p. 100).

24. Ken Cook, interview with author, Washington, D.C., May 24, 1992.

25. Robert C. Paehlke, *Environmentalism and the Future of Progressive Politics* (New Haven: Yale University Press, 1989).

26. Michael Colby, "Environmental Management in Development: The Evolution of Paradigms," *Ecological Economics* (1991): 193-213. See also B. Devall and G. Sessions, *Deep Ecology: Living as if Nature Mattered* (Salt Lake City: Peregrine Smith Books, 1985).

27. Allen V. Kneese and Charles L. Schultze, *Pollution, Prices and Public Policy* (Washington, D.C.: Brookings Institution, 1975), 45.

28. Barry G. Rabe, *Fragmentation and Integration in State Environmental Management* (Washington, D.C.: Conservation Foundation, 1986), 16.

29. Landy, Roberts, and Thomas, *The Environmental Protection Agency*, 259; and U.S. Environmental Protection Agency, Office of Policy Analysis, Office of Policy, Planning, and Evaluation, *Unfinished Business: A Comparative Assessment of Environmental Problems: Overview Report* (Washington, D.C.: EPA, 1987), xiii.

30. U.S. Environmental Protection Agency, Science Advisory Board, *Reducing Risk: Setting Priorities and Strategies for Environmental Protection: Relative Risk Reduction Project* (Washington, D.C.: EPA, 1990), pt. 1.

31. See, for example, *Environment 2010: The State of the Environment Report* (Olympia: Washington Department of Ecology, 1989), and *The Comparative Risk Bulletin*, the newsletter of the Northeast Center for Comparative Risk at the Vermont Law School in South Royalton.

32. Landy, Roberts, and Thomas, *The Environmental Protection Agency*, 279.

33. On comparing and communicating risk, see Richard N. L. Andrews, "Risk Assessment: Regulation and Beyond," in *Environmental Policy in the 1990s*, ed. Norman J. Vig and Michael E. Kraft (Washington, D.C.: CQ Press, 1990), 167-186.

34. Landy, Roberts, and Thomas, *The Environmental Protection Agency*, 13.

35. U.S. Environmental Protection Agency, Science Advisory Board, *Reducing Risk: The Report of the Strategic Options Subcommittee: Relative Risk Reduction Project* (Washington, D.C.: EPA, 1990), pt. 4, app. C, 131-132.

36. *Environmental Opinion Survey* (Washington, D.C.: Environment Opinion Study, 1991), 2.

37. See Stephan Schmidheiny, with the Business Council for Sustainable Development, *Changing Course: A Global Business Perspective on Development and the Environment* (Cambridge: MIT Press, 1992), and Frances Cairncross, *Costing the Earth: The Challenge for Governments, the Opportunities for Business* (Boston: Harvard Business School Press, 1992).

38. Herman E. Daly and John B. Cobb, Jr., *For the Common Good: Redirecting the Economy Toward Community, the Environment, and a Sustainable Future* (Boston: Beacon Press, 1989), 19.

39. D. H. Meadows, D. L. Meadows, J. Randers, and W. W. Behrens, *The Limits to Growth* (New York: Potomac Associates; Universe Books, 1972).

40. Sandra Batie, "Sustainable Development: Challenges to the Profession of Agricultural Economics" (Presidential address to the American Agricultural Economics Association, Baton Rouge, La., July 30, 1989). See also H. Jeffrey Leonard and contributors, *Environment and the Poor: Development Strategies for a Common Agenda* (New Brunswick, N.J.: Transaction Books, 1989).

41. World Commission on Environment and Development, *Our Common Future* (New York: Oxford University Press, 1987), 310.

42. Batie, "Sustainable Development," 18.

43. Colby, "Environmental Management in Development," 201.

44. Canadian Council of Resource and Environment Ministries, *Report of the*

National Task Force on Environment and the Economy, September 1987.

45. For example, the Environmental Defense Fund has opened wide-ranging, long-term dialogues with McDonald's and with General Motors. *Wall Street Journal*, August 20, 1992, B1.

46. Tom Horton and William E. Eichbaum, *Turning the Tide: Saving the Chesapeake Bay* (Washington, D.C.: Island Press, 1991), 113-114.

47. Ibid., 104-127.

48. Colborn et al., *Great Lakes: Great Legacy?* (Washington, D.C.: Conservation Foundation, 1990), 16-21.

49. A 1981 study compared the health of pregnant women and their offspring who ate Lake Michigan fish with women who did not. The length of the gestation period, birth weight, and cognitive development of the infants were among the factors adversely affected by fish consumption. Ibid., 172-173.

50. See John J. Berger, ed., *Environmental Restoration: Science and Strategies for Restoring the Earth* (Washington, D.C.: Island Press, 1990).

51. Irwin Mussen notes, "The need exists, and probably will persist, at most levels of public service to articulate a process for maintenance of existing and continuous forging of new networks—ad hoc or permanent—for creative, joint action programs." Irwin Mussen, "Toward a New Federation for Environmental Restoration: The Case of Air Quality Through Intergovernmental Action—From Community to Global." Ibid., 368.

52. "Four Key Battles," in *Turning the Tide: Saving the Chesapeake Bay* (Washington, D.C.: Island Press, 1991).

53. "An Ecosystem Approach to Great Lakes Policy," in Colborn et al., *Great Lakes: Great Legacy?* 1-13.

CHAPTER THREE

An Overview of State
Environmental Policy

When the federal government reduced its budgetary and philosophical commitments to environmental protection in the 1980s, how did states respond? Did they follow the federal lead and cut back? Or did they step forward? And when states did step forward with new environmental initiatives, what kinds of problems did they address? What tools did they use?

These are not easy questions to answer because information about state environmental policy is fragmentary. There is voluminous information about environmental conditions in the fifty states, but these data do not tell much about state efforts to improve environmental quality. For example, that Los Angeles has the worst air quality of any large city in the United States does not mean that the city has adopted weaker policies than other cities; it means only that the city has not succeeded in solving air quality problems. And although there is extensive information about state processes—such as number of permits issued, violations, fines, and so on, this information is also an incomplete guide. The goals of environmental legislation are not to issue permits or fine violators; legislation seeks to improve environmental quality. Thus a small number of violations and fines could be a sign either of weak enforcement and a loss of environmental quality or of widespread compliance and an improvement in environmental quality.

The data described in this chapter measure state policies. We focus on what states are trying to do, rather than on what they have accomplished. Although the data have obvious limitations, they provide evidence that results are not what might have been predicted in the early 1970s, when tough federal statutes were put in place because state environmental policies were weak. It appears that many states have increased their budgetary commitment to environmental protection, and many have stepped forward with independent initiatives. Furthermore, the data suggest that states and localities are trying to address the unfinished business of using tools that catalyze and give incentives, structures that link and integrate, and procedures that engage and promote learning. Many of these independent state and local initiatives use nonregulatory tools to address problems such as nonpoint pollution, sensitive ecosystems and lands, and pollution prevention.

FEDERAL AND STATE ENVIRONMENTAL BUDGETS

The federal government spends more than states on protection of the environment. But in real dollars (adjusted for inflation), federal spending is lower now than it was at its peak in the late 1970s, and state spending has become more important. Furthermore, although the data are incomplete, there is very strong evidence that when the federal government cut back its spending on environmental protection in the 1980s, states stepped forward to pick up the slack.

As of 1991, federal spending was about $18.2 billion for environmental and natural resource programs, including $6 billion for EPA.[1] This figure includes not only the budget for operating EPA's regulatory programs but also money for special programs for cleaning up toxic waste sites and building pollution control facilities. State spending is smaller than federal spending—only $9.6 billion per year as of 1991. A portion of this is accounted for by federal grants, primarily from the EPA, the U.S. Department of Agriculture, and the U.S. Department of the Interior.[2]

Although the federal government is still the senior partner, states are increasingly important. We often look back to the Reagan administration as the period when the federal government began to back off its commitment to environmental protection. However, as Figure 3-1 shows, the total EPA budget crested in 1977 (in real dollars)—well before Ronald Reagan took office.

Figure 3-1   EPA Budget Outlays 1971-1993 (in 1987 Dollars)

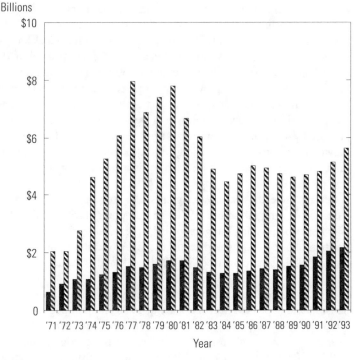

Billions

Operating Budget   Total Budget

Notes: Budget outlays were adjusted by the average of price indexes for government spending on pollution abatement, regulation and monitoring of pollution, and research and development on pollution abatement; 1976 transitional quarter is omitted.

Sources: U.S. Environmental Protection Agency, *Summary of the Budget* (Washington, D.C.: Office of the Comptroller, 1971-1993); Gary L. Rutledge and Mary L. Leonard, "Pollution Abatement and Control Expenditures, 1972-90," *Survey of Current Business,* June 1992, 25-41; and Gary L. Rutledge and Mary L. Leonard, "Pollution Abatement and Control Expenditures, 1987-91," *Survey of Current Business,* May 1993, 55-62.

Federal spending on wastewater treatment accounts for a large portion of the decline in total EPA spending. For two decades the federal government provided grants for the construction of municipal wastewater treatment plants. This program began in 1972 and peaked in 1976 at $9 billion. By 1990 it had channeled $50 billion to localities, with municipalities and states providing a 25 percent match for each federal grant.[3] However, the Clean Water Act Amendments of 1987 phased out this assistance. Over a seven-year period ending in 1994, the act promised $8.4 billion to capitalize state revolving loan funds if states provided 20 percent in matching funds. Localities borrow from these funds, and repayments will be used to finance loans for new construction projects.

Setting aside the wastewater grants, the story is much the same— a decline starting in the late 1970s and dropping further in the 1980s. The last two operating budgets for EPA prepared by the Carter administration allowed little growth, and the EPA operating budget hit bottom in 1984 at 75 percent of its 1981 peak and regained the peak in 1991.

EPA grants to states shrank even more sharply than EPA's other expenses. Grants peaked in real dollars in 1975 and bumped along in the 1980s at about 60 percent of the peak. In 1991 and 1992, EPA grants to states jumped to almost 75 percent of the peak (Figure 3-2).

When federal spending on EPA regulation, wastewater treatment, and many other environmental programs was dropping in the 1980s, state spending appears to have increased. It is difficult to tell the story precisely for two reasons. First, some states have been much more willing than others to appropriate more funds than EPA requires to win federal dollars to operate federally mandated environmental programs. Second, there are no time series data of state spending on environmental management since the 1970s. Collection of these data ceased as a result of initial budget cuts made by the Reagan administration. However, the Congressional Budget Office (CBO) has prepared estimates of the extent to which states relied on EPA grants for financing state programs before 1986. According to the CBO, federal dollars accounted for only 33 percent of state spending on water programs in 1986 (down from 49 percent four years earlier) and 40 percent of hazardous waste programs (down from 76 percent). There was no significant change in

Figure 3-2   Federal Grants to State and Local Programs (in 1987 Dollars)

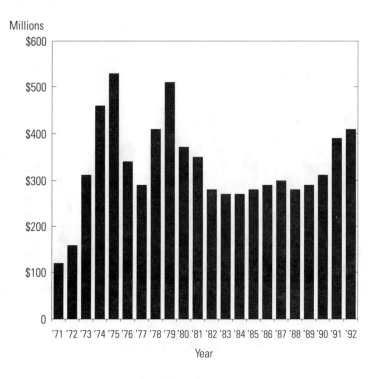

Millions

Sources: U.S. Environmental Protection Agency, *Summary of the Budget* (Washington, D.C.: Office of the Comptroller, 1971-1993); Gary L. Rutledge and Mary L. Leonard, "Pollution Abatement and Control Expenditures, 1972-90," *Survey of Current Business,* June 1992, 25-41; and Gary L. Rutledge and Mary L. Leonard, "Pollution Abatement and Control Expenditures, 1987-91," *Survey of Current Business,* May 1993, 55-62.

the reliance of state air programs on federal grants (Figure 3-3). Since 1986, we know that state spending on environmental and natural resource activities has almost doubled (Figure 3-4, p. 57).

The budget squeezes of the early 1990s hit both state and federal environmental programs. President Clinton's first proposed budget for EPA

Figure 3-3   Grants to States as a Percentage of Total State Budgets, by Program

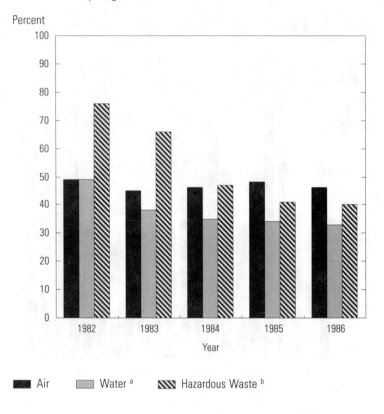

Percent

Year

■ Air   ▨ Water [a]   ▨▨ Hazardous Waste [b]

[a] Includes water quality programs; some drinking programs may not be included.
[b] Includes both hazardous and solid waste programs.

Source: Congressional Budget Office, Staff Working Paper, *Environmental Federalism: Allocating Responsibilities for Environmental Protection* (Washington, D.C., September, 1988).

Figure 3-4   State Expenditures on Environment and Natural Resources
(in 1987 Dollars)

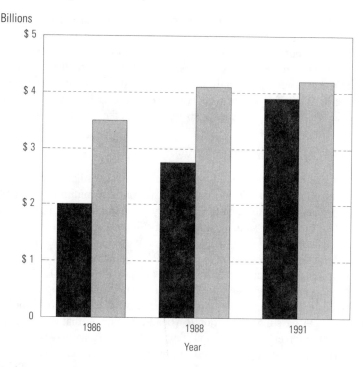

Billions

$5

$4

$3

$2

$1

0

1986   1988   1991

Year

■ Natural Resources   ▢ Environment

Sources: R. Steven Brown and L. Edward Garner, *Resource Guide to State Environmental Management* (Lexington, Ky.: Council of State Governments, 1988), 93; R. Steven Brown, John M. Johnson, and Karen Marshall, *Resource Guide to State Environmental Management,* 2d ed. (Lexington, Ky.: Council of State Governments, 1991); R. Steven Brown, Karen Marshall, Corey Miller, and Ellen Quinn, *Resource Guide to State Environmental Management,* 3d ed. (Lexington, Ky.: Council of State Governments, 1993); Gary L. Rutledge and Mary L. Leonard, "Pollution Abatement and Control Expenditures, 1972-90," *Survey of Current Business,* June 1992, 25-41; and Gary L. Rutledge and Mary L. Leonard, "Pollution Abatement and Control Expenditures, 1987-91," *Survey of Current Business,* May 1993, 55-62.

recommended a $1.5 billion cut between FY 1993 and FY 1994. Solid data about state spending on environmental agencies in those years are not available, but it is clear that some states cut environmental budgets.

In sum, trends in state and federal spending contradict the assumption that states will act only when forced to do so by the federal government. When federal budgets were cut in the late 1970s and early to mid-1980s, most states stepped forward to take up the slack.

THE FOCUS OF STATE ENVIRONMENTAL POLICY

Although environmental agencies in many states have gained significant support from state tax dollars, far beyond the minimum required to win EPA grants to operate regulatory programs, federal programs are still at the core of state agency concerns in most states. When the directors of state environmental agencies gather, the agenda is dominated by federal-state issues, such as new EPA regulations and prospects for changes in federal law. When state officials meet with EPA officials, there is much discussion of how the regulatory partnership is working.

For example, in discussions with EPA, state officials often complain that EPA pays more attention to "bean-counting"—that is, to the number of enforcement actions and fines that state regulators levy—than to such goals as compliance and improved environmental quality. There are debates about whether EPA standards are consistent across different programs (for example, Superfund, regulation of underground storage tanks, or hazardous waste programs); politically and financially feasible (for example, requirements for elaborate and costly testing that may be out of the reach of small public water systems, or design of stormwater sewers for annual, five-year, or ten-year maximum flows); flexible enough to allow states to design programs that fit local circumstances; and effective (for example, the safety of on-board systems for trapping gasoline vapors in motor vehicles or new federal standards for wetlands). There is pulling and tugging about whether federal officials are indecisive or heavy-handed and whether state agencies have the budgets, political support, and will to resist the pleas of polluters for lenient enforcement of environmental laws.[4]

At the margin, where states are innovating, the picture seems to be different. Although federal regulatory legislation dominates the day-today business of state and federal officials, existing legislation leaves large areas completely or partially uncovered. As we shall see, most states are independently tackling these gaps in environmental problems that the federal regulatory structure does not address adequately, including nonpoint pollution, pollution prevention, and protection of land from a variety of types of pollution. In these cases, states do not rely heavily on federal funding. They often use nonregulatory strategies—sometimes in concert with regulation, but often outside a regulatory framework.

SOURCES OF INFORMATION
ABOUT STATE ENVIRONMENTAL POLICY

The evidence about state policies and programs is scattered and incomplete. Some fundamental information is missing. For example, perhaps the most basic descriptive question about state-EPA relations is whether the EPA has delegated to states the authority to enforce the thirteen regulatory programs where such delegation is permitted by law. The EPA has never compiled a document detailing which states have primacy for the various EPA programs.

Information is missing because the regulatory system is complex and fluid. For many programs, it is possible to delegate partial authority—that is, for some program elements but not others. The status of delegation changes from time to time as regulations change and as states and the EPA respond. Thus, compiling a list of state primacy is much more difficult than filling in yes or no answers to thirteen questions for each of the fifty states. For a snapshot detailing which states have assumed primacy for which programs, one would have to consult each of the EPA program offices in Washington, and probably the regional offices and the states as well.[5]

Several organizations, including the EPA, do try to monitor independent state initiatives taking place outside the specific requirements and provisions of federal law. This chapter is based primarily on the *1991-92 Green Index: A State-by-State Guide to the Nation's Environmental Health,* compiled by Bob Hall and Mary Lee Kerr of the Institute for Southern Studies; the *Environmental Success Index,* compiled in 1990 by Renew America; and information gathered on state environmental and energy policies.[6] The indexes provide useful information despite their limitations.

The *Green Index* is an effort to paint a comprehensive picture of state environmental policies and programs.* It is a compilation and interpretation of information gathered by many organizations, including EPA, associations of state environmental officials, environmental groups, and trade magazines that publish annual "state of the state" reports summarizing state policies and programs. The *Green Index* includes 206 indicators of environmental quality and 50 indicators of policies and programs in each of the fifty states.

There are two major problems with the *Green Index*. The first is that it is an inexact guide to the quality of state performance. It is based on yes or no answers—either a state has adopted a policy or it has not. As the report cautions, this information is an inexact measure of whether a state is actually accomplishing something significant. States often pass legislation and then fail to appropriate funds. But appropriations are not a good measure either. Some effective programs are quite inexpensive, whereas well-funded programs may amount to little more than window dressing.[7]

The second problem is with the timeliness and accuracy of the data. Collection is a monumental effort, and there are a number of cases in which the data are outdated and perhaps inaccurate. Although the authors of the *Index* did evaluate the sources of data, their report is nevertheless a compilation of work by others. They did not double-check each entry.

Renew America has taken a different approach, focusing on the most successful efforts to address environmental issues, primarily at the state and local levels. Its data base includes information about 866 "successful" state and local, as well as public and private, initiatives. The information in the Renew America data base has been double-checked and may be somewhat more reliable, but the compilation is less systematic than the *Green Index*.† Every year since 1990, Renew America has attempted to identify the most noteworthy initiatives taking place out-

---

*The publisher of the *Green Index* is the Institute for Southern Studies, a liberal nonprofit organization based in North Carolina. The institute is actively involved in local and regional organizing efforts and has published various reports on environmental problems, including a book on successful local activism.

†Renew America is a Washington-based nonprofit environmental organization that has specialized in documenting state activities across a wide range of environ-

side of Washington, D.C., in the area of environmental management. The organization has sought to examine a full range of program areas, it has cast its net broadly in seeking nominations, and it has subjected them to rigorous review.‡

---

mental issues. For several years this organization rated the performance of the fifty states in specific program areas. In compiling their reports, Renew America built relationships with environmental activists in every state. A great deal of the literature on state environmental programs is based on the Renew America studies. Many political scientists have analyzed relationships between Renew America rankings and such factors as political culture, party affiliation, patterns of political organization, federal and state funding for environmental programs, and industrial structure. This literature is rich and suggestive; for a review, see James P. Lester and Emmett N. Lombard, "The Comparative Analysis of State Environmental Policy," *Natural Resources Journal* 30 (1990): 301-319.

In my contacts with environmental activists in Washington and in the states, I have heard several complaints about the Renew America rankings and about the awards that have been given to the highest-ranking states. This is not surprising, given the diversity of opinion among environmentalists and the inherent difficulty of ranking complex state programs. Renew America has since given up its effort to rank states and instead is gathering data on successes. To detour around disagreements about whether Renew America has gathered the right stories, I have treated all of the cases in the same way, whether or not Renew America has given them awards. Perhaps more important, this book rests its case not only on the successes that Renew America has documented but also on detailed case studies of state initiatives whose success is sometimes problematic. Furthermore, the discussion of civic environmentalism does not attempt to rank the performance of different states, but rather to describe a new style of environmental policy and politics that is developing in virtually every state, to a greater or lesser extent.

‡The process of gathering and screening nominations for the index were as follows: Renew America published several thousand brochures asking for nominations of success stories from the private or public sector at the federal, state, or local level. Most of the nominees nominated themselves. Each nominee filled out an application, and Renew America staff interviewed five local references, including local environmentalists, to verify the information submitted. Three of the five had to rank the case above 5 on a 1-10 scale to be included in the index. Renew America also discarded applications that were incomplete, for which there was disagreement among reviewers about the merit of the undertaking, or which were deemed unworthy by state contacts or by a national review panel.

In 1990, the result was a list of 866 nominees, 81 of whom were selected for awards or merit citations. All 866 were included in the published *Environmental Success Index*. Of these, 395 involve efforts by state or local governments, federal agencies, or public-private groups organized partly by public officials and receiving significant public funding; the remaining 471 involve wholly private activities by citizen groups, businesses, or individuals. The 395 public sector cases are the primary focus of this analysis.

The Renew America list has some clear strengths. It includes a mix of federal, state, and local efforts as well as some information about how different levels of government and different types of organizations work with each other. Each entry provides a fairly rich description of the program or initiative.* The list does not include all of the independent state and local governmental or private initiatives taken in recent years, or even necessarily the best ones. Since it catalogs only nominees for awards, it includes neither examples of state or local neglect of important problems nor examples of programs that were launched but failed.

In short, the Renew America data base is best seen as a snapshot of many, but not all, of the independent initiatives taken at the state and local levels to improve environmental quality. But together with the *Green Index* and other scattered information about state environmental initiatives, we can put together a broad picture of the kinds of environmental problems that states are addressing, the tools that states are using to address environmental issues, and the roles of vari-

---

*Renew America files for all 866 cases, including the original applications and program descriptions submitted by the nominators, as well as the comments of the independent experts with whom Renew America consulted, were examined. In several cases this review was supplemented by additional information about a project—who the sponsor was, what the nature of the program was, what other groups were directly involved in the initiative, and what problem the initiative sought to address. However, information about the effectiveness of the program was often incomplete, consisting only of claims and opinions. Furthermore, information about how a program was established was often sketchy. It was usually clear which organizations were formally involved in managing a program (for example, which organizations were contributing funds to operate a public-private partnership), but it was less clear which organization provided the motivating force to create partnerships.

ous levels of government and of private organizations in state and local initiatives.

WHICH PROBLEMS ARE STATES ADDRESSING?

State and local initiatives occur in all areas of environmental policy. The assessment of activism in different areas depends on which measures are used (Table 3-1). Renew America and the *Green Index* both report high levels of state activity in waste management and water quality. Both list relatively few state innovations in reducing air pollution. However, whereas the *Green Index* shows only a few measures of state activity in energy policy and land management, Renew America reports a great deal of innovative activity in these two areas.

When one looks beneath these broad patterns, examining the kinds of environmental problems that states and localities addressed and the tools that they used, both indexes point to the same finding. That is, the majority of recent state and local initiatives have addressed the unfinished business of environmental problems, those of nonpoint pollution, protection of ecosystems and environmentally sensitive lands, and prevention of pollution. To combat these problems, states and localities are using nonregulatory tools quite extensively. The data also suggest that states and localities are involving many new players in their environmental initiatives. The story is not simply about regulators versus polluters; it is about a complex array of partnerships.

Land Protection

According to the Renew America data, land protection is the focus of the largest amount of innovation by states. The Renew America data also include several cases of land protection by local governments, public-private partnerships, and federal agencies that manage land, including the Tennessee Valley Authority and the Bureau of Land Management.

The Renew America data include numerous nonregulatory efforts to protect specific parcels of land. The tools used most often include public works, acquisition, and volunteer programs. Examples include an effort cosponsored by the state government, local governments, and the private sector to clean up and build a bike path along the Platte River in

TABLE 3-1

STATE ENVIRONMENTAL PROGRAMS AND INNOVATIONS

	Land	Waste	Water	Energy	Air	Environmental Education	Other
Renew America [a]							
State initiatives	40	20	25	22	7	17	6
Other government initiatives	52	55	30	47	6	35	5
Green Index [b]							
Number of policy areas in the index	3	22	9	3	7	0	6
Average number of states active in each policy area	7	11	22	21	22	—	22

Sources: Renew America data base, Washington, D.C., 1990; Bob Hall and Mary Lee Kerr, *1991-1992 Green Index: A State-by-State Guide to the Nation's Environmental Health* (Washington, D.C.: Island Press, 1991), 142-145.

[a] Table headings as defined by the interest group Renew America:
  Land: Beautification, food safety, forest management, growth management, public lands, open space, range conservation, soil conservation, wildlife conservation.
  Waste: Hazardous materials, pesticides, radioactive waste, solid waste reduction, solid waste recycling.
  Water: Drinking water protection, fish conservation, groundwater protection, surface water protection.
  Energy: Energy pollution control, renewable energy, energy efficiency, transportation efficiency.
  Air: Air pollution reduction, greenhouse gases.
  Environmental education: Education for the public, school-based instruction.

[b] Table headings as defined by the *Green Index:*
  Land: Growth management, coastal zone management, sustainable agriculture.
  Waste: Recycling, land fills, toxic wastes.
  Water: Water pollution
  Energy: Energy and transit.
  Air: Air pollution and auto tests.
  Other: Mandatory seat belts (thirty-five states), workplace safety (thirty-five states), indoor air pollution (twenty-four states), biotechnology regulation (seven states), organic farming (two measurements: eight states and twenty-one states).

Denver; several cooperative efforts between the Nature Conservancy and states to raise funds for purchasing sensitive lands; the "Don't Mess with Texas" volunteer "adopt-a-highway" antilitter campaign, which was organized by the Texas Department of Highways (and has been copied in many other states); and many state and local efforts to preserve agricultural land and open space through the purchase of land or easements.

The *Green Index,* in contrast, shows a relatively low level of state activism on land management issues. The explanation may be that the *Green Index* emphasizes regulatory activity, and there are fewer clear cases of innovative state regulation of land use. Historically, the power to regulate land has been delegated by states to local governments. In recent years, several states (nine according to the *Green Index*) have adopted growth management legislation that mandates tougher controls on development, protection of critical lands, and efforts to ensure that adequate public infrastructure is available in areas being developed.

The Renew America data include three of these state growth management efforts, in Maine, Vermont, and Oregon. All of these states require—and provide assistance to—local governments to prepare land use plans and associated zoning regulations that take into account the problems of sensitive environmental areas as well as the need for open space. The legislation in Maine and Vermont, like other state growth management legislation passed in the 1980s, addresses the availability of low- and medium-cost housing in rapidly growing areas. Other states, notably Florida, also require that local plans ensure that funds are available for public infrastructure (including highways) before new developments are begun.

Private not-for-profit groups have been organized in several states to support growth management by monitoring state and local decisions and raising funds to help protect critical lands. The Renew America nomination for Oregon was both for legislation, passed in 1973, and for the 1000 Friends of Oregon, the model for many similar organizations.

Waste Management

Both the *Green Index* and the Renew America list show a high level of activism on waste management. The Renew America data indicate that states are active in this area, especially with efforts to control toxic wastes, but local governments are also quite active, especially with regard to solid waste.

According to both indexes, the most common form of innovation in waste management is public support for recycling of solid waste. Often—in about two-thirds of the Renew America cases—recycling programs are voluntary and use nonregulatory tools. Voluntary programs might provide special containers for disposal of glass, paper, or aluminum, or include special pickups of recyclable materials. There are several examples of successful public education efforts to encourage recycling. There are also many examples of mandatory requirements for separating recyclables from other wastes. In fact, there are more examples of purely regulatory efforts in the waste area than in other parts of the Renew America data.

One of the older programs involving mandatory recycling is in New Berlin Township, New Jersey. The director of the local public works department developed a comprehensive effort to recycle plastics, vehicle batteries, glass, newspapers, and used motor oil. Over 60 percent of the town's trash was diverted from the landfill, and 95 percent of the population participated in the program. More recently, Seattle and other cities have organized voluntary recycling programs that rely on sliding scales of fees, provision of special bins for recyclable materials, and public education. Other municipalities have combined mandatory recycling with nonregulatory assistance and encouragement.

Although many recycling efforts are sponsored by local governments, states have also become involved. They mandate local efforts, provide assistance to local governments, and set goals for waste reduction and recycling. For example, Oregon provides tax credits for the procurement of recycled materials. Minnesota provided financial support for a recycling and solid waste reduction program in Winona, which was nominated for a Renew America award.

The *Green Index* found numerous nonregulatory state efforts to control solid waste, but the authors were not satisfied. They saw the failure to regulate as a drawback of state policies.

> Even in the best-ranking states, laws challenging industry to reduce production of poisons are among the last to make it through the legislature. By contrast, recycling programs that cost industry little and elicit broad support become law first. Forty-three states have passed some sort of recycling legislation, compared to 16 with toxic reduction laws.[8]

The Renew America data do include examples of state efforts to manage toxic wastes using both regulatory and nonregulatory means. The federal Resource Conservation and Recovery Act mandates cradle-to-grave documentation and control of the production, use, transportation, and disposal of hazardous wastes. States have assumed primacy for enforcement of many elements of this federally designed system.

In addition, in the last few years EPA has made grants to most states to support small-scale pollution prevention programs, and several states have created programs independently. The first statewide pollution prevention legislation was established in North Carolina before EPA began its pollution prevention efforts. The legislation was inspired and modeled in part on the voluntary programs of the 3M Company. The Renew America list includes several voluntary technical assistance programs in North Carolina, as well as similar programs operated by the New York Environmental Facilities Corporation and state agencies in Rhode Island and California.

More recently, some states have created hybrid toxic use reduction programs, which combine voluntary and regulatory tools. In addition to providing technical assistance or grants to firms, this legislation requires industries that use toxins to set goals for reductions, provides for state monitoring of progress, and allows citizens some form of access to information about the reduction in the use of toxins by nearby firms.

Water Quality

Both indexes emphasize water quality as an important area for state and local action. To understand the nature of state activities in this area, one must understand the basic structure of federal water pollution law. The federal regime for managing water pollution regulates discharges from point sources such as industrial plants, municipal sewage treatment plants, underground storage tanks, and wells for injecting wastes into the ground. Federal law requires EPA to issue—or delegate to the states responsibility to issue—permits for point source discharges. Federal law also authorizes the U.S. Army Corps of Engineers (or states, if their programs qualify) to permit projects to dredge or fill rivers or to alter wetlands. In contrast, there are no federal statutes providing for permits for nonpoint source pollutants such as stormwater runoff in urban areas or the movement of agricultural chemicals into surface water

or groundwater. The Clean Water Act provides that, instead of requiring permits, EPA shall assist states, with limited funds and various kinds
of technical assistance, in preparing areawide plans to manage nonpoint
pollution.[9]

The *Green Index* stresses states' willingness to assume primacy in issuing National Pollution Discharge Elimination System point-source
permits and operating other federal water pollution regulatory programs. However, the index also tallies state efforts to design individual
programs to manage groundwater and to encourage reductions in the
use of chemicals in agriculture.

The Renew America data include only one state water program that
is purely regulatory, along with several programs that combine regulatory and nonregulatory efforts. The Florida Surface Water Improvement and Management (SWIM) plans are one example of a hybrid
program. (One of these plans is discussed in detail in Chapter 5.) Another hybrid example in the Renew America data base is the joint effort
by several Great Lakes states, Canadian provinces, the EPA, and the
government of Canada to address toxic waste contamination of sediments and water in the Great Lakes. In many locations, federal requirements for eliminating discharges into the lakes have not been enforced.
Parties to the Great Lakes effort agree to strive for a "zero-discharge"
policy for toxins. The program also includes building a trust fund of
$100 million to support research into toxic contamination of the lakes,
as well as public education efforts, the adoption of common standards
for declaring fish too contaminated to be eaten safely, and other forms
of cooperation between parties.[10]

Several states have made efforts to protect groundwater and to encourage low-chemical "sustainable" agriculture. These programs rely
heavily on public education, monitoring, and public works. Chapter 4
describes the Iowa program, which includes taxes on chemicals, research, technical assistance, and demonstrations of sustainable low-
chemical agriculture but very little regulation of farming practices.
Other states, notably Wisconsin, have regulatory standards and requirements for farmers as well as nonregulatory assistance and education.

The Renew America data also include a number of other cases of
hybrid and nonregulatory programs. The Rensselaerville Institute-New
York State Self-Help Support Program is one such hybrid. It is a part-

nership of the nonprofit institute with three state agencies to provide low-cost loans and technical assistance to small towns that mobilize volunteer programs to repair or build new public water supply systems. This program has recently extended its operations to Oklahoma and other states; it has received significant private foundation funding.

Energy Conservation

Both indexes find many state and local efforts to encourage energy conservation or to promote the use of renewable sources of energy. However, the data may be misleading. With a few outstanding exceptions, most state energy programs rely almost entirely on Department of Energy grants or oil overcharge funds, so it is not clear that there is a long-term state commitment to these programs.*

State energy programs cited in the two indexes generally involve targeted efforts to promote energy conservation through public education and through grants and technical assistance to private industry. Many states also operate weatherization programs with federal funding. One of the more fully developed state programs is the North Carolina Alternative Energy Corporation, a nonprofit organization included in the Renew America list, which was organized with state support and state funding. It has several nonregulatory programs, including assistance to the poultry industry on efficient factory lighting, to the woodworking industry on timber drying, and to air conditioning and heating contractors on the installation of energy-efficient heat pumps.

A few states, notably California and New York, have invested significant state money in energy conservation and renewable energy. Several of their programs are included in the Renew America data. California spends more than the federal government on research about methanol, a substitute for gasoline. Arizona has invested heavily in solar energy.

---

*Oil overcharge payments originate from fines that federal courts have levied on major petroleum companies for overcharging during periods when the prices of gas and petroleum were regulated by federal law. Some of the fines were very large, amounting to billions of dollars. The courts allow the federal government to pass some of these funds through to state governments to encourage energy conservation and other activities that are presumed to benefit the consumers who were overcharged.

States have recently begun to use another set of tools to promote energy conservation and renewable energy sources. State public utility commissions regulate the rates for investor-owned electrical and gas utilities, and several have adopted policies and incentives to encourage "integrated resource planning," which involves assessing alternatives to conventional fossil fuel and hydropower production of electricity, as well as "demand-side management," which involves efforts to reduce the demand for energy by promoting conservation. The Conservation Law Foundation's work with commissions and utilities in New England, as well as demand-side management efforts by the Bonneville Power Administration (a federal agency in the Pacific Northwest), are included in the Renew America data base. Chapter 6 describes activities by public utility commissions in California, Wisconsin, and other states, and includes a case study of recent activities in Colorado.

Air Quality

The story of independent state initiatives in air quality is impressive, albeit brief. State action focuses more on tough regulation than on nonregulatory measures. The *Green Index* finds a fair amount of state activity to applaud; but of three measures of state activity in air quality, two are actually reports of state implementation of federal regulatory programs (Table 3-2, p. 72). The Renew America data include only 13 state or local efforts to improve air quality (of the 395 cases). Four involve making information available about the danger of radon gas in homes or schools. Six involve efforts to reduce areawide air pollution and center on transportation. The remaining three were narrow in scope and not particularly impressive.

The Renew America data do capture two of the most important state- and local-level initiatives on air quality. One is the plan recently adopted by the South Coast Air Quality Management District (SCAQMD) to control air pollution in the Los Angeles basin. California has long been a leader in measuring, evaluating, and regulating air quality. Congress has frequently drafted federal legislation that directly copies California state law or programs created by regional authorities in the Los Angeles basin.[11] The new SCAQMD plan is a regulatory regime that also includes nonregulatory measures such as technical assistance for small businesses that emit air pollutants and support for van pooling and mass transit. The plan is designed to meet federal requirements for attaining clean air goals in the region.

The Renew America list also includes action in Denver, Colorado, where state and local officials designed, and the state adopted, mandatory use of oxygenated gasoline for cars during the winter months, when certain air quality problems are especially severe. This step helped Denver meet federal requirements to find adequate measures to meet air quality standards. Renew America data do not include another recent effort that should be mentioned. In the Northeast, seven states jointly adopted the requirement that all cars sold in these states meet California requirements for emissions controls, which are more stringent than federal requirements. Together with California, these states constitute almost half of the market for new cars sold in the United States.

A fourth example of state air quality initiatives involves the adoption of regulatory standards and procedures for controlling air toxins. Although the 1970 Clean Air Act required that EPA take these steps, over the following twenty years federal standards were adopted for only eight of many hundreds of pollutants. In the absence of effective federal action, more than a dozen states moved independently to set standards and establish permitting systems for air toxins. In 1990, Congress amended the Clean Air Act and rewrote the section on air toxins completely. EPA must now establish emission standards for 189 substances over the next ten years. Existing state programs will have to comply with new federal procedures and requirements.[12]

THE TOOLS OF STATE ENVIRONMENTAL POLICY

The two indexes suggest that environmental activities at the state and local levels involve a wide variety of tools, including many nonregulatory tools. The nonregulatory tools used in the 395 Renew America public sector cases are listed in Figure 3-5.

The most commonly used tools incorporate routine governmental services such as teaching about environmental concerns in the public schools, changing waste management systems to encourage recycling or waste minimization, and instituting public works to protect lands or improve water quality in streams and lakes. Fully half of the tools governments use in these cases force changes in routine government services.

TABLE 3-2

NUMBER OF STATES WITH *GREEN INDEX* PROGRAMS

State Program

Assistance to Private Sector/ Individuals (policy/no. of states)	Services (policy/no. of states)	Hybrid [a] (policy/no. of states)	Administration of State Regulations (policy/no. of states)	Administration of Federal Regulations (policy/no. of states)
		Waste		
Buy recycled goods (20)	Grants/loans for recycling (34)	Statewide recycling (30)	Mandatory recycling (7)	Superfund plan (24)
Goals for buying recycled goods (15)	Set recycling goals (28)	Bottle return law (10)	Mandatory source separation (7)	
Tax aid for recycling (17)		Limit disposable diapers (4)	Landfill cleanup standards (12)	
Public disclosure of toxic waste (20)		Newsprint reuse (10)	Right to sue on toxic waste (15)	
Fund public disclosure of toxic waste (21)		Protect toxic waste workers (36)	Strict liability on toxic waste (31)	
		Toxic waste reduction law (16)		

(Continued on next page)

TABLE 3-2 *(CONTINUED)*

		State Program		
Assistance to Private Sector/ Individuals (policy/no. of states)	Services (policy/no. of states)	Hybrid [a] (policy/no. of states)	Administration of State Regulations (policy/no. of states)	Administration of Federal Regulations (policy/no. of states)
		Waste		
		Plan and report toxic waste reductions (13) Reduce toxics (3)		
		Air		
			Halt acid rain (6)	Fees for air emissions (37)
			Control air toxics (35)	Local auto tests (37)
			Ozone protection (15)	State auto tests (6)
			Halt global warming (12)	Certify auto tests (17)
		Water		
Test groundwater in landfills (37)	Protect groundwater (37)		Groundwater toxins (29)	Issue NPDES[b] permits (38)

(Continued on next page)

TABLE 3-2 *(CONTINUED)*

		State Program		
Assistance to Private Sector/ Individuals (policy/no. of states)	**Services (policy/no. of states)**	**Hybrid** [a] **(policy/no. of states)**	**Administration of State Regulations (policy/no. of states)**	**Administration of Federal Regulations (policy/no. of states)**

		Water		
			Wetland protection (16)	Regulate federal water quality sites (30)
			Ban phosphates (11)	Water pre-treatment program (26)
			Pesticide permits (8)	

		Land		
Assist sustainable farming (6)			Growth management plan (9)	
			Coastal zone management (5)	

(Continued on next page)

TABLE 3-2 *(CONTINUED)*

State Program				
Assistance to Private Sector/ Individuals (policy/no. of states)	**Services (policy/no. of states)**	**Hybrid** [a] **(policy/no. of states)**	**Administration of State Regulations (policy/no. of states)**	**Administration of Federal Regulations (policy/no. of states)**
Energy				
	Fund mass transit (33)		Least-cost energy (17)	
	Halt global warming (12)			
Other				
Certify organic food (8)			Biotechnology (7)	
Assist organic marketing (21)			Seat belt law (35)	
			Indoor pollution (24)	
			Workplace safety (35)	

Source: Bob Hall and Mary Lee Kerr, *1991-1992 Green Index: A State-by-State Guide to the Nation's Environmental Health* (Washington, D.C.: Island Press, 1991).

[a] Hybrid programs use regulatory and nonregulatory tools and often take the form of private sector-state government partnerships.

[b] NPDES: National Pollution Discharge Elimination System.

In many Renew America cases, governments sought to catalyze private action, usually through efforts to educate the public at large about environmental issues such as energy conservation or solid waste disposal, and through volunteer programs often associated with the protection of specific lands. Governments also provide technical assistance and grants to private firms, subsidize research, and purchase lands for conservation purposes. (For a discussion of the classification of the tools listed in Figure 3-5 and of the use of tools in recent literature on public policies and state-federal relationships, see Appendix B.) These nonregulatory tools were in all but forty of the Renew America public sector cases involving classic regulation (Table 3-3, p. 78). There are 307 efforts that use nonregulatory tools only, 48 that involve a mix of regulatory and nonregulatory tools, 18 that are pure regulation, and 22 others that are primarily support activities such as improved governmental planning or intergovernmental cooperation. In the complete Renew America data base of 866 cases, 86 clearly fit the traditional mode of environmental protest-regulation-cleanup. The list includes 54 citizen protests, the 18 regulatory initiatives just mentioned, and 14 cleanups by firms that had polluted lands or water. (Renew America also documented 403 cases of wholly private initiatives, including 254 efforts by citizen groups to do such things as purchase land, provide environmental education, or clean up litter; 43 examples in which corporations built small parks or provided other public services; and 104 private business ventures such as solar energy firms and chemical-free farms.)

The *Green Index* focuses more direct attention on state regulatory measures than the Renew America data do. Of the fifty policy areas included in the *Green Index*, nine involve participation by the state in EPA regulatory programs and twenty involve independent state regulatory initiatives. The other twenty-one *Green Index* policies involve substantial nonregulatory activities, either on their own (twelve policies) or via hybrid policies, which blend regulatory and nonregulatory elements. The nonregulatory policies in the *Green Index* include state grants, loans, tax incentives, and procurement policies for recycling; testing of groundwater; and certification of organic produce and financial assistance to low-chemical farming. The index shows that nonregulatory state initiatives were found in as many states as were regulatory initiatives (Table 3-2).

Figure 3-5 Tools Used by Governments in Nonregulatory Initiatives

SERVICE

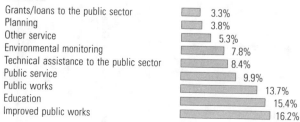

Grants/loans to the public sector	3.3%
Planning	3.8%
Other service	5.3%
Environmental monitoring	7.8%
Technical assistance to the public sector	8.4%
Public service	9.9%
Public works	13.7%
Education	15.4%
Improved public works	16.2%

SUBSIDY

Tax credits	.3%
Government procurement	1.0%
Emission tax	1.5%
Other subsidy	3.3%
Land acquisition	7.3%
Grants/loans to the private sector	8.4%
Research	9.6%
Technical assistance to the private sector	10.4%

CATALYTIC

Mediation	.3%
Deregulation	.5%
Example setting	.8%
Goal/target setting	1.5%
Voluntary certification	1.5%
Catalytic grants	2.0%
Volunteer programs	3.0%
Other catalytic	5.1%
Educating the public	27.3%

Source: Renew America data base.

TABLE 3-3

THE RENEW AMERICA INDEX

Program	Federal	State	Local	Government Public Schools/ Universities	Public-Private Partnerships	Other	Total
Regulatory	2	7	8	0	1	0	18
Hybrid[a]	4	17	19	2	3	3	48
Nonregulatory	39	112	86	23	46	1	307
Support[b]	2	10	3	2	0	1	18
Other	1	2	1	0	0	0	4
Totals	48	148	117	27	50	5	395

Activity	Big Corporations	Small Corporations	Individuals	Nongovernment Private Schools/ Universities	Civic-N[c]	Environmental Groups	Other	Total
Cleanups	14	0	0	0	0	0	0	14
Protests	0	0	3	0	3	47	1	54
Other	66	66	9	12	23	202	25	403
Totals	80	66	12	12	26	249	26	471

Source: Renew America, *Environmental Success Index* (Unpublished data, Washington, D.C., 1990).
[a] Hybrid: programs that use regulatory and nonregulatory tools, such as private sector-state government partnerships.
[b] Support: planning, training, data management.
[c] Civic-N: civic and neighborhood associations.

WHO IS INVOLVED?

The two indexes suggest that all states have taken significant steps toward framing independent environmental initiatives. The governmental initiatives in the Renew America *Index* represent forty-seven of the fifty states. In the *Green Index*, every state has at least nine of the fifty policies in place, and the average state has nineteen.

However, activism is concentrated in certain states. From information in these two sources, it appears that the states that have the toughest regulatory climates also have the most nonregulatory and hybrid initiatives. States seem to supplement strong regulations with incentives and assistance to encourage citizens and private firms to be aware (Table 3-4).

TABLE 3-4

STATE ENVIRONMENTAL POLICIES AND STATE-LOCAL INNOVATION

Ranking of State Policies	Government and Public-Private Programs	Private Initiatives
Twelve "greenest" states (Calif., Conn., Mass., Me., Mich., Minn., N.J., N.Y., Ore., R.I., Vt., Wis.)	41.0%	38.6%
Thirteen "next most green" states (Del., Fla., Hawaii, Iowa, Ill., Md., Mo., N.C., N.H., Ohio, Pa., Va., Wash.)	23.5%	36.5%
Thirteen "less green" states (Colo., Ga., Idaho, Ind., Kan., Ky., La., Mont., N.D., Neb., N.M., S.C., Texas)	17.2%	16.1%
Twelve "least green" states (Ariz., Alaska, Ala., Ark., Miss., Nev., Okla., S.D., Tenn., Utah, W.V., Wyo.)	16.2%	8.7%

Sources: Bob Hall and Mary Lee Kerr, *1991-1992 Green Index: A State-by-State Guide to the Nation's Environmental Health* (Washington, D.C.: Island Press, 1991); Renew America index.

Note: Percentages reflect the fraction of Renew America cases found in each group of states.

As mentioned above, Renew America does not confine its attention to states. Of the 395 governmental initiatives, only 148 are sponsored by state agencies, and another 27 were organized by public colleges and universities, mostly affiliated with state governments. In addition, state agencies are involved in many initiatives that others started. Most of the Renew America cases involve some kind of partnership or joint effort among different levels of government or in a formal organization created jointly by a public agency and a private corporation or nonprofit organization. State agencies play important roles in most of these partnerships, even if the party responsible for initiating or managing the activity is a local government or a public-private partnership. States provide funding for one-third of the local efforts and almost two-thirds of the public-private initiatives. Thus, state agencies are directly involved in at least 243 (62 percent) of the examples on the Renew America list, either as the responsible party or as a funder. The federal government and private corporations are also involved in state, local, and public-private undertakings, although they are partners less often than are states (Table 3-5, p. 81).

SUMMARY

Although only scattered information is available about state spending and policies, this information suggests that the assumptions that drove the federal government to preempt state laws in the 1970s no longer hold. That is, states *are* willing to spend their own dollars and enact their own policies, without being forced by the federal government to do so. Virtually all states have taken some steps to go beyond federally imposed requirements, and some have taken the lead in several areas. Independent state initiatives are especially notable in the areas of waste management, land protection, and water quality. Only a few states have moved outside the scope of federal air quality statutes (except with regard to air toxins). On average, states seem to be more willing than the federal government to increase spending on environmental protection.

Often state and local initiatives fit into the pattern of civic environmentalism described in Chapter 1. The initiatives use nonregulatory approaches to environmental management. They involve providing public services in new ways, catalyzing private action, and subsidizing corporate

TABLE 3-5

SPONSORS AND FUNDERS OF RENEW AMERICA INNOVATIONS

Funders	Sponsors						Total Cases Funded
	Federal Agencies (48 cases)	State Agencies (148 cases)	Local Governments (117 cases)	Public-Private Organizations (50 cases)	Public Schools/ Universities (27 cases)	Other (5 cases)	
Federal agencies	48	33	24	17	10	3	135
State agencies	5	145	41	31	17	4	243
Local governments	1	14	108	16	4	1	144
Public-private organizations	0	0	0	5	0	0	5
Public schools/ universities	0	8	9	4	13	0	34
Businesses	4	12	12	33	8	1	70
Trade associations	1	2	0	4	1	0	8
Foundations	0	2	1	13	3	1	20
Citizen groups	1	4	6	15	2	1	29
Individuals	0	0	4	11	1	0	16
Sales	0	2	9	2	0	0	13
Other	0	0	2	1	0	1	4

Source: Renew America data base, Washington, D.C., 1990.

Notes: Sponsors initiate environmental innovations, and funders pay for them. These figures may underestimate the involvement of states and federal agencies in local and public-private initiatives. In some cases, all of the funding sources may not have been reported. Also, it is likely that some of the support provided by states originated in federal grants.

or individual behavior through grants or technical assistance. Sometimes these nonregulatory measures are explicitly linked to regulatory requirements, and the effect is a hybrid set of policies employing a wide array of tools. At other times nonregulatory efforts are substitutes for regulation. They may also be a means of avoiding the more intractable challenge of reducing flows of hazardous substances into the environment. To say that states are a creative force in environmental policy is not to say that they could assume full responsibility for environmental management. In many ways, their initiatives build on federal law. Nonregulatory carrots often presume that somewhere there is a regulatory stick.

The picture of civic environmentalism that emerges from this survey is suggestive but woefully incomplete. How do officials coordinate the use of diverse nonregulatory tools with regulation in hybrid initiatives? Why are states and localities organizing new collaborative relationships with each other, with federal agencies, and with the private sector? How do these partnerships work out in practice? And do the new kinds of environmental tools and the focus on new issues change the shape and dynamics of political struggle? For answers to these questions, we must turn from dry secondary data to case studies. The following three chapters provide examples of how civic environmentalism works in the real world of politics. The first case study (Chapter 4) focuses on nonpoint pollution in Iowa. The second and third (Chapters 5 and 6) focus on the two other dimensions of the unfinished business of environmental policy—protecting endangered ecosystems and preventing pollution.

NOTES

1. *Budget of the United States Government, FY 1991* (Washington, D.C.: Government Printing Office, 1991).
2. Council of State Governments, *Resource Guide to State Environmental Management* (Lexington, Ky.: Council of State Governments, 1993).
3. Dennis Melamed, "As the Feds Bow Out, Communities Seek New Ways to Pay for Clean Water," *Governing,* July 1990, 19.
4. Meeting of state EPA directors with EPA Administrator William Reilly, October 1991, Tysons Corner, Virginia.
5. Personal communication with Mary McCarthy O'Reilly, EPA Office of Regional Operations and State/Local Relations, January 1992.

6. Bob Hall and Mary Lee Kerr, *1991-1992 Green Index: A State-by-State Guide to the Nation's Environmental Health* (Washington, D.C.: Island Press, 1991); and Renew America, *Environmental Success Index* (Unpublished data, Washington, D.C., 1990).

7. See Thomas Dye and Dorothy Davidson, "State Energy Policies: Federal Funds for Paper Programs," *Policy Studies Review* 1, no. 62 (1981): 255.

8. Hall and Kerr, *1991-92 Green Index*, 138.

9. A. Myrick Freeman III, "Water Pollution Policy," in *Public Policies for Environmental Protection*, ed. Paul R. Portney (Washington, D.C.: Resources for the Future, 1990), 97-150.

10. Theodora E. Colborn et al., *Great Lakes: Great Legacy?* (Washington, D.C.: Conservation Foundation; and Ottawa, Canada: Institute for Research on Public Policy, 1990), 3-5.

11. Sheldon Kamieniecki and Michael R. Ferrall, "Intergovernmental Relations and Clean-Air Policy in Southern California," *Publius* (Summer 1991): 143-154.

12. Steven M. Hoffman and Kristin Sigford, *State Air Quality Control Programs: A Comparative Assessment* (St. Paul, Minn.: Project Environment Foundation and University of St. Thomas, 1991), 36-40.

CHAPTER FOUR

Doing Things in the Right Order: Reducing the Use of Agricultural Chemicals in Iowa

In June, rural Iowa is an American idyll of green fields and small towns. But the landscape is hardly natural; 90 percent of Iowa is farmland, with 75 percent of this acreage planted in row crops such as corn and soybeans.[1] Iowa has perhaps the most developed countryside of any American state.

Iowa's farmlands are among the most productive on earth, but there is, as the *Des Moines Register* announced in 1986, an "ugly side of a bountiful harvest."[2] Iowa farmers spend about a billion dollars every year on farm chemicals, especially nitrogen fertilizers and herbicides like atrazine. These chemicals create environmental problems. About 130,000 rural Iowans drink water from private wells that have nitrate levels that exceed federal health advisory limits; during the summer of 1991, the public water supplies in Des Moines and Iowa City were periodically declared unsafe for consumption by infants.[3]

The increased use of farm chemicals has been profitable for Iowa. Farmers have doubled their use of herbicides and chemical fertilizers since the early 1960s, and yields have climbed from 60 bushels of corn per acre in 1960 to over 120 bushels in 1980.[4] Given the importance of chemicals to Iowa's powerful farm industry, one might predict that the state would be reluctant to address the environmental effects of farm chemicals.

However, Iowa has acted, and its efforts have won wide praise. In 1989 Renew America named Iowa the leading state in water quality, citing the 1987 Iowa Groundwater Act, and in 1992 the EPA gave a pollution prevention award to the interagency Iowa Consortium on Agriculture and Groundwater Quality. Iowa's accomplishments are particularly noteworthy because no federal law has forced the state to act.

This chapter tells the story of farm chemicals in Iowa and examines how closely the story fits the hypotheses outlined in previous chapters about the focus, tools, and politics surrounding independent state initiatives in environmental policy. The story of farm chemicals in Iowa is a clear example of how civic environmentalism works. The issue of farm chemicals is a good example of the unfinished business that we expect states to address. Iowa has relied almost exclusively on nonregulatory tools. In doing so, the state has experienced sharp confrontations, especially during the passage of the landmark Groundwater Protection Act of 1987, but the aggressive tactics of chemical interests clearly backfired. For several years, the politics surrounding this issue has been a quieter matter of negotiation and collaboration.

The story of farm chemicals in Iowa also illustrates the limits of civic environmentalism. Iowa now faces a turning point. Although sales of fertilizers based on chemical nitrogen have decreased by about 15 percent, the environmental problems caused by agricultural chemicals have not yet been solved. Some Iowa farmers have cut back their use of chemicals, but others still use large amounts, especially of pesticides. Perhaps Iowa agriculture will move to a path of sustainable development, where economic and environmental goals can both be achieved on a large scale. However, the immediate future of state efforts to promote sustainable agriculture is unclear. Several of the projects started in 1986-1987 have been completed, and an important source of funds for such programs is disappearing. Should Iowa continue its nonregulatory approach? If so, someone must assemble a political coalition to restore funds for these programs. If that does not happen, one might conclude that Iowa's nonregulatory, collaborative approach to sustainable agriculture will not pay off in the long run. Is regulation the next step for Iowa?

David Osterberg and Paul Johnson, legislators who sponsored the 1987 act, say that Iowa is on the right path. "Regulations do not make sense until most people are doing what you want them to do," says Osterberg.[5] "I think we are doing things in the right order," adds Johnson.[6]

GETTING THE ISSUE ON THE AGENDA

Environmentalists have long been concerned about the effects of chemicals on wildlife and human health. Rachel Carson's *Silent Spring*, which received wide public attention in the early 1960s, presented evidence that accumulations of DDT were causing serious reproductive problems in insects and birds. Also in the 1960s, Barry Commoner expressed concern about the buildup of farm chemicals in rivers in Illinois. However, for many years, both farmers and the agricultural experts at Iowa State University assumed that the chemicals used most widely in Iowa would not contaminate drinking water, if they were applied properly. Although herbicides like atrazine killed weeds in cornfields, experts told farmers that atrazine did not accumulate in the soil or water because it quickly broke down into harmless compounds. It might not be wise to rinse pesticide containers next to a well used for drinking water, or to drink from a stream running through a field that had just been sprayed, especially if a quick rain shower might have washed chemicals into the stream. However, the risk of nonpoint pollution by farm chemicals, arising from widespread application and general filtration into groundwater or runoff into streams, seemed nonexistent.

Confidence in farm chemicals began to break down at the end of the 1970s. In 1979, aldicarb was discovered in wells near potato farms on Long Island. Soon after, atrazine was found in dozens of drinking wells owned by farmers and municipalities in Iowa; obviously, it did not break down as quickly as the experts had thought. About the same time, milk processors in eastern Iowa began telling farmers that their milk contained excessive amounts of nitrates, which might be coming from chemical fertilizers.

First Steps by Agency Bureaucrats

When the first evidence of farm chemicals in groundwater appeared in Iowa, several state agencies quickly focused on the problem, centering their attention on the karst region of the northeastern part of the state. This area is relatively hilly, with thin soils over a layer of fractured limestone. In many places, water that soaks into the soil dissolves the limestone, causing the surface to collapse in sinkholes. Surface water flows into the sinkholes, then into aquifers that feed springs in the valley bottoms. Chemicals were detected both in wells and in the springs.

Several people and agencies in the area were concerned about groundwater quality. The manager of a state fish hatchery that gets its water from springs suspected that something in the water was hurting the fish. A local soil and water conservation district was concerned about the contamination of wells. The state was preparing a regional water quality plan, with funding from EPA and support from the U.S. Soil Conservation Service, pursuant to section 208 of the Clean Water Act. Usually such studies focused on the pollution of rivers and streams by sediment or surface runoff, but in response to concerns voiced at public hearings, this study focused on groundwater.

When chemicals were detected in the area, the problems were first thought to be local and caused by the unique geology. That is, people assumed that the contaminated water had traveled quickly through the aquifer from a nearby sinkhole to the spring or well. However, when Bernie Hoyer, George Hallberg, and others at the Iowa Geological Survey looked closely at available data, they found that some of the contaminated wells were far from sinkholes. It appeared that the chemicals might be traveling long distances in underground aquifers and were not breaking down into harmless components during the process. This raised the possibility that much of Iowa's groundwater might become contaminated by agricultural chemicals, even outside the karst region.

In 1981, eight agencies pooled resources for a close look at the Big Springs watershed, where they hoped to pin down the causes and extent of the problem. Much of the research was conducted by the Iowa Geological Survey, with funding from the U.S. Soil Conservation Service, the EPA, and the state water quality program. In addition, several federal and state agencies provided technical support and services. A year of work in the Big Springs basin convinced the participants that groundwater in the basin was contaminated. To pursue the work further, the agencies created the Ad Hoc Karst Committee.[7]

Many of the key participants in the Ad Hoc Karst Committee are still active players, and the direction that the committee took set the tone for later legislation. (The players, a chronology of events, and key programs are listed in Tables 4-1, 4-2, and 4-3, respectively.) An effort was made to bring all interested public agencies into the group, including researchers from the Iowa Geological Survey; regulators from the state water quality program, and occasionally from EPA; state and federal agencies that promote soil conservation; the U.S. Agricultural Stabilization and Conservation Service, which manages federal farm price support programs; and the Cooperative Extension Service, which is based at Iowa State University and is responsible for educational activities. The Iowa Farm Bureau Federation and the Iowa Fertilizer and Chemicals Association (IFCA), which is the trade association for dealers who sell chemicals, were also invited; the IFCA came regularly.

As Hallberg explains, from the start the Ad Hoc Committee tried to avoid disagreements over turf. "Everyone put their resources on the table, and we tried to identify gaps and come up with a coordinated plan and agree on points of authority." [8] In taking this approach, the group could draw on longstanding friendships and working relationships. For example, Hallberg had worked with committee members from the extension service on preparing soil maps in the early 1970s. The committee was cochaired by two officials who were seen to be neutral parties, because they would not be recipients of grants for studying the problem and would not be called on to design a regulatory response. One cochair represented the local water conservancy district in northeast Iowa, and the other cochair was the director of agricultural programs for the extension service, which would become active only when it was clear what could be told to farmers about how to avoid polluting the groundwater.

Reaching Out for Federal Help

From the start, the group aggressively sought attention and support for its efforts, and in the classic pattern of environmental policy, turned to the federal level for help. In Washington, as in Iowa, officials were eager to learn more about the extent of chemical pollution in the groundwater. George Hallberg recalls: "EPA and USDA [U.S. Department of Agriculture] often invited us to Washington to present the Iowa perspective.

TABLE 4-1

KEY PARTICIPANTS IN THE IOWA CASE

Legislators	Rep. Paul Johnson, Decorah
	Rep. David Osterberg, Mount Vernon
	Rep. Ralph Rosenberg, Ames
State Agency Officials	George Hallberg and Bernie Hoyer, senior geologists, Iowa Geological Survey, Iowa Department of Natural Resources
	Darrell McAllister, chief, and Ubbo Agena, environmental scientist, Surface and Groundwater Protection Bureau, Iowa Department of Natural Resources
	Jim Gulliford, director, Division of Soil Conservation, Department of Agriculture and Land Stewardship
Iowa State University	Vivian Jennings, associate director (until 1985), Iowa Cooperative Extension Service (ICES)
	Jerry DeWitt, associate director (since 1985), ICES
	Jerry Miller, ICES
	Dennis Keeney, director, Aldo Leopold Center for Sustainable Agriculture
	Fred Blackmer, professor of agronomy
	Steve Padgitt, professor of sociology

(Continued on next page)

They were hungry for solid technical information. I always took advantage of the occasion to talk to people. They usually said, 'This is great stuff, but I don't have any money. See so-and-so down the hall.' " [9]

Hallberg was receiving a practical lesson in the politics of groundwater at the federal level. As he was finding out, many federal agencies had an interest in groundwater but few had significant resources to do anything about it, and none had direct authority for the pollution of groundwater by agricultural chemicals. A 1983 study found 44 groundwater programs in the U.S. Department of Interior, and a 1987 study found 270 programs within the EPA.[10] For groundwater there was only

TABLE 4-1 *(CONTINUED)*

Federal Officials	Lyle Assell, assistant state conservationist, U.S. Soil Conservation Service
	Julie Elfving, nonpoint source program coordinator, Region VII Office, U.S. Environmental Protection Agency
Agribusiness	Winton Etchen, executive vice president (until 1989), Iowa Fertilizer and Chemical Association (IFCA)
	Dan Frieberg, executive vice president (since 1989), IFCA
	Iowa Farm Bureau Federation
	Dow Chemical Company
	Monsanto Company
	Ciba-Geigy Corporation
Iowa Environmentalists	Lyle Cruzen, Sierra Club
	Cindy Hildebrand, Audubon Council
	Judy Hoffman, League of Women Voters
	Duane Sand, Iowa National Heritage Foundation

a disorganized group of program offices and specialists, only a few of which had resources to share.

Groundwater is the end of the line for many pollutants. For example, scrubbers at electrical generating stations collect pollutants from smokestacks, and the ash is sent to landfills. If the landfills leak, the poisons that would have been in the air end up in the groundwater. Similarly, municipal sewage plants remove pollutants from wastewater. But several pollutants are concentrated in sewage sludge, and if the sludge is dumped on the land, these pollutants may leak into groundwater.

TABLE 4-2

CHRONOLOGY OF THE IOWA CASE
EPA Activities and Other Federal-Level Events

1984   EPA publishes initial groundwater strategy.
        Initial grants under section 106 of Clean Water Act to prepare groundwater
        strategies.
1985   First farm bill to require soil conservation as a condition of receiving price
        supports.
1986   Publication of National Research Council report on groundwater.
1987   Publication of National Groundwater Policy Forum Report.
1990   First farm bill to include regulatory activities (concerning soil erosion) for U.S.
        Soil and Water Conservation Service.
        President's Water Quality Initiative.
1991   EPA publishes groundwater strategy and pesticide and groundwater
        strategy.

Iowa Initiatives
1974   Pesticides first detected in groundwater in Iowa.
1978   Iowa Geological Survey starts research in Northeast Iowa on farm
        chemicals.
1981   Northeast Iowa River Basin Study starts.

(Continued on next page)

Federal laws directly address the contamination of groundwater by toxic wastes, nuclear wastes, and landfills. Several federal laws also touch on the phenomenon of agricultural chemicals that find their way to drinking water supplies via groundwater or surface flow. However, the legal framework for farm chemicals, and other nonpoint sources, is full of gaps, and no regulatory program addresses the problem directly.

For example, the Clean Water Act provides federal support for state planning and research activities directed toward nonpoint pollution, such as the pollution that might be caused by the application of chemicals to crops. The 1987 amendments to the Clean Water Act required states to submit plans to manage nonpoint pollution, but the amendments did not state that the plans must be implemented. The act may

TABLE 4-2 *(CONTINUED)*

1984	Formation of Ad Hoc Karst Committee; later called the Iowa Consortium on Agriculture and Groundwater Quality.
1985	In state water plan, legislature requires report on groundwater by January 1987.
1986	Big Spring Demonstration Project starts with partial funds.
	Des Moines *Register* runs six-part series on groundwater.
	Legislature establishes Agriculture Energy Management Advisory Council (AEMAC).
	Integrated Farm Management Demonstration Project established by AEMAC.
1987	Groundwater Protection Act.
1988	Water Protection Projects and Practices Act.
	Last meeting of the consortium.
1989	Department of Natural Resources report asks for authority to enforce standards; legislature fails to act.
	Creation of Resource Enhancement and Protection Act.
	Secretary of Agriculture and Land Stewardship cuts atrazine use.
1990	Energy Efficiency Act.
1992	Oil overcharge funds run out; funding for nonregulatory programs declines.

give EPA authority to regulate discharges to groundwater—this has been litigated with mixed results—but EPA has not pushed the point.[11] In 1984, EPA published its first groundwater policy statement, and since 1985 the agency has provided funds to protect groundwater. However, the 1984 policy focused on research and classification rather than on mandating specific steps that states must take to protect groundwater from contamination by farm chemicals.

The Safe Drinking Water Act also touches on groundwater issues. It requires that the EPA and state governments ensure that public water supplies are free of dangerous amounts of chemicals. Under this act, EPA sets standards for maximum acceptable levels of agricultural chemicals in drinking water. However, there were no standards for many chemicals

TABLE 4-3

KEY PROGRAMS AND STATUTES IN THE IOWA CASE

Big Spring Basin Demonstration Project, 1986-1992
Integrated Farm Management Demonstration Project, 1986-1992
Iowa Groundwater Act of 1987
Aldo Leopold Center for Sustainable Agriculture, Iowa State University, 1988-present
Model Farms Demonstration Project, 1989-1993
Water Protection Projects and Practices, 1989-present
Resource Enhancement and Protection Act, 1989-present

that are widely used in Iowa—for example, there was no standard for atrazine until 1982. EPA also has the authority to designate wellhead protection areas and aquifers that are "sole sources" for drinking water. EPA provides funds to protect these areas, and no federal agency is allowed to support projects that would damage these aquifers; but once again EPA lacks clear authority to prescribe management practices.

There are federal regulatory statutes that apply to sources of contamination other than farm chemicals, such as leaking underground storage tanks and toxic waste dumps. The Federal Insecticide, Fungicide, and Rodenticide Act (FIFRA) is also regulatory. It requires that pesticides be registered and labeled to protect workers who handle the pesticides and consumers who might eat vegetables with traces of pesticide. The EPA bureau that administers FIFRA may have the legal authority to consider the pollution of groundwater when it registers pesticides and decides what information must be written on the label about using a chemical. However, until recently this bureau has generally focused on food safety and the proper handling of chemicals, not on water pollution. Also, the bureau lacks a mechanism to ensure that farmers use chemicals as directed on the label; farmers and independent firms that apply pesticides are merely registered. FIFRA does not address fertilizers.

Thus, when George Hallberg went to Washington, he could find many people who were interested in Big Spring, and a few with money for studies and demonstrations, but no one with the clear authority to design a policy response for the problem.

As it became clear that farm chemicals might be polluting groundwater outside the karst region and that there was widespread interest in this possibility, the Ad Hoc Committee changed its name to the Iowa Consortium on Agriculture and Groundwater Quality and began to talk about solutions. In keeping with the collaborative spirit of the group, and in light of the strong orientation of the extension service and many other participants toward voluntary methods like education and cost sharing, the group steered away from regulatory answers. The consortium's response took the form of a proposal for a $6.8 million Big Spring Demonstration Project, which would include research on best management practices for farming to reduce contamination of the aquifer, education of farmers, and evaluation of how education and research influence the attitudes and behavior of farmers. With state and federal grants for some of these activities, the project began a projected seven-year life in 1986.

THE LEGISLATURE ACTS

Three years after state agencies formed the Ad Hoc Committee, the Iowa legislature first addressed the issue of groundwater pollution. Over the next five years, the result was a series of bills and appropriations. The legislators who pushed these efforts worked closely with the state and federal agencies and built on the base they had laid.

The Leaders and Philosophy
That Drove Iowa Legislation

The legislative process affords many opportunities for individuals and groups to influence outcomes, so it would be inaccurate to say that any one individual was responsible for Iowa's legislation. But more than any other legislator, Paul Johnson focused his attention on agricultural chemicals. Johnson was at the center of legislative debates about chemicals for six years. His background and ideas had a strong influence on Iowa's policies on this issue.

Johnson is a farmer from the karst region who lives about fifty miles north of Big Spring. He is neither a typical farmer nor a typical legislator. He grew up in a town in South Dakota and had studied natural resources management at the University of Michigan. He had a deep interest in ecology but decided, before writing his doctoral dissertation, that he wanted to farm instead.

> At Michigan, we talked a lot about ecology and the environment, but only with respect to wild lands. No one was looking at the ecology of farmland. I decided that if I wanted to work on ecology and agriculture, I had to become a farmer first. So my wife and I did a systematic search of places that we might settle, looking for a town in the Midwest where we would want to raise our family, and we decided on Decorah. We like its hills, and the proximity to the Mississippi River, and the fact that it has a local college, which adds a lot to the town.[12]

In 1984, after more than a decade of farming, Johnson was certain that agriculture in Iowa could remain quite successful with the use of fewer chemicals. He decided to run for the legislature to work toward the goal of reducing chemical use. Although he was a Democrat in a Republican district, he won easily. One of his first moves upon arriving at the state capitol was to propose a one dollar per pound tax on pesticides, which would raise the price by about one-third.

Johnson became a friend of Don Avenson, who also came from northeast Iowa and was the powerful speaker of the House. Avenson told Johnson that to propose a pesticide tax would be political suicide. The bill did die quickly, but Johnson persisted. He became a close friend of, and during the session shared a room with, David Osterberg, an outspoken liberal who came from eastern Iowa. Osterberg had become interested in groundwater partly because his hometown had a small Superfund site, with contaminated groundwater. Ralph Rosenberg, another liberal, who represented the hometown of Iowa's land grant university (Ames), also became interested in farm chemicals; as chair of the House Committee on Environment and Energy, he helped arrange an interim committee to study the issue of farm chemicals and groundwater after the 1985 and 1986 legislative sessions.

As they began working on the issue, Osterberg, Johnson, and Rosenberg met the members of the Consortium on Agriculture and Groundwater Quality. Together, and with increasing support from Speaker Avenson, they built a coalition with other legislators who were interested in farm chemicals and other sources of groundwater contamination, such as hazardous wastes, underground storage tanks, and solid waste landfills. The coalition of legislators and entrepreneurial members of the consortium, which began to emerge in 1986, was the driving force behind legislation for several years.

From the start, Johnson, Osterberg, and Rosenberg decided not to push for a regulatory strategy. They did look closely at the experience of Wisconsin, where in 1984 the legislature had adopted a regulatory groundwater program. Wisconsin established a two-tiered system of standards for groundwater quality. The top tier is equal to the levels set by EPA under the Safe Drinking Water Act. The law provides for regulatory action before water quality becomes degraded to the point of being dangerous to health. So regulators set lower preventive action limits, usually at 10 percent, 20 percent, or 50 percent of the EPA level. In areas where concentrations have reached the lower limits, state agencies have authority to restrict the use of agricultural chemicals.

Johnson and Osterberg decided against the Wisconsin approach. There were practical reasons to think that a regulatory regime would be difficult to impose. For example, in 1985 there was a great deal of uncertainty about the extent of groundwater pollution. Iowa had not yet completed an inventory of water quality in rural wells. If a chemical were discovered in a watershed, a regulatory statute might allow agencies to restrict the use of the chemical in that area but not in an adjacent county, where the geology might be quite different. However, farmers from the contaminated watershed might easily drive to the next county to buy the chemical. To enforce restrictions, the state would have to hire people to monitor the purchase and use of chemicals. Since Iowa has about 100,000 farmers, the enforcement staff might have to be quite large.

In addition to such practical concerns, Osterberg and Johnson had deeper, philosophical reasons for rejecting a regulatory approach. Johnson feels that setting standards—so many parts per billion of a substance in drinking water as the acceptable level of risk—is the wrong way to approach the problem.

Some want to focus on how much pollution hurts people. But we do not have to answer that question now. We do know that we don't have to farm the way we do. Theoretically, there is lots of room to reduce the application of chemicals without sacrificing productivity, although we do not know exactly how to go about making that happen. It seems obvious that, if we put our minds to it, we can find a better way to farm. At least we should start there.[13]

Johnson was echoing the ideas of one of the two schools of thought after Earth Day—the school that was uninterested in passing new federal statutes and believed the answer to environmental problems lay in changes in attitudes and lifestyle.

David Osterberg's starting point was different, but quite compatible. As he sees it, regulation will not work until most people are already doing things the right way. "When new ideas come along, some people adopt them quickly; the majority come along a little later; and a few hold out until the end. This is how farmers will change their use of chemicals. It does not make sense to regulate until there is already substantial compliance. We are not there yet." [14]

In addition to their unfavorable attitudes about regulation in this case, Johnson and Osterberg agreed on a second idea that helped shape Iowa's policies. They thought it appropriate to trust government, not as a single entity, but as a collection of voices. Osterberg explains that when one is trying to change citizens' perceptions and behavior, it is more effective if citizens hear from lots of different people. So he has made it a matter of practice to build institutions inside state government, and often within state universities, to express new ideas.

As Johnson remembers it, in 1984 the land grant system, including Iowa State University, county extension agents, and other related activities, were not dealing with the important question of alternative ways of farming. "All that research, all those bright people, but very few asking the right questions." Furthermore, as he saw it, "You cannot make people change without trusting them. We have made government the enemy, but it is not. People in the bureaucracy are the only ones who are working for the common good." [15]

These ideas meshed neatly with the ideas that motivated the key members of the consortium. As explained by Jerry DeWitt, who was active in the karst region in the early 1980s and is now involved as the top official in the Iowa Extension Service for agriculture, "We are the people who were raising a clamor about the environment in the 1960s and 1970s. We did not have influence then, but we had zeal and ideals. Now we have power, and we are doing things." [16]

1986: The Agricultural
Energy Management Advisory Council

In Johnson's first year, there was little legislative action about groundwater or farm chemicals. But steps were taken that were important for the future. One step was a change in the name and the legislative authorization for the Department of Agriculture.

The top priority of Gov. Terry E. Branstad, a Republican first elected in 1982 and still in office when this book was written, was the reorganization of state government from dozens of independent agencies into a much smaller number of departments. One of the agencies slated for elimination was the Department of Soil Conservation, which together with the U.S. Soil Conservation Service provided technical support to local soil conservation districts as well as education and cost sharing for on-farm improvements that would reduce soil erosion, such as the construction of terraces. The question arose: Where should the division be placed? Inside the Department of Agriculture, which promoted agriculture through marketing programs? Or inside the Department of Natural Resources, comprising environmental regulators and the division of fish and game, which wanted farmers to reduce erosion so that more rivers could support fish? Johnson's answer was immediate: inside the Department of Agriculture, the agency the farmers would listen to and trust. However, he wanted it clear that the division would promote good land stewardship, so he sat down with Jim Gulliford, the division head and a member of the consortium, and wrote the legislative statement of objectives, including the charge to "encourage a relationship between people and the land that recognizes land as a resource to be managed in a manner that avoids irreparable harm." [17] The department also received a new name, the Department of Agriculture and Land Stewardship. This step was mostly symbolic, but other steps were more concrete. In 1985, the consortium prepared its seven-year plan for the Big Spring Project. In addition, the group began preparing to take the issue statewide.

Two studies of public water supplies, in 1985 and 1986, found evidence of contamination outside the karst region. In the Little Sioux Valley of western Iowa, 42 percent of the public water supply wells tested had detectable concentrations of pesticides.[18] George Hallberg spent a month during the summer of 1985 at the extension service offices at Iowa State University assembling a package that would include several university programs and departments in a multifaceted statewide program of education for farmers, demonstration projects, monitoring, and evaluation. The package was a typical consortium product—supplying a role for everyone involved and funding for many.

Then Hallberg, joined by Johnson, Osterberg, and several others, went looking for funds. They soon heard about oil overcharge funds, which had been collected by the U.S. Department of Energy after a federal court ruled that Exxon had violated federal price ceilings and should compensate the public. By federal law, the funds were available for such public purposes as operating state offices of energy conservation, insulating public schools and other public buildings, and weatherizing homes of poor people.

In 1986, the Iowans pressed their case for the funds, arguing successfully that fertilizer was made from natural gas, that pesticides were a by-product of refining petroleum, and that the consortium's program would save energy by encouraging farmers to use fewer chemicals. Osterberg and Sue Mullins, a Republican state legislator from a district with groundwater quality problems, wrote a letter to the secretary of energy, asking if oil overcharge funds could be used for the consortium's programs. When the answer was noncommittal, Hallberg and the director of the state energy program prepared a proposal and visited federal offices in Washington. Governor Branstad's office also contacted the Department of Energy and sought support from the Iowa Farm Bureau Federation for using oil overcharge funds for groundwater programs. The governor, who was up for reelection, announced that he would see that the U.S. Department of Energy accepted the proposal. The legislature created an Agricultural Energy Management Advisory Council to supervise the use of oil overcharge dollars in the Integrated Farm Management Demonstration Program designed by Hallberg and others. The 1986 legislation passed with little controversy; technically it amounted to no more than a way to manage federal dollars. However, the legislation allowed the first big expansion of the consortium's activities.

The 1987 Groundwater Protection Act

Although oil overcharge funds were fueling more activities, the legislature had not set out policies about groundwater contamination. In the process of articulating such a policy in 1987, there was a fierce battle in the legislature.

The story of the 1987 act began quietly, when in 1985 the legislature had enacted a state water plan. The plan dealt with surface water but also included a little noted provision that the Department of Natural Resources should submit a strategy for groundwater. During 1986, Bernie Hoyer of the Iowa Geological Survey spent several months in the Department of Natural Resources headquarters office, writing the strategy. Several other members of the consortium kept in close touch with the process.

Meanwhile, public interest in groundwater pollution was building. The Department of Natural Resources held small group meetings to discuss groundwater with citizens, and the legislative interim committee held public hearings. Congress was debating—and ultimately failing to pass—groundwater legislation. Closer to home, the *Des Moines Register* and the *Cedar Rapids Gazette*, two widely read newspapers, ran front-page series on the pollution of groundwater by farm chemicals. The *Register* series described pollution in the Big Spring Basin and reported on birth defects in Australia and on the death of an infant in South Dakota that had resulted from nitrates in drinking water. The series reported that chemical companies claimed that their chemicals were not harmful; scientists admitted that their understanding of the health effects of chemical pollution was incomplete. But the *Register* also printed an alarming account of a "farm family worried about drinking others' chemicals" and ran a feature with tips on buying bottled water.[19]

Meanwhile, the consortium arranged for an Iowa State University professor to survey public opinion about groundwater pollution. He found that many farmers were worried that farm chemicals were contaminating their own drinking water; the survey showed that 86 percent of all Iowans thought that groundwater contamination was a serious problem and would support steps to resolve the problem. Only 11 percent dismissed groundwater pollution as unimportant.

The strategy that Hoyer and others prepared for the legislature did not focus only on farm chemicals. The report described how leaking underground storage tanks, household hazardous wastes, and businesses that produced hazardous wastes all contributed to the threat to groundwater. As legislators and consortium members look back at the debate in 1987, they stress the scope of the debate. The message was that everyone, not just farmers, was to blame for part of the problem. And everyone was at risk. This helped make groundwater protection an issue of general public welfare. Legislators could tell their constituents, "We are not picking on farmers, or industry, or anyone else. This is a problem that everyone is causing." Ralph Rosenberg, chair of the committee that developed the bill in the House, created four subcommittees, each chaired by a different legislator, as a way to build broad support and to tackle all sources of contamination.

However, the debate in the legislature was dominated by the issue of farm chemicals. The Iowa Fertilizer and Chemical Association (IFCA) attacked the groundwater report, and the legislation that would implement it, head on. Winton Etchen, its executive vice president and top full-time employee, argued that there was no firm evidence that farm chemicals were causing health problems. An Iowa State professor who was a member of the IFCA board argued that "it is my scientific opinion that . . . normal use does not ordinarily cause measurable contamination of wells." [20] As the legislature debated a bill based on the strategy, IFCA lobbied aggressively. In addition, every week the large national chemical companies flew highly paid (or at least well dressed) lobbyists into Des Moines to attend hearings and look for ways to deflect the legislation.

The battle became quite bitter. The Iowa State professor on the IFCA board was not allowed to testify, and Sue Mullins, a Republican legislator who was an active supporter of the groundwater bill, filed a formal complaint against Etchen. The complaint charged that Etchen had distributed a leaflet that misrepresented her position as favoring the elimination of all farm chemicals. The debate was a classic hard-nosed confrontation, typical of fights about major environmental legislation. But three features were atypical.

The first atypical feature was that the bill did not call for the regulation of agricultural chemicals, although it included tighter controls on the registration of applicators and registration of agricultural drainage wells.* The central feature was instead a wide array of taxes and fees—on pesticides, chemical fertilizer, dealers of farm chemicals, household hazardous waste retailers, underground storage tanks, and solid waste disposal. As originally proposed by the Department of Natural Resources, this revenue was to support $230 million of programs over ten years to protect groundwater, including expanded education and technical assistance for farmers, research, monitoring, and evaluation.[21] As enacted, the package provided for between $38 and $46 million of programs over five years and also created the Aldo Leopold Center for Sustainable Agriculture at Iowa State University. The center was to conduct research, and in cooperation with the extension service, to educate farmers about all aspects of alternative farming practices, including new ways of cultivating and rotating crops as well as reduced use of chemicals. The center was named after an Iowan who was a distinguished scientist, an early spokesman for environmental protection, and an advocate of wilderness preservation. There would also be centers on other aspects of groundwater pollution at the University of Iowa and the University of Northern Iowa.

The second atypical feature is closely related. In legislative battles, environmentalists often ask for tough numerical standards on pollution, and industry protests that the standards are too extreme or should be dropped altogether. However, this time, since the environmentalist legislators were not asking for regulation of the use of farm chemicals, they did not push for standards. Instead, they supported a provision favoring nondegradation of the state's groundwater. This was a clear statement of principle; but without standards, there was no way to enforce it. On the other side, IFCA vigorously defended standards. Since it held the position that the levels of contamination were so low as not to be worth attention, the IFCA was confident that any standard that would be politically feasible in Iowa would have no practical effect.

---

*The legislation did include significant authority to regulate other sources of groundwater contamination, such as leaking underground storage tanks and solid waste landfills. Also, a companion bill included regulatory authority to prevent pollution of groundwater by hazardous waste.

There were two additional reasons for industry's support of standards and environmentalists' opposition to them. First, the executive branch was controlled by a Republican governor, who had appointed to the Environmental Protection Commission several members who were seen as friends of industry. Second, other legislation provided that the state could not adopt any environmental standards that were tougher than federal standards, which were nonexistent.

The third atypical feature was the peripheral role of environmental groups and of the most powerful spokesmen for the industry that was causing the pollution. The most important nonparticipant was the Iowa Farm Bureau Federation. It is an immensely powerful force in Iowa politics. It boasts 120,000 members, more members than there are farmers in the state. This is partly because the Farm Bureau sells insurance and counts everyone who buys insurance as a member. It has a large staff of lobbyists and in 1988 had the second largest political action committee in the state.[22]

The Farm Bureau was not entirely inactive. It lobbied strongly and successfully against proposals to prohibit agricultural drainage wells. (These wells are common in north central Iowa, where the soils are particularly rich but become waterlogged unless they are drained. Farmers have constructed tile channels under the fields, which lead to wells that drain water through bedrock and into deep aquifers. Some environmentalists call this mainlining chemicals.) The Farm Bureau also pushed for a provision explicitly stating that a farmer is not legally liable for polluting groundwater if chemicals are applied in accordance with instructions on the label. With this point won, the Farm Bureau was publicly neutral about the bill, if quietly uneasy, especially about the imposition of fees. Following its lead, commodity groups, such as the corn growers and the soybean growers, were also neutral.

In short, by meeting key demands of the most powerful farm groups, adopting a strictly nonregulatory approach, and riding a wave of media stories (which emphasized that everyone shared the blame for polluting groundwater), Johnson, Osterberg, Rosenberg, and their allies had isolated out-of-state chemical manufacturers and the in-state dealers. It was the public against the chemical industry. As Winton Etchen said later: "In the closing days of the legislature, it was us against the world and we did not come out looking too good."[23]

Another group noticeable for its low-profile role was the environmentalists. The leadership in the struggle clearly came from the six legislators, with support from the consortium members. The environmental movement was not a strong force in Iowa. The only people available to lobby the groundwater bill on a continuing basis were two part-time volunteers—Cindy Hildebrand of the Audubon Society and Judy Hoffman of the League of Women Voters. These two were at the capitol every day, and others joined them at times. Their role, however, was not to lead the charge but to help the six legislators keep track of events. For example, after the House passed its version of the bill, the more conservative Senate adopted a long list of amendments. Hildebrand attended the committee meeting at which this happened and stayed up all night analyzing the amendments. The next morning, she gave the package to Johnson and Rosenberg, who decided where to compromise and where to hold firm. Thus the environmentalists acted primarily as staff to the six legislators, rather than as leaders of citizen groups. The key decisions were made by the legislators.

The debate came to a dramatic climax. Paul Johnson had a mild heart attack and went to a hospital for a short stay. In March, just before the bill was passed, 400 IFCA members—a fifth of all members—came to the state capitol and filled the rotunda, buttonholing legislators. After the Senate passed a watered-down bill, a conference committee met. After lengthy negotiations, one of the final points of difference was the question of standards. The Senate members were firmly committed to some kind of standards. The House members were opposed. When this point could not be resolved, Avenson called for a break. When the committee reconvened, Avenson proposed a study of standards. Johnson and Rosenberg objected loudly. Turning to the senators, Avenson offered to force the package through the House, over objections by Johnson and Rosenberg, if the Senate would concede other points. Impressed, the senators agreed and the deal was done.

Further Legislative Actions
in 1988, 1989, and 1990

The Iowa Groundwater Protection Act of 1987 has not been amended significantly. However, the legislature did consider the issue of standards once more, and it has added to the funds for nonregulatory programs.

In 1988, the legislature fine tuned the act, for example, by removing the requirement that retailers who sell small quantities of chemical fertilizers and pesticides, such as lawn and garden stores, report their sales. The chemical industry pushed for wholesale amendments but was unsuccessful. In 1989, the Department of Natural Resources completed its study of standards and suggested that it be given the authority to create a two-tier system like Wisconsin's. If the lower-tier levels were exceeded, the department suggested that it be given authority to ban a chemical and to ask the manufacturer of the chemical to come up with a plan and also to finance implementation of the plan. There would be no possibility of any financial burden on farmers, dealers, or taxpayers.[24] There was a vigorous debate about standards at public hearings organized by the Department of Natural Resources, but the legislature took no action on the department's recommendation.

In 1988, 1989, and 1990, the legislature created new programs and added to the pool of funding. One important step was shoring up funding for the Leopold Center. When the revenues from fees on chemicals were below expectations, general funds supplemented the center's budget. In addition, the legislature created new programs that extended activities into all parts of Iowa and allowed additional organizations to become involved. In 1988, the legislature created a new program for the Division of Soil Conservation, to provide cost sharing for farmers who invested in improvements that would reduce sedimentation or chemical pollution of ground or surface waters. These funds were available to local soil and water conservation districts. In 1989, Governor Branstad asked the department to design a program, similar to the Big Spring Project, for other parts of the state.* George Hallberg and other members of the consortium designed the Model Farms Demonstration Project, which created five new multifaceted programs. By 1991, the Cooperative Extension Service had the full-time equivalent of twenty-two people working on various efforts that were explicitly designed to

---

*The Integrated Farm Demonstration Project (IFDP) was actually the third generation after the Big Spring Project. The second generation was the Butler County Project, which was similar to Big Spring but located in north central Iowa, where the problem was not fractured limestone but agricultural drainage wells. IFDP was modeled on both the Big Spring and Butler County projects.

reduce the use of farm chemicals, including eight on campus, eleven at field projects, and four media specialists.[25]

In 1989, the Democratic-controlled legislature enacted the Resource Enhancement and Protection (REAP) Act, a multipurpose environmental program to be funded from lottery proceeds. A portion of REAP moneys went to groundwater programs. In 1990, 1991, and 1992, as the state ran into ever more serious budget problems, Governor Branstad proposed cutting REAP and, in 1991, diverting the fees on farm chemicals to the state's general fund. Democrats in the legislature stalled most of the cuts in REAP. Both Republican and Democratic legislators resisted the diversion of fees on farm chemicals. The idea was pushed off the table for good when fishermen mobilized to oppose *any* diversion of Department of Natural Resources fees, particularly their fishing license fees, which are a major source of revenue for the state's hatchery, habitat enhancement, and wildlife management activities.

DECISION TIME FOR IOWA

It is difficult to estimate the exact amount that Iowa has invested in research, education, and demonstration, because so many programs were funded and because both federal and state-supported programs with broader purposes were tilted toward the goals of reducing the use of farm chemicals. The total investment may have been as high as $10 million per year at the peak.

The peak has passed, at least for the present. As in other states, the recession and new federal mandates have squeezed state budgets. In addition, the oil overcharge funds have now been almost exhausted. The oil overcharge funds were to be spread over five years, and as the federal government deregulated oil prices, no more overcharge funds were collected. By the summer of 1992, only small amounts remained for completing the evaluations and final reports of the Big Spring Demonstration Project, the Integrated Farm Management Demonstration Project, the Model Farms Demonstration Project, and similar activities. Some new federal funds have appeared to replace the oil overcharge dollars. New sources include EPA funding for nonpoint source water protection projects under Section 319 of the Clean Water Act and U.S. Department of Agriculture funds from President Bush's Water Quality

Initiative, which supported projects like those in Iowa. However, these new funds are smaller, and there are many claimants. It is clearly time to take stock of what has been accomplished and to reassess Iowa's policy and funding strategies.

Accomplishments

There are several ways to measure the accomplishments of Iowa's nonregulatory programs—such as activities completed, attitudes changed, new farming practices, and cleaner water. From the citizen's point of view, the bottom line might be water quality: Can farmers now drink water from their wells, and can townspeople trust public water supplies? Unfortunately, this question is not easy to answer because long-term data about water quality are so difficult to obtain. Furthermore, the data that do exist are not particularly encouraging.

For example, pesticide levels at the Big Spring Basin dropped steadily for several years after 1985, but in 1991 and 1992 concentrations increased. No one is quite sure why. Perhaps pesticides that had accumulated in the groundwater remained there during the drought years of 1987-1989 and were flushed out in the abnormally wet years that followed. The picture for nitrates is also confusing. In early 1992, Dennis Keeney of the Leopold Center published a study comparing nitrate levels in the Des Moines River in the 1980s with nitrate levels in 1945, the only year preceding the extensive use of chemical fertilizers when many data on water quality were gathered. The data show that the average concentration of nitrates was about the same in the 1980s as in 1945. Once again, no one is quite sure why. Perhaps more nitrates did flow off the land but have been stored in large masses of algae rather than in the water. Or the explanation may be that once nitrates reach the river, they look the same, whether they came originally from chemical fertilizer, manure, sediment, or plants like hay and soybeans that turn minerals in the soil into nitrates. Perhaps changes are canceling themselves out—as the volume of nitrates moving into the rivers from chemical fertilizer goes up, nitrate levels from manure and hayfields are going down. In 1945, there was less chemical fertilizer but more cattle, more hayfields, and more soil erosion.[26]

The conclusion to be drawn from these ambiguous data is not that

Iowa's efforts have been fruitless. Rather, the data suggest that it may take a long time, measured perhaps in decades, for farm chemicals to wash out of the waters of Iowa.

Another test might be a change in the use of farm chemicals in Iowa. This is the measure that Paul Johnson would use; as explained above, his goal was that farmers might farm differently. The evidence on this point is somewhat clearer. Since 1985, the use of nitrogen-based chemical fertilizers in Iowa has dropped steadily, even though fertilizer has become less expensive.[27] Meanwhile, the use of fertilizer has kept rising in Illinois, Iowa's rival in corn production. However, average yields for corn in Iowa kept pace with yields in Illinois. Translated into dollars, this meant that Iowa farmers spent about $80 million less for fertilizer over the two years of 1989 and 1990, without reducing their income.[28] The story for pesticides and herbicides is less dramatic because it is less clear. As measured in pounds, sales of these chemicals declined in Iowa as in many other states. For example, sales of herbicides for corn dropped by 17.5 percent from 1985 to 1990, and sales of herbicides for soybeans dropped by 25.3 percent.[29] However, the reasons may be that farmers bought smaller amounts of more powerful chemicals and planted fewer acres of corn.

The reduction in the use of nitrogen was uneven. Iowa's various groundwater programs were planned to reach about 2 to 3 percent of Iowa farmers directly. Available data suggest that about half of these farmers reduced their use of nitrogen. Meanwhile, about 40 percent of their neighbors and less than 25 percent of other farmers used less fertilizer.[30]

Changes in Attitudes

Another way to measure the impact of the Groundwater Protection Act, and the options for next steps, is to consider changes in attitudes about farm chemicals. Sometimes in politics, attitudes about a problem and political alignments change more rapidly than the problem itself. This has clearly happened in Iowa on the issue of farm chemicals. The public positions of some of the key participants in the debates of 1987 have shifted dramatically. One might even say that the supporters of the Groundwater Protection Act have won virtually a complete political victory.

The most dramatic shift involves the IFCA. Winton Etchen did not surrender after the 1987 Groundwater Protection Act passed. In the 1988 election campaign, IFCA helped to recruit a primary opponent to Sue Mullins and contributed to opponents of Johnson, Osterberg, Avenson, Rosenberg, and Jack Hatch, another legislator who had worked hard for the groundwater bill. Etchen told the press that IFCA would do whatever it could to defeat the six, and he encouraged IFCA members to work against the legislators. The Farm Bureau also contributed to the campaigns of the opponents of the five Democratic legislators, but this was nothing out of the ordinary, as the bureau usually supported Republicans. On the other side, environmentalists in Washington, D.C., organized a small fundraiser for the legislators who had led the fight for the groundwater bill.

Only one of the six legislators was defeated. Mullins lost the primary to a more conservative Republican, who outspent her five to one and who opposed abortion rights. Mullins says that the groundwater issue was just one of many issues that hurt her in the primary. The conservative Republican who replaced her lost the general election to a Democrat.

Osterberg and Avenson were also hurt somewhat by IFCA's efforts. Osterberg had been unopposed in the previous election, and this time his opponent spent 40 percent more than he did. Osterberg won 55 percent of the vote and is still in the legislature, but he remembers 1988 as a particularly tough race. Avenson also faced a well-financed opponent, and his margin was cut from 65 percent in 1986 to 53 percent in 1988. The other legislators were not hurt by IFCA's efforts. Johnson's margins rose slightly, from 58 percent to 60 percent. The two other legislators, who were from liberal Ames and Des Moines, profited from IFCA's open opposition; it helped them raise money and increased their victory margins.[31]

Etchen did not fare so well. After the election, he was persuaded to resign his position. To replace him, IFCA chose Dan Frieberg, a farmer who had participated in one of the programs funded by the Agricultural Energy Management Advisory Council. By the time Frieberg took over, there was no longer much doubt that atrazine was present in water supplies in many parts of the Midwest. Frieberg took a much more conciliatory line than Etchen on environmental issues.

IFCA publications took a very different tone on environmental issues. For example, the spring 1991 issue of the IFCA newsletter encouraged dealers to inform farmers about a newly developed test to indicate whether a cornfield needed a fresh application of chemical fertilizer in the spring.

The public positions of chemical manufacturers has also changed. For example, in 1989, Ciba-Geigy, the manufacturer of atrazine, encouraged the Iowa secretary of agriculture to reduce allowed amounts of atrazine to be applied. Application rates were cut from 4 pounds per acre to 3 pounds in seventy-seven counties, and to 1.5 pounds in twenty-two counties with sinkholes and agricultural drainage wells. This was less of a sacrifice by Ciba-Geigy than it might appear. Since its patent on atrazine had just expired, other manufacturers were producing the chemical, and Ciba-Geigy was marketing new, patentable products that combined atrazine with other chemicals. Also, with other producers in the field, Ciba-Geigy would not be risking lawsuits by admitting that atrazine was polluting water, because it would be difficult for anyone to prove that the atrazine in a specific well was a Ciba-Geigy product.

Some thought the secretary's ruling did not go far enough. Osterberg was furious that the secretary did not impose tighter restrictions in southern Iowa, where atrazine had been found widely in surface water. Nonetheless, industry had clearly changed its stance from the days when its lobbyists prowled the rotunda of the state capitol echoing Winton Etchen's claim that pesticides did not pollute groundwater.

There have also been important shifts in attitudes at Iowa State University and elsewhere in the agricultural establishment. In 1987, when a legislator told a distinguished professor of agronomy about the proposal to establish a center at Iowa State and name it after Aldo Leopold, the professor asked who Aldo Leopold was. Five years later, the same professor assigned *Sand County Almanac*, Leopold's poetic book on ecology, as required reading for an introductory course. In 1992, Dennis Keeney ran for president of the American Society of Agronomy against a well-known scientist who works for the Tennessee Valley Authority, which has long promoted the use of chemical fertilizers; Keeney won. Paul Johnson has become a member of the National Academy of Science's Board on Agriculture.

The willingness of the IFCA and others to accept the proposition that farm chemicals might be an environmental problem has opened the door to cooperation between the IFCA and its former adversaries. In 1991, the IFCA proposed legislation to clean up groundwater pollution that had been caused by spills on the property of chemical dealers. David Osterberg became an active sponsor of the bill, which would have provided state funds to help subsidize the cleanup. The Farm Bureau opposed the bill because it would have been financed by another tax on chemicals and thus would have ultimately been paid for by farmers. The bill died. However, communications between Osterberg and the IFCA remained open.

For the most part, farm chemicals and groundwater have dropped off the legislative agenda, replaced by other issues. Paul Johnson decided not to run for reelection in 1990 and was defeated when he ran for the state senate in 1992. Ralph Rosenberg, David Osterberg, and other leaders in the 1987 battle turned their attention to other environmental issues. So when the oil overcharge funds began to run out in late 1991, the consortium could not arouse much interest in the legislature. Just before the 1992 session, consortium members tried to use the evidence of declining sales of chemical fertilizer to lobby for new state appropriations to replace the oil overcharge money. Sixteen program managers and Iowa State professors coauthored a report that was released to the press and was featured on the front page of the *Des Moines Register*. Along with the facts about the use of nitrogen, the report included an estimate that for an investment of about $11 million of state and federal money in work on fertilizers, Iowa farmers were saving eight to ten times as much.[32] The report also said that if the state did not replace the oil overcharge money, momentum might be lost. The *Register* reported that scientists felt that nitrogen use could eventually be cut by 40 percent without a reduction in yields.[33]

However, the political reality was that the state could not afford to replace the oil overcharge funds. David Osterberg pushed hard to maintain funding for REAP and to restore staffing to the regulatory programs of the Department of Natural Resources, which had shrunk by over forty positions as a result of repeated hiring freezes and the difficulty of hiring new staff at the state's low pay scale. He says his third priority would have been to replace oil overcharge funds, but there was simply no hope of success, so he did not try.

Unlike legislators, who deal with many issues, the state and federal officials who helped bring the issue of farm chemicals and water quality to public attention are still working on water quality issues. However, among those who had pioneered Iowa's groundwater policies, one sometimes senses a mood of fatigue. In George Hallberg's words, "The issue kind of exploded on us in 1987, and now some of us are rather fried. We have come to a new plateau, and we are concerned that we take the time here to complete things, to write up the reports and be clear about what we have learned." [34]

Although they may be tired, most of the key members of the consortium are still actively involved. The consortium itself has not held formal meetings since 1989, when large funds began to roll into new programs. Members of the consortium explain that the new funds created many opportunities for members to keep in touch through meetings and through publications about the programs. For example, when the Department of Natural Resources or the Division of Soil Conservation considered applications for project funding, the advisory committee that reviewed the proposals included most of the key players from other agencies. Furthermore, a core group of five, including Jerry DeWitt and Jerry Miller from the extension service, George Hallberg of the Iowa Geological Survey, Lyle Assell of the U.S. Soil Conservation Service, and Jim Gulliford of the state Division of Soil Conservation, are close friends and have met for several years on an informal but regular basis to exchange information and discuss possible next steps.

Although the issue has dropped off the legislative agenda, the dealers and chemical manufacturers now admit that chemicals are a problem, and the issue may come up again. After all, as explained above, the problem of water pollution by farm chemicals has not been solved. In the summer of 1992, Dan Frieberg helped to organize an ad hoc task force of agricultural interests that will reexamine the issue. The committee is called the Nutrient Management Task Force. Its members include the Farm Bureau; IFCA; the corn growers and soybean growers; the pork, beef, and poultry associations; the association of grain and feed dealers; a professor from the Iowa State University Department of Agronomy; and a representative of the Iowa Department of Agriculture and Land Stewardship.

The members of the consortium are not included. Their report, published in late 1992, acknowledged the problems created by chemicals, endorsed the consortium's programs, and called for more practical research but explicitly opposed raising taxes on fertilizer.

Next Steps in Iowa

There are at least three possible directions state policy could take on farm chemicals and water quality. One would be to pursue a reinvigorated state-funded program of research, demonstration, and education. Jerry DeWitt, George Hallberg, and others of the consortium say that the next step must be to rev up the effort that began with the 1986 and 1987 acts to reach more farmers and make larger reductions in the use of chemicals. The key would be forging a closer link with dealers. A recent master's thesis at Iowa State University, by a student who was working at the Leopold Center, found that nearly 80 percent of the cooperatives, which comprise 60 percent of IFCA's membership, make less than one-third of their gross sales from farm chemicals.[35] A larger portion of their sales and profits comes from storing grain, selling farm equipment, and other services. This suggests that perhaps the co-ops and other dealers are not unalterably wed to making their profits on sales of chemicals. Perhaps dealers could make profits on selling information about how to use chemicals.

It may not be easy to convert dealers into purveyors of information. For example, consider the matter of testing soil to determine whether farmers should add chemical fertilizer. Many dealers now offer free tests for phosphorus and potassium, as a way to attract customers. However, for nitrogen, most dealers, and also the extension service, calculate the amount of nitrogen to be applied on the basis of the desired yield, rather than on the basis of a soil test, which would indicate how much nitrogen is already in the soil. So dealers would have to add a new service and start charging for soil tests.

There are also technical problems with using soil tests. The usual practice in Iowa is for farmers to apply manure and chemical nitrogen in the fall, after harvest. This means that winter snow and rain may wash some chemicals into streams and groundwater. If there were a way to test soil in the spring, after the corn plants emerge from the soil, farmers could apply smaller amounts of fertilizer, or none at all, depending on how much nitrogen remained in the soil. Over the past decade, with funding from the Iowa Fertilizer and Chemical Association before 1985 and from Big Spring, the Integrated Farm Management Project, and the Leopold Center more recently, Fred Blackmer of Iowa State University adapted a spring soil test for nitrogen. However, the test is not cheap; separate tests must be taken for every ten acres; and farmers are busier in the spring and thus may not have time to make the tests or to apply fertilizer. Furthermore, if the weather is wet after the corn emerges, the fields may be so muddy that equipment cannot get into the fields before the corn grows so tall that fertilizing equipment cannot enter the fields.

Moreover, Blackmer says that the spring nitrogen test can never be widely successful as a purely private sector product. Because of its cost, and because farmers need results very quickly, the only feasible way to use the test is to develop a detailed data base for a large area of multiple farms, using information about soils and historical yields. Then after observing the weather and making spot tests, it would be possible to quickly decide how much each field should be fertilized. Such a system, says Blackmer, would operate much more efficiently if one person did the spring nitrogen tests for an area the size of half a county. This would seem to suggest the need for a large governmental role or for a public-private partnership.

In short, the first possible direction for Iowa's policies on farm chemicals and water quality requires some kind of rearrangement of how dealers and public agencies handle information about the use of farm chemicals. At this point, several experts at Iowa State are studying various technical and economic questions, and some other participants in the consortium are designing programs to experiment with different ways of organizing public and private roles in the farm chemical information business.

The second option would be to replace Iowa's nonregulatory programs with a tough regulatory regime. Several of the key authors of the 1987 act are not philosophically opposed to regulation, just convinced that regulation was the wrong place to start in 1987. Perhaps now, when farmers have learned about the damage caused by chemicals and about how low-chemical agriculture works in practice, they may be willing to accept some kinds of regulation. Paul Johnson explains:

The Groundwater Act started a *process.* Education, research, and demonstration sometimes lead to regulation. People are willing to be regulated once they know what it's all about. When people are aware, and when we know we are regulating the right thing, we can move to regulation to deal with the 10 percent of the people who will never go along. For example, we may be ready now to regulate abandoned drainage wells or to require that farmers leave filter strips of trees and shrubs along streams.[36]

However, the Farm Bureau and other powerful farming interests are deeply hostile to the idea of regulating farming. Although there may be significant new regulatory initiatives, it is hard to see how proenvironmental forces could push through a full-scale regulatory regime if they are not able to sustain funding for less controversial nonregulatory programs. Thus a serious turn to regulation would require intervention by the federal government.

Some see signs that federal mandates for regulation are coming, perhaps from EPA but more likely from Congress. EPA recently announced a new groundwater strategy, as well as a strategy on pesticides and groundwater. These steps by EPA may encourage states to move toward regulation. According to the EPA groundwater strategy, states are expected to design their own programs, but EPA is pushing states to adopt the elements of a comprehensive system for managing groundwater. EPA has made grants to associations of state environmental officials to form a task force to identify the elements of a comprehensive system. So far, the design does not require regulations, but it certainly pushes states in that direction. The EPA description of a comprehensive system would include a way to classify aquifers according to their likely future use, health-related standards for groundwater quality, and permits for emissions into groundwater. Currently Iowa has none of these elements, except for permits for discharges from municipal wastewater and coal combustion facilities.*

EPA has also made it clear that it expects a comprehensive state program to be a formal matter, with written memoranda of understanding

---

*The EPA description of a comprehensive system also includes a geographic information system that would map different classifications of groundwater according to their vulnerability to pollution. Iowa does have a mapping system, but it might not meet EPA standards.

about the responsibilities of various agencies. The members of the consortium are very resistant to this idea. They are reluctant to be quoted on this point, but one said:

> Our bosses are all politicians, and they don't always agree. The governor is a Republican; the secretary of the Iowa Department of Agriculture and Land Stewardship is a Democrat; the regents of Iowa State University are independent of both; and we work closely with federal agencies. If we tried to write down how those of us at the working level get things done, our bosses and their lawyers would have to review the document, they would see problems, and it would be hard to keep on cooperating the way we do.

Outside Iowa, many state officials are skeptical about the EPA groundwater strategy. In the words of Kevin Kessler of Wisconsin,

> Virtually all states share the concern that the newest EPA groundwater strategy is too much top-down. It gives lip service to recognizing states. It talks about the criteria for an adequate system to manage groundwater quality, but EPA does not have the authority to say what these criteria are. They can provide advice; that's all. And states see little incentive to pay attention to what EPA says anyway, almost none. There is very little money in it for states. If you want a federal groundwater protection program, this will require a new federal law.[37]

Recognizing the patchy legal authority for a federal role in groundwater, the EPA strategy is to say that if states conform to the elements of a comprehensive groundwater management system, then EPA will allow states more flexibility in air, water, and waste programs, areas in which federal law is clear and states must comply.

While the EPA groundwater strategy is debated, another possible vehicle for introducing regulation has appeared. In 1991, the Coastal Zone Management Act was amended to require that states submit plans that would ensure that nonpoint pollution, including runoff from farmlands, does not pollute coastal estuaries. This act does not apply to Iowa, but proposals have been made to amend the Clean Water Act to make similar requirements.

Others want a tougher approach. Ken Cook, a soil scientist and leading environmentalist on farm issues, says that the Coastal Zone Management Act approach would lead only to "another round of planning and paperwork by state-level officials."[38] He has asked that Congress amend the Clean Water Act to have states decide how much of a reduction in pollution is necessary in different watersheds and what share each landowner would be responsible for. Then landowners would be required to prepare plans for how they will meet the requirements. This approach, says Cook, would create a market for consulting services to farmers on how to reduce pollution to meet the required standards. Thus the goal for Cook, too, is to change how dealers, crop consultants, and other private sector consulting services function.

There is a third possible direction for Iowa policy to take. Perhaps nothing will change: the fees will continue to support a lower level of nonregulatory programs; no new state funds will be appropriated; and no federal action will force regulation. Yet the momentum of the past decade may continue for at least a while. State-imposed fees still yield over $2 million each year. If, as Paul Johnson and many others say, it is possible to farm profitably by reducing the use of chemicals, perhaps these programs and market forces will solve a good part of the problem of water pollution by farm chemicals in Iowa.

CONCLUSION

The story of Iowa's efforts to reduce pollution by farm chemicals is a clear illustration of how state-centered civic environmentalism works. The issue is an example of the unfinished business of environmental governance; it involves a nonpoint problem, with numerous polluters and with many technical uncertainties about how pollution occurs. The federal regime to address this pollution is full of gaps; Congress considered tough groundwater legislation several times in the 1980s but was unable to agree on a response. So Iowa stepped forward to tackle this unfinished business.

As suggested in Chapter 1, the Iowa approach emphasizes nonregulatory tools, including subsidies, education, technical assistance, and research. At the beginning, the chemical manufacturers and the chemical dealers refused to admit that there was a problem, but their confrontational tactics backfired, and the politics surrounding the issue settled down into the quieter collaborative style that was predicted in Chapter 1.

This story illustrates both the strong points and the limits of civic environmental politics. Iowa's approach has been an administrative success. The collaborative approach and the emphasis on nonregulatory tools allowed state officials to implement an extensive, multifaceted program that involved all relevant public agencies and several nonprofit organizations, even though the authority to address this form of pollution is highly fragmented. Informal collaboration found a path around the many rivalries between the elected officials who headed the agencies that participated in these programs. The programs reached 2 percent of all Iowa farmers personally, including a farmer who later became head of the chemical dealers' association, which had once denied that farm chemicals were causing environmental problems.

Iowa's approach has also been a political success so far. By emphasizing that groundwater pollution is a civic issue, where all industries and all citizens share some of the blame for pollution, the consortium and the six legislators were able to build a broad public interest coalition that defeated well-financed industry lobbyists and enacted the 1987 Groundwater Protection Act. Then their key opponent (Winton Etchen) was forced from office, and the industry shifted its position and admitted that its chemicals were causing problems. By their willingness to find a role (and funding) for all agencies that might be interested in the issue, and to create programs in all parts of the state, the leaders of Iowa's groundwater efforts built a coalition that attracted federal dollars and resisted most of the budget cuts that other programs have suffered in recent years. The state's groundwater programs have won national awards, and several Iowans—notably Keeney, Johnson, and Hallberg—have been recognized for their leadership.

However, Iowa's approach also has limits. The problem of farm chemicals in Iowa's waters has not been solved; the problem is too complex and too big to be solved in the ten years since the Ad Hoc Karst Committee was formed or in the five years since the Groundwater Protection Act. And a major source of funding has been exhausted. So a key question is whether the Iowa initiative has political staying power. As of mid-1993, the answer to this question is not clear.

Until now, the political force behind Iowa's initiatives has been a relatively small group of insiders, including employees of state agencies and the land grant university, some federal officials, and a few key legislators. These people are linked by ties of friendship and long-term collaboration and by a common commitment to environmental values.

However, the real power holders in Iowa, such as the governor, the Farm Bureau, the secretary of the Department of Agriculture and Land Stewardship, and university officials, may not be as committed as the insiders to the groundwater programs or to the enterprise of solving the problem of pollution by farm chemicals.

The most serious limitation of Iowa's programs so far is that they lack scale. This is not necessarily a criticism; it makes good sense to start with research and demonstration. However, both Paul Johnson and key members of the consortium say that the next step should be to reach many more farmers and achieve much deeper cuts in the use of farm chemicals. The task that lies ahead is to integrate environmental values more fully into the business decisions made by Iowa farmers and by the many organizations that support the agricultural sectors, especially dealers in farm equipment and supplies, including farm chemicals. Thus the next step is to make sustainable development work, to manage farming routinely so as to achieve both economic and environmental goals. This could mean much closer working relationships between the advocates of low-chemical farming and the chemical dealers. The critical factor may be whether agricultural co-ops and other chemical dealers can profit enough from selling information about the efficient use of farm chemicals to make up for reduced sales of chemicals. The collaborative style of Iowa's initiatives so far has opened the door to working with the dealers, but it remains to be seen whether the dealers, the Farm Bureau, and other agribusiness interests are ready to move through the door. Perhaps the threat of legislation modeled on the Coastal Zone Management Act amendments or Ken Cook's proposals will encourage agribusiness interests to support an expansion of Iowa's nonregulatory programs. Or perhaps federal regulation is unavoidable. As one consortium leader put it, "The farming community accepts the validity of the work that we have done, but their commitment to do something at significant scale is lacking. Patience and money are running short in Washington. I would not be surprised to see regulation in the next Farm Bill."

The next case study tells a somewhat different story. In Florida, a progressive water management agency was moving slowly to address an environmental problem, and the federal government intervened dramatically and forcefully to push the problem to the top of the agenda.

NOTES

1. U.S. Soil Conservation Service, Iowa Association of Soil and Water Conservation District Commissioners, and Iowa Department of Agriculture and Land Stewardship, Division of Soil Conservation, *Lines on the Land* (Washington, D.C.: Government Printing Office, 1991), 24.

2. Larry Fruhling, "Water in Iowa Tainted by Farming Chemicals," *Des Moines Register,* May 4, 1986, 1.

3. "Iowa State-Wide Rural Well-Water Survey" (Iowa City: University of Iowa, Center for Health Effects of Environmental Contamination, n.d.), 1.

4. Larry Fruhling, "Missing Nitrogen: Fertilizer Threatens Iowa Groundwater," *Des Moines Register,* May 6, 1986, 6A. See also National Research Council, Board on Agriculture, Committee on the Role of Alternative Farming Methods in Modern Production Agriculture, *Alternative Agriculture* (Washington, D.C.: National Academy Press, 1989), 41, 45.

5. David Osterberg, interview with author, Decorah, Iowa, May 21, 1992.

6. Paul Johnson, interview with author, Des Moines, Iowa, May 20, 1992.

7. Bernard E. Hoyer, "Policy Perspectives on Groundwater Protection from Agricultural Contamination in Iowa," Iowa Geological Survey, Iowa City, n.d., unpublished paper.

8. George Hallberg, interview with author, Iowa City, May 20, 1992.

9. Ibid.

10. Cited in David Getches, "Groundwater Quality Protection: Setting a National Goal for State and Federal Programs," *Chicago-Kent Law Review* 65, no. 2 (1989): 392.

11. Ibid., 400.

12. Paul Johnson, interview with author, Decorah, Iowa, May 21, 1992.

13. Ibid.

14. David Osterberg, interview with author, Des Moines, Iowa, May 20, 1992.

15. Ibid.

16. Jerry DeWitt, interview with author, Des Moines, Iowa, May 18, 1992.

17. Iowa Statutes, Chapter 159.2 (2).

18. Richard D. Kelley, "Synthetic Organic Compound Sampling Survey of Public Water Supplies," Iowa Department of Water and Air Management, Des Moines, April 1985; and Richard D. Kelley and Monica Wnuk, "Little Sioux River Synthetic Organic Compound Municipal Well Sampling Survey" (Iowa Department of Water and Air Management, Des Moines, March 1986). See also Richard D. Kelley, "A Brief Historical Review of the Events Leading up to the Iowa Groundwater Act" (Des Moines, n.d.). There had also been studies in the Little Sioux Valley in 1984, but the

results of those studies and of the 1985 test were challenged because the tests were said to be improperly designed. The 1984 results were not confirmed, but the 1986 results did support the 1985 findings.

19. Melinda Voss, "Farm Family Worried About Drinking Others' Chemicals," *Des Moines Register*, May 8, 1986, 1, and "What Consumers Do About Water," 17.

20. Quoted in Steven Joseph Doherty, "The Politics of the 1987 Iowa Groundwater Protection Act" (Master's thesis, Iowa State University, 1990), 60.

21. Bernard E. Hoyer, James E. Combs, Richard D. Kelley, Constance Cousins-Letherman, and John H. Seyb, *Iowa Groundwater Protection Strategy: 1987* (Des Moines: Iowa Department of Natural Resources, 1987), 1.

22. Doherty, "The Politics of the 1987 Iowa Groundwater Protection Act," 99.

23. Ibid., 71.

24. James Combs, Don Koch, Richard D. Kelley, Lisa Smith, Monica Wnuk, and J. Edward Brown, *The Role of Standards in Iowa's Groundwater Protection Program: A Report to the Iowa General Assembly* (Des Moines: Iowa Department of Natural Resources, 1989), ix.

25. Information provided by the Cooperative Extension Service. The numbers do not add up, which illustrates the difficulty of estimating exactly what resources are dedicated to the complex multiagency effort that Iowa has mounted.

26. "Nitrates in the Des Moines River: Not a New Problem," *Leopold Letter* 4, no. 1 (Spring 1992): 10-11.

27. George R. Hallberg et al., *A Process Evaluation of Iowa's Agricultural-Energy-Environmental Initiatives: Nitrogen Management in Iowa*, Technical Information Series 22 (Des Moines: Iowa Department of Natural Resources, 1991), 18. Virtually all of the university and state employees who managed consortium projects cosigned this report.

28. Ibid., 19, 22.

29. These figures are in pounds of active ingredients. Iowa State University Extension Service, *A Survey of Pesticides Used in Iowa Crop Production in 1990*, No. PM1441 (Ames: Iowa State University Extension Service, 1991).

30. Ibid., 2.

31. Doherty, "The Politics of the 1987 Iowa Groundwater Protection Act," 92-95.

32. Hallberg et al., *A Process Evaluation of Iowa's Agricultural-Energy-Environmental Initiatives*, 2.

33. Dan Looker, "Iowa Farms' Nitrogen Use Drops," *Des Moines Register*, December 6, 1991, 1, 2A.

34. George Hallberg, interview with author, Iowa City, May 20, 1992.

35. Eileen Gannon Williams, "Evaluating Future Strategies for Iowa Farmer-owned Cooperatives in Supplying Agricultural Products and Services: An Assessment of Integrated Crop Management Services" (MBA thesis, Iowa State University, 1991), 61.

36. Paul Johnson, telephone interview with author, September 3, 1992.

37. Kevin Kessler, telephone interview with author, May 11, 1992.

38. Ken Cook, interview with author, Washington, D.C., July 17, 1991.

CHAPTER FIVE

Leadership in the Everglades:
The Politics of Restoring an Ecosystem

In 1988 the U.S. attorney for the Southern District of Florida sued the state of Florida and the South Florida Water Management District. He charged that failure to enforce state law was allowing polluted water from sugar cane farms to flow into the Everglades National Park and the Loxahatchee National Wildlife Refuge. "This is like a cancer, and the cancer is spreading south [into the park]," said Michael Finley, superintendent of the Everglades National Park.[1]

The Water Management District rejected these claims and called the lawsuit an unwarranted interference in state antipollution efforts.[2] Three years later, after the district had spent $6 million on the fees of a Washington law office that was defending the suit, the newly elected governor of Florida announced to a federal judge that he wanted to "surrender." "I've brought my sword," said Lawton Chiles. "I want to find out who I can give my sword to." [3]

This would seem to be a classic case of confrontational environmental politics, illustrating the fact that federal legal action is often necessary to force state regulators to take on a powerful industry, such as the $1.5 billion sugar industry in Florida. However, as we will see, there is much more to the story. The rhetoric of surrender is familiar but ultimately misleading. The tools and confrontational politics of regulation are only part of the story of the Everglades lawsuit. If the Everglades ecosystem is to be restored, the politics of restoration will probably be a consensual politics of investment rather than an adversarial politics of regulation. And the state, rather than the federal government, is the key. In the words of the Florida regional director of the Wilderness Society, "the

law establishing Everglades National Park calls on the [U.S.] Department of the Interior to protect the objects and processes of its natural
life, forever. The park's 'forever' lies more with the South Florida Water Management District than with federal authority." [4]

Thus, the answer to the governor's question, "Who should I give my
sword to?" may be: himself and his appointees. Federal officials can
force the issue onto the state's agenda and bring important resources to
bear, but they cannot resolve the issue. Protection of the Everglades will
require leadership by state and local officials, and it will center on state
and local processes.

Furthermore, restoration will require much more than the strict enforcement of regulations. Cleaning up the water that flows from farmland into the Everglades and mitigating the effects of pollution from
farms are only part of the solution. If the Everglades ecosystem is to be
protected, and if a portion of the Everglades is to be restored, the massive public works project that controls the flow of water in South Florida
must be reengineered, and additional public works will be required. In
addition, there will have to be changes in how public water supply agencies go about their business; they will have to institute higher tap fees
and other such measures to encourage the more efficient use of water.
The bill for new public works could be well over a billion dollars. The
central questions facing Florida are similar to the questions facing Iowa
farmers: Are there ways that economic development can be consistent
with achieving environmental goals? Is there a sustainable development
future for South Florida?

THE SCIENCE AND POLITICS OF RESTORING AN ECOSYSTEM

The Everglades is an ecosystem in danger. Half of the primeval Everglades has been drained and is now covered by farms or suburban sprawl.
The remainder is wild, but the system has been fundamentally altered.
The vast flocks of wading birds that made the Everglades famous have
been reduced to 10 percent of their original size; twenty-six species of
animals are threatened or endangered; and large acreages have been in-
vaded by exotic plant species or transformed fundamentally.[5]

Ecologically, the Everglades is unique. Politically, it is distinctive
in two important ways. First, although the Everglades is very large—

Figure 5-1   The South Florida Water Management System

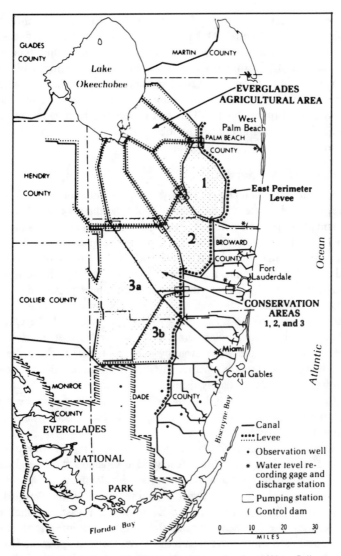

originally it covered most of southern Florida—it lies entirely within one state (Figure 5-1). In contrast, consider the Chesapeake Bay, the Great Lakes, or the Columbia River system. Second, federal, state, and local governments are at the brink of investing a billion dollars to restore a large part of the Everglades to its original ecological condition. No other effort to restore an endangered ecosystem has progressed quite this far. This fact makes the Everglades an excellent case for examining the politics of managing endangered ecosystems.

Complexity of the Ecosystem

Like many other endangered ecosystems, the situation in the Everglades is complex; there is uncertainty about the threats to the ecosystem and about possible solutions; and authority to take action is highly fragmented. Before European settlement, the Everglades was a shallow "river of grass" that flowed slowly 230 miles from central Florida to the southern tip of the peninsula. It took a year for water to move down through the watershed. From the northern end, near present-day Orlando, the Everglades ran from small lakes and swamps through the broad flood plain of the meandering Kissimmee River to Lake Okeechobee, which is thirty miles across but only twelve feet deep. The south shore of the lake was a swampy pond apple forest. From there, water flowed imperceptibly across vast, flat wet prairies of saw grass filled with small islands barely rising above the water and bordered by deep pools and drier lands hosting isolated wetlands. From the saw grass, the Everglades emptied into mangrove forests and then into the shallow Florida Bay.[6]

The Everglades is linked hydrologically to coastal regions where Miami and other cities are located. A low ridge separates the Everglades from the east coast of Florida. But the urban development has sprawled over this ridge far into the Everglades, and the water of the Everglades flows under the ridge. Beneath the Everglades is a vast, flat shelf of porous limestone. Much water sinks through the rock into the shallow Biscayne aquifer, which lies beneath the coast as well as under the Everglades. Some of this water bubbles up along the coast in springs. Elsewhere, the Biscayne aquifer flows directly into the sea. Nineteenth-century boatmen wrote of tossing buckets into upwellings of sweet fresh water in Biscayne Bay, a large expanse of saltwater that lies east of Miami and is separated from the Atlantic Ocean by small islands and reefs.

Today the cities of South Florida draw their drinking water from shallow wells punched into the Biscayne aquifer. So the physical links between the Everglades and the coast have spawned an economic dependence. In order to replenish their drinking water and to keep saltwater from intruding into their wellfields, the coastal cities depend on a natural flow from the Everglades through the limestone into the aquifer. Water from the Everglades also drains into estuaries, keeping them fresh.

In addition to considering the terrain, the aquifer, and the estuaries, one must understand basic facts about South Florida's climate in order to grasp the ecology and politics of the Everglades. The area is wet; an annual average of over 50 inches of rain is largely compressed into a six-month rainy season. However, in some years, there can be as much as 100 inches of rain, and in others the region experiences drought. During the dry season and periods of drought, Lake Okeechobee and the Everglades are vast reservoirs, releasing water slowly to keep the saw grass wet and to feed the Biscayne aquifer. In the past, when hurricanes hit the primeval Everglades, the lake and the saw grass prairies would overflow, and floods swept into areas that are now suburbs and cities. Thus the Everglades is actually a variety of ecosystems linked via aquifers, floods, and manmade water management structures to the South Florida coast.

Uncertainty About the Facts

Knowledge about the Everglades is growing, but essential facts are still in dispute. Wildlife experts have discovered that the pattern of variation between wet and dry seasons is important for wildlife. For example, wood storks nest during high-water season, and their eggs hatch as the water level drops. Then, during the dry season, when fish are concentrated in narrow channels, parents of young birds have easy feeding. Enormous flocks of these birds helped make Everglades National Park famous.

Scientists have only recently built computer models to describe how wet the primeval Everglades was and where the water went. How deep was water in the saw grass prairies before humans altered them one hundred years ago? How deep were the pools? Did Lake Okeechobee flow into the saw grass prairies often or only after heavy rainfall? Scientists debate vigorously these questions and others.

The most controversial scientific issue in recent years has been the question of how phosphorus affects the Loxahatchee National Wildlife Refuge and the Everglades National Park. This was the central scientific issue in Florida's massive litigation effort.

There is agreement about some basic facts. South of Lake Okeechobee, on top of the limestone shelf, lies a layer of muck made of decomposed vegetation. Near the southern edge of Lake Okeechobee, the muck is twelve feet thick. Farther to the south, the muck is much shallower and does not always cover the underlying rock. The muck is wonderfully rich in nitrogen and phosphorus. Once drained, the thicker muck soils can support extensive agriculture. However, when the muck dries out, it slowly oxidizes, and most of it turns into gas or is dissolved in water, leaving a residue of minerals. When the muck is drained and farmed, the land subsides as much as an inch per year in some places.

Phosphorus is one of the elements that is freed when the muck is cultivated and oxidizes. Thus lands south of Lake Okeechobee that have been drained and now support a large sugar industry and substantial acreage in vegetable farms are contributing to an environmental dilemma. Water draining south from the sugar cane plantations contains elevated amounts of phosphorus.

Here agreement ended and controversy began. In 1988 there was a spirited debate about how changing amounts of nitrogen and phosphorus in the water were affecting Lake Okeechobee and the saw grass prairies. The prairies are an oligotrophic ecosystem—that is, a low-nutrient environment. This means that when phosphorus is added to the water, it provides a fertilizer that boosts the growth of the kinds of vegetation that can absorb the phosphorus and grow quickly. Specifically, cattails supplant saw grass, and different kinds of algae form. The marsh becomes muddier, there are fewer fish, and thus there are fewer birds. The algae stinks.

Scientists at the South Florida Water Management District and the Everglades National Park think that phosphorus is the most significant reason cattails replace saw grass south of the lake. Scientists who work for the sugar industry have disagreed about the extent and rate of growth of cattails. They cite other explanations for the presence of cattails, such as fire and changes in the hydroperiod—scientific shorthand for level, timing, and direction of water as it flows through the Everglades.[7] Representatives of the sugar industry also note that cane fields are not the only sources of phosphorus. For example, they say that sediments underneath Lake Okeechobee are rich in phosphorus and that strong winds create waves that stir up the silt.

Phosphorus, as well as nitrogen from dairies north of the lake, has degraded the quality of water in Lake Okeechobee. North of the lake and west of the Kissimmee River, there are large phosphate mines. Where should efforts to protect the quality of water in the lake and in the saw grass prairies south of the lake be focused? With phosphorus or hydroperiod? With whose phosphorus? Where should the hydroperiod be changed? And what steps would be most cost effective?

THE HISTORICAL SETTING

Soon after he took office as assistant attorney general of the United States, Richard Stewart asked Dexter Lehtinen, U.S. attorney for South Florida, to come to Washington, D.C., to brief him on the Everglades lawsuit. "Dexter brought this book" *[pointing to a thick and attractive coffee table volume]*, "and started his explanation in the nineteenth century. Right away, I knew this would not be an easy case," Stewart said later.[8]

Early Years

When the United States purchased Florida from the King of Spain in 1821, the Everglades became federal land. Florida became a state in 1845. In 1850, Congress passed the Swamp Lands Act, which gave ownership of "overflowed lands" in the Everglades to the state of Florida on the condition that some of the lands might be drained, settled, and used for agriculture. The state sold vast tracts at low cost to railroads, which borrowed funds by issuing bonds and promised to open the land for settlement. Most of the railroads went bankrupt during the Civil War, and the railroad bonds became worthless. Many private ventures did drain tracts, but most failed financially. Hamilton

Disston, a Philadelphia native, spent millions and died bankrupt in 1896.

In the early twentieth century, state and local governments took over the task of converting the Everglades to productive use. Napoleon Bonaparte Broward was elected governor of Florida in 1905 on a platform of "drain the Everglades." He helped organize the Everglades Drainage District, which operated from 1906 to 1929, when it, too, went bankrupt. A road was built in the 1920s from Miami to the west coast of Florida; the road was a major barrier to water flow into the southernmost saw grass prairies and the mangrove swamps along the coast of Florida Bay. By 1948, the district and the state had cut 440 miles of canals and drained some of the richest muck soils south of Lake Okeechobee.

At the same time as the state, local governments, and private businesses were investing public dollars in draining the Everglades, sentiment was building for preserving at least a portion of the ecosystem. In the early 1900s, civic groups in Miami campaigned to preserve sanctuaries for wild birds and to discourage women from wearing hats with long plumes taken from birds in the Everglades. In 1941, the daughter of a *Miami Herald* journalist published *The Everglades: River of Grass,* a lyrical description of the wonders of the ecosystem and a condemnation of efforts to drain it for commercial and industrial purposes.[9] The book helped to fuel a campaign to create a national park in the south end of the Everglades. The campaign was finally successful in 1947, when Congress created the Everglades National Park at the tip of the Florida peninsula. The state of Florida donated 850,000 acres and used $2 million of its own funds to purchase private lands inside the park's boundaries.[10]

The Flood Control Project

In 1948, the state and the federal government joined in a major new effort to transform the ecosystem. In 1947, two hurricanes hit the Everglades, and flood waters swept across southern Florida, covering downtown Fort Lauderdale, northwest Miami, and vast areas of farmland. These floods provided the catalyst for congressional approval of the Central and South Florida Project for Flood Control and Other Purposes.

The prime purpose of the project was flood control.[11] The U.S. Army Corps of Engineers built 1,400 miles of levees and canals so that flood waters would pass around farms and coastal cities and be carried swiftly into the Everglades or directly to the sea. North of Lake Okeechobee, the project included digging a channel for the Kissimmee River so that it could carry flood waters away more swiftly, and so that the Kissimmee flood plain could be drained and farmed. The corps also expanded an existing dike along the southern shore of Lake Okeechobee to keep the lake from flooding towns and farms. An eastern perimeter levee was built for sixty miles from west of Miami to west of Palm Beach to protect the coastal areas from flooding. East of the perimeter levee, most lands remained in private hands, and the corps dug canals to encourage drainage, farming, and urban development.

West of the perimeter levee, much of the land is still owned by the state. State lands were made into Water Conservation Areas (WCAs), large pools that could retain flood waters, replenish the Biscayne aquifer, and accommodate recreation, fishing, airboating, and other uses. To make up for harm the project would do to wildlife habitat, the northernmost WCA was leased by the district to the U.S. Department of the Interior and became the Loxahatchee National Wildlife Refuge.

In addition to flood control for urban areas, the other major purpose of the Central and South Florida project was the creation of the Everglades Agricultural Area (EAA) south of the lake and adjacent to the refuge. Over 700,000 acres, an area almost the size of Rhode Island, was drained and leveed. Gigantic pumps were built to pump irrigation water into the EAA from Lake Okeechobee during the dry season and droughts and to move water out of the EAA during the rainy season after torrential summer thunderstorms. This water was diverted either north, into the lake, or south, into the WCAs and canals that eventually lead to the park or to the Atlantic Ocean.

When the project was completed in 1962, it put an end to the river of grass that characterized the primeval Everglades. The completed project was the culmination of a long process of construction that cut off the flow of water from the northern half of the Everglades, in the Kissimmee River valley and Lake Okeechobee, into the southern half of the system. South of the lake, levees stopped the sheet flow of water across the saw grass prairies into the park. Water was allowed to flow only through canals and a few structures along the edge of the WCAs. The regulation schedules prepared by the U.S. Army Corps of Engineers controlled how much water flowed into Everglades National Park and when it would arrive. The natural hydroperiod was replaced by an artificial regime.

As with all corps projects, there was a local sponsor. The state of Florida passed legislation creating the Central and Southern Florida Flood Control District, which helped assemble land for the project and which now operates most of the pumps and canals under guidelines established by the corps. The district's board of directors was named by the governor, and it was given authority to levy a small property tax on landholders to pay for its operations. As Miami, Fort Lauderdale, and other towns along the coast boomed, these taxes provided increasing revenue to the district. The state created four additional water management districts in other river basins, but the district in South Florida was the richest and most powerful because it managed the flood control project.[12]

The Emergence of Sugar
and Modern Environmentalism

Two momentous changes occurred in the Everglades in the 1960s and 1970s. The first took place after the revolution in Cuba, when the United States placed an embargo on Cuban exports of sugar and other products and imposed quotas on the import of sugar from other countries. This spurred rapid expansion of farming in the Everglades Agricultural Area. Between 1960 and 1975, sugar acreage increased nearly sixfold. With over 421,000 acres planted, sugar is the primary crop in the EAA.[13]

The second major change was the intensification of interest in environmental values in South Florida and the nation. As noted, sentiment in favor of protecting the Everglades was not a new phenomenon. Environmental values had received some attention when the Central and South Florida project was authorized. Benefits from fishing and hunting were included in the cost-benefit calculations (although they were overshadowed by projected benefits from the EAA).

In the mid-1960s, many of the same groups (and some of the same individuals) who had fought to protect plumed birds and to create Everglades National Park fought again to stop construction of a massive "jetport" in the Big Cypress Swamp west of Miami. The successful struggle against the jetport was an important event in heightening national interest in environmental issues.

Beginning in the late 1960s, some changes in the Central and South Florida project occurred in response to rising concern about environmental values. In 1967, the corps and the district built a new canal to bring water around the levee on the north boundary and into the center of the park. In 1972, Congress passed legislation guaranteeing minimum flows of water from the project's canals and structures into the Everglades National Park. The levee on the north side of the park was breached to allow some semblance of the original sheet flow into the park. Farther north, there was widespread public dissatisfaction with the ditch that the corps had dug as a new channel for the Kissimmee River, and in 1978 the state proposed that the ditch be filled and the old riverbed restored.

Environmental revolution also brought changes to the institutions governing the Everglades. In 1972, the Flood Control District was given responsibilities for regulating water quality and administering new state laws governing drainage of wetlands. In 1976 it was rebaptized the South Florida Water Management District.

The Phosphorus Issue

Water quality in the Everglades first became an issue in the 1970s, but concern focused on Lake Okeechobee, not on water flowing south to the park. Large algae blooms had begun to appear in Lake Okeechobee after 1977. To bring political attention to the problem, an activist fisherman dumped a bag of muck and algae on the governor's desk. Scientists working for the district said that the largest and most obvious cause of the problem was nutrients—nitrates and phosphorus—that flowed into the lake from dairy farms along the Kissimmee River.

Water entering the lake from the Everglades Agricultural Area also contributed between 12 percent and 14 percent of the phosphorus entering the lake. About one-third of the water pumped from the EAA went into Lake Okeechobee; the rest was pumped south. In 1979 the district, the state, and the corps of engineers agreed to stop pumping from the EAA as one element of an interim action plan to clean up Lake Okeechobee.

Of course, runoff that would have gone north into the lake had to be pumped south instead, into the Water Conservation Areas. As early as 1974, scientists on the district staff wrote reports suggesting that adding phosphorus to the WCAs could encourage the growth of cattails and that phosphorus might reach Everglades National Park and affect conditions there. However, the reports were not circulated widely and the district and the state did nothing to reduce the flow of phosphorus-laden waters from the EAA to the WCAs, the park, and the refuge. Such action would have required confronting the powerful sugar industry. This would have been much tougher than tackling the Kissimmee River dairies. The sugar industry is much larger, exerts great political power, and was accustomed to receiving support from governmental agencies and to resisting public criticism.

In 1987, the issue of water quality in areas south of the lake began to gain serious attention. The legislature passed the Surface Water Improvement and Management (SWIM) Act, which required that Florida's water management districts prepare plans to avoid and reverse degradation of the state's waters. SWIM set targets for how much phosphorus might enter Lake Okeechobee, specified a model to measure flows, required that the district prepare a plan for the lake, and set up a technical advisory council to study the effects of phosphorus on the WCAs and other areas south of the lake. The district could also prepare SWIM plans for other areas with significant problems. The act included a provision that directly addressed the issue of phosphorus and the park. It said the water management districts "shall not divert waters to ... the Everglades National Park in such a way that state water quality standards are violated [or] that the nutrients in such waters adversely affect indigenous vegetation communities or wildlife." [14] However, the decision about whether to prepare a SWIM plan for the Everglades was left to the district.

ORIGINS OF THE LAWSUIT

On October 12, 1988, Dexter Lehtinen, acting U.S. attorney for South Florida, filed suit against the district and the state of Florida. The lawsuit charged, among other things, that the district had failed to obtain state water quality permits for the pumps that discharged waters from the EAA south into the WCAs.

Fearing pressure from Washington to stop the suit, Lehtinen did not give the normal thirty days' notice to defendants. Indeed, Lehtinen and his allies in federal offices in Florida did not tell their superiors in Washington that they planned to file suit. To some observers, including Lehtinen's allies, the lawsuit was "tainted in its inception.... He clearly violated the administrative manual for operation of the U.S. attorney's office." Later, the sugar industry raised a legal challenge to the lawsuit on these grounds. Lehtinen, however, did not hide his independence. The timing, he said, was deliberate—a few weeks before the presidential election. "The environment was a big issue in the campaign, and Dukakis [the Democratic candidate] was taking big hits on the pollution in Boston Harbor. So how could [the U.S. Department of] Justice come out and say, 'No you shouldn't have filed it.' That's tantamount to saying you should kill the Everglades. No way they could do that." [15]

The lawsuit was a radical challenge to a well-understood and deeply entrenched way of doing business. As many analysts have explained, large, federally supported water projects are a classic example of developmental politics, involving investments of public dollars, or if you will, subsidies of private or local interests, by the federal government. These projects are orchestrated by an iron triangle, including a local sponsor closely tied to private interests (such as agriculture) that stand to benefit from the project; the U.S. Army Corps of Engineers; and the congressional committees that authorize the projects. Relations between these partners are usually managed without a great deal of public controversy and conflict. The politics is an insiders' game, traditionally played by a small number of engineers, businesspeople, and politicians in a back room. However, for many water projects and other major federal investments, concern about environmental values has undermined the power of the iron triangle and fragmented the political system. New players and new interests struggle to break into the back room politics.[16]

The Central and South Florida Flood Control Project is a typical example of these broad patterns. The story of the lawsuit is the tale of a flamboyant political entrepreneur who recognized new political realities and mobilized new players. The result was to polarize the political system and then paralyze it during two and a half years of bitter combat. A chronology of the lawsuit is shown in Table 5-1 (p. 140).

On one side of the struggle were Lehtinen, the superintendents of the Everglades National Park and the Loxahatchee National Wildlife Refuge, several environmental groups, and eventually the Department of Justice staff in Washington. On the other side were the district, the sugar industry, and usually Gov. Bob Martinez and his Department of Environmental Regulation. Two key players in the original iron triangle were strangely quiet. The U.S. Army Corps of Engineers was formally, but reluctantly, in Lehtinen's corner. Congressional committees and local members of Congress have been only marginal players until quite recently. Key players in the litigation and settlement are listed in Table 5-2 (p. 142). The story of how the new players entered the battle and what they brought helps to explain how power had fragmented and why the lawsuit resulted in deadlock for almost three years.

Lehtinen and His Allies

It is tempting to describe the lawsuit strictly in terms of the personalities involved, especially Dexter Lehtinen. Certainly Lehtinen's flamboyant and uncompromising style irritated many of the other principals. He grew up near the Everglades in a rural area south of Miami, had been a state senator, and was serving on the Senate's natural resources committee when the SWIM Act was passed. Although he is very well connected politically—he is married to Ileana Ros-Lehtinen, a Cuban-American Republican who was elected to the U.S. House of Representatives from southern Dade County in a special election in August 1989—the U.S. Senate never took action on his nomination as U.S. attorney.

Newspapers explain that senators were concerned about complaints of Lehtinen's fiery temper and incidents of domestic violence.[17] He was also charged with allowing political considerations to influence his management of the U.S. attorney's office. In 1992, faced with pressure from the White House and the Justice Department and with a report criticizing public statements he made exonerating the Broward County sheriff before the end of an investigation into corruption, he resigned.

Just as significant as Lehtinen's personality are the circumstances he faced. Once the suit was filed, all parties stated that they wished to avoid a trial, which promised to be both time consuming and expensive. There were several efforts to settle the suit, but none of them gained sufficiently wide support to be successful. The result was an impasse, enormous legal bills, and increasing bitterness among all those involved. If Lehtinen's personality seems important, it is because authority was so fragmented that no agency or official was clearly responsible for resolving the dispute.

When Lehtinen became acting U.S. attorney, in early 1988, he sought ways to expand his office's role in environmental issues. He met with local environmentalists and asked them what single most important thing he could do for the environment. Their response was quick. The Everglades was the obvious issue, and the focus should be the sugar industry and other agricultural uses. Environmentalists had been seeking ways to take on the sugar industry for many years. They had asked the EPA to determine whether the pumps from the EAA to the WCAs required a permit under the Clean Water Act. But because the act did not cover runoff from farmland, EPA held that the pumps were exempt. Bob Dreher of the Sierra Club Legal Defense Fund and Jim Webb, regional director of the Wilderness Society, had been considering other ways to challenge the pumps, such as suing the EPA or the corps of engineers.[18] However, when Lehtinen and Assistant U.S. Attorney Suzan Ponzoli began working on a lawsuit against the state and the district, the environmentalists decided not to proceed with their own action. The U.S. attorney's office had far more resources than they could command.

It was clear from the outset that drafting a complaint would be tricky. The technical facts about how phosphorus was affecting the ecosystem were complex and controversial. It seemed evident to federal officials that phosphorus was causing cattails to grow; however, the legal team had a great deal of work to do to document this well enough to prove it in court. An equally difficult challenge would be crafting a legal argument that would not require suing the corps of engineers as well as the state and the district. The corps still owned the pumps that drained the EAA into the WCAs. But they were operated by the district under contract.

When the lawsuit was filed, environmental attorneys intended to stay out. Bob Dreher of the Sierra Club Legal Defense Fund explained that his annual budget for expenses related to litigation was only $10,000, far too little to cover even the costs of photocopying the many documents that the suit eventually spawned. Furthermore, even if Dreher invested time and money in the litigation, the federal government would clearly be the dominant force in setting legal strategy.

However, the environmentalists were invited to join the suit in early

TABLE 5-1

CHRONOLOGY OF EVENTS IN THE EVERGLADES CASE

Construction of the Everglades Agricultural Area

1906	Formation of the Everglades Drainage District.
1947	Creation of Everglades National Park (ENP).
1948	Congress approves the Central and Southern Florida Project for Flood Control and Other Purposes.
1960s	Revolution in Cuba; growth of sugar industry in the Everglades Agricultural Area (EAA).
1972	Congress guarantees minimum flows of water into ENP.

Early Development of the Phosphorus Problem

1979	Decision to pump stormwater from the EAA into Water Conservation Areas instead of into Lake Okeechobee.
1983	Gov. Bob Graham starts the "Save Our Everglades" program.
1987	Passage of the Florida Surface Water Improvement and Management (SWIM) Act.

Filing of the Lawsuit

Spring 1988	Dexter Lehtinen nominated U.S. attorney for South Florida.
October 1988	Lawsuit filed: *U.S. v. South Florida Water Management District.*
November 1988	Florida Audubon intervenes; other environmental groups follow.
December 1988	Amended complaint filed.

Litigation

December 1989	Judge rejects district's motion to dismiss.
April 1990	Federal agencies file joint comments on Everglades SWIM plan.
September 1990	Governor Martinez announces compromise.
November 1990	Lawton Chiles elected governor, defeating Martinez. U.S. files motion for limited summary judgment.

Settlement

January 1991	Chiles promises to settle lawsuit within six months.
February 1991	"Summit" ends with no progress.
March 1991	Negotiations begin with scientists addressing water quality.
April 1991	Five new members join district board.
May 1991	Governor Chiles appears in court and "surrenders."

(Continued on next page)

TABLE 5-1 *(CONTINUED)*

May 7, 1991	Marjory Stoneman Douglas Act signed.
July 8, 1991	Settlement agreement announced.
December 1991	Judge orally approves settlement.
March 1992	Written order accepting settlement agreement.

Statement of Principles

March 1992	District approves SWIM, including design of artificial wetlands.
	Sugar Cane League offers plan to clean up phosphorus and files legal challenge to SWIM.
Summer 1992	Adoption of rules for on-farm best management practices (BMPs).
December 1992	Mediator hired.
March 1993	FloSun and U.S. Sugar offer new settlement proposals.
	Secretary Babbitt commits to making Everglades a test case.
May 1993	Technical group proposal unveiled.
July 1993	Secretary Babbitt announces statement of principles.
	District announces tax increase.
October 1993	Details of statement of principles to be announced.

November, shortly after the election. The outgoing assistant attorney general had summoned Lehtinen to Washington to discuss the lawsuit. Bob Dreher was asked late one Friday afternoon if he could file papers to join the suit before ten o'clock the following Monday morning. If environmental groups were parties to the litigation, it would be harder for the assistant attorney general to demand that the suit be dropped. Dreher worked over the weekend and filed the papers at nine. At ten of ten, Dreher received a call and reported that environmental organizations were now official parties to the litigation. Reassured, the federal attorneys from Florida went into the meeting with their Washington superiors. The suit was not dropped.

Lehtinen found other allies in Mike Finley, superintendent of the Everglades National Park, and Burkett Neely, manager of the Loxahatchee National Wildlife Refuge. Their agencies became Lehtinen's clients, and Finley and Neely both were highly visible proponents of the

TABLE 5-2

SELECTED PARTICIPANTS IN THE EVERGLADES LITIGATION

Federal Government	Bruce Babbitt, secretary of interior (1993-present) George Frampton, assistant secretary of interior (1993-present) Assistant attorneys general: Roger Marzulla (1988-1989); Richard Stewart (1988-1991); Steve Herman, senior attorney Dexter Lehtinen, U.S. attorney for South Florida (1988-1991) Suzan Ponzoli, assistant U.S. attorney for South Florida William Hoeveler, U.S. district court judge Superintendent, Everglades National Park (ENP): Mike Finley (1985-1989); Bob Chandler (1989-1991) Michael Soukup, director of research, ENP Burkett A. Neely, Jr., manager, Loxahatchee National Wildlife Refuge (LNWR) Mark Maffei, wildlife biologist, LNWR
State of Florida	Governor: Bob Graham (D) (1979-1987); Bob Martinez (R) (1987-1991); Lawton Chiles (D) (1991-present) Buddy MacKay, Lieutenant Governor (D) (1991-present) Secretary, Department of Environmental Regulation (DER): Dale Twachtmann (1987-1991); Carol Browner (1991-1992) Dan Thompson, attorney, DER Richard Harvey
South Florida Water Management District	Executive director: John Wodraska (1985-1991); Timer Powers (interim, 1991); Tilford Creel (1991-present) Chairman of the board: James Garner (1987-1991); Alan Milledge (1991-1993); Valerie Boyd (1993-present) Tom MacVicar, deputy executive director

(Continued on next page)

TABLE 5-2 *(CONTINUED)*

	Steve Walker, general counsel (until 1991)
	James Rogers, outside counsel, Skadden, Arps, Meagher, and Flom (1988-1991)
Sugar Industry	Nelson Fairbanks, president, U.S. Sugar
	Flo-Sun (owned by the Fanjul family)
	Talisman Sugar, subsidiary of St. Joe Paper
	George Wedgworth, president, Sugar Cane Cooperative of Florida
	Curtis Richardson, Duke University wetlands ecologist, consultant to the Florida Sugar Cane League
Environmental Community	James Webb, regional director, Wilderness Society
	Paul Parks, FOREVERGLADES, Florida Wildlife Federation
	Charles Lee, Florida Audubon Society
	Nathaniel Reed
	Marjory Stoneman Douglas
	Bob Dreher, Sierra Club Legal Defense Fund, Washington, D.C.
	Tim Searchinger, Environmental Defense Fund, New York
	Brian Culhane, chairman, Everglades Coalition, Wilderness Society, Washington, D.C.
	Tom Martin, director, National Audubon Society Everglades Campaign

lawsuit. The problem of water quality in the refuge was immediate. Since the refuge lay on the eastern edge of the EAA, it received water directly from cane fields. Six thousand acres of saw grass had been taken over by cattails, and refuge staff were convinced that phosphorus in drainage from the EAA was the cause.

The effects of phosphorus on the park were less clear. The park boundary lies forty miles south of the pumps that drain the EAA. There have been no large-scale conversions to cattails in the park. However, park scientists had studied the problem for several years and were concerned. Park Superintendent Finley had already established himself as a visible public spokesman for the park and had appeared at meetings of the district board to press the case for various measures that would improve the flow of water into the park.

While Lehtinen was exploring the possibility of litigation, Finley was negotiating with the district and the corps of engineers about the flow of water to an area in the eastern portion of the park. When the water was deep in this area, it seeped into farmland further east, outside the park boundary in a place called the frog pond. When several board members resisted his requests that water be directed to this part of the park, which would harm farming but keep the water level high enough to support vegetation and wildlife on park lands, Finley was irritated. Some think this incident compelled Finley to support the suit. Finley and Neely helped Lehtinen and Ponzoli with technical information about water problems, and Finley strongly supported the suit when it was filed.

The Defendants and the Sugar Industry

The defendants in the litigation were the South Florida Water Management District and, secondarily, the state Department of Environmental Regulation. (In 1993, the Department of Environmental Regulation and the Department of Natural Resources merged to form the Department of Environmental Protection.) During the period of deadlock, which lasted for over two years, the state usually played a passive role. Meanwhile, the sugar industry, the real target of the lawsuit, fought to forestall any change.

The South Florida Water Management District is proud of its power, its professionalism, and its accomplishments. In the mid-1980s, the district built a new headquarters office in West Palm Beach. In the large, two-story lobby are comfortable chairs and an impressive video display that includes a large multicolored map of current weather conditions across southern Florida.

Off the lobby is the board room. The nine board members sit on a platform with the district's executive director, facing a phalanx of district officials. There are chairs behind for 200 guests and a press gallery at the rear. The proceedings are videotaped and televised on two giant screens inside the board room. There is also a television in the lobby, for guests who wish to monitor the discussion while chatting.

The building and its fittings bespeak wealth and power. The wealth comes from the power of the district to tax property. Its levies are a minor portion of anyone's tax bill, but since the district covers eleven full counties and portions of five others, the total is impressive: $240 million per year. And the district has not even levied the full millage allowed by state law.

Power comes from the district's wealth, from its range of responsibilities, from its independence, and from its competence. The district's boundaries include an entire watershed within which it has powers to regulate drainage and water quality as well as to manage the flood control project.[19] The district staff is protected from direct political influence by the nine-member board. Members are appointed for four-year terms, so they enjoy a measure of independence. The members meet once a month, usually for two days, and they approve numerous small contracts and other details of district operations. They have the opportunity to guide the district in great detail. But the board members are not paid, so it is an unusual board member who has the time, as well as the expertise and inclination, to second-guess the staff.

The power of the district, and particularly that of its staff, also derives from competence. The district pays well and has a large staff of skilled engineers and scientists. For professional skill, the district can match the local offices of the U.S. Army Corps of Engineers, the park, the refuge, and the Florida Department of Environmental Regulation. No one disputes that the project, which the corps and the district built and which the district manages, has been successful in accomplishing its two primary objectives—flood protection and promotion of agriculture. (The project has not yet been tested by a major hurricane since it was built, but no one suggests the system would fail to prevent flooding. Hurricane Andrew's path in 1992 was farther south and did not test the system.)

Prior to the lawsuit, the district enjoyed a reputation for being relatively progressive on environmental issues. John Wodraska, its director from 1984 to 1991, claims that it is harder to get a district permit for altering a wetland than to get a permit from the corps of engineers for the same purpose. In his view, the district is far ahead of the EPA on many issues.

Although some state regulators and many environmentalists would protest that the district almost always ranked flood control and protection of agriculture ahead of environmental protection, they could not dispute that the district had a strong track record in mediating disputes and coming up with progressive solutions. The district completed one of the first negotiations in the nation to determine how much water a native American tribe was entitled to receive under treaties and other agreements with the federal government. (The Seminole tribes, which signed the agreement, and the Miccosukee tribe both own tracts in the Everglades. The Miccosukee lands are sandwiched between the northern boundary of the park and the southernmost WCA at a sensitive part of the Everglades.) The district also developed plans for the largest environmental restoration project to date and paid for a pilot demonstration along the Kissimmee River. To win state approval for this plan, the district engaged in a formal mediation process with ranchers, dairies, and other parties in the Kissimmee valley.

The district is proud of the "rainfall plan," which was developed to address hydroperiod problems in the southeast portion of the Everglades, where the Shark River Slough enters the park's northeast corner. In the early 1980s, the park service wanted water to flow through this area in greater volume and at seasons that mimicked historical flows. Several large farms and residents of the area were concerned that if the district allowed more water to flow through its gates and canals, their lands would be flooded.[20] As with the Kissimmee plan and the Indian water rights, the district negotiated with farmers, residents, and other agencies. The plan allows for much larger flow into the park than many residents and farmers were willing to tolerate before the mediation process. In short, on the eve of the lawsuit, the district was confident of its powers and its reputation. Its critics called it arrogant, but if it was, perhaps this was understandable.

When the federal suit was filed, counsel to the district examined it and reported that it was legally weak. The district had heard rumors of litigation and had taken steps to prepare. A court ruling in the 1970s had said that water passing through a dam was not a point source and thus was not subject to regulation under the federal Clean Water Act. There were reports that national environmental groups were considering litigation to determine that the pumps that drained the EAA were not covered by this ruling and thus did need permits. The district had prepared for this contingency by signing a $50,000 contract with the Washington, D.C., office of Skadden, Arps, Meagher, and Flom, a large law firm, which would respond to such a suit. (Skadden Arps was chosen because the board wanted a top-rated firm and could not find another, in Florida or Washington, that lacked conflicts of interest because of longstanding relationships with the sugar industry or with other potential parties to the suit.)[21]

James Rogers and Steve Walker, the lead attorney from Skadden Arps and the district's in-house counsel, respectively, said that Lehtinen's legal case was very weak. The complaint advanced some unusual claims. It argued that the federal government, as well as state and local governments, could enforce laws against public nuisances, and that pollution constituted such a nuisance. It argued that since the federal government owned the park, the government had the right to protect the park from damage under the property clause of the Constitution. This was an argument that lawyers with environmental groups, including Jim Webb, had been studying for some time and were hoping to advance. If it were upheld, it might allow the federal government to challenge state water laws throughout the West.

The role of the U.S. Army Corps of Engineers was a major weakness of the lawsuit. The corps engineer responsible for supervising the project had not been consulted about the lawsuit before it was filed, and if the corps acknowledged its responsibility for the pumps, the case might collapse. If Lehtinen were forced to include the corps as a defendant because it owned the pumps and set the regulation schedules for them, then he would have no case because the federal government could not sue itself. The whole matter would be an internal administrative issue, not an issue for the courts.

As well as being legally questionable, the lawsuit offended the district's top officials. Although the legislature had not directed the district to prepare a SWIM plan for the Everglades, the district had made a commitment to do so. By rejecting the SWIM process at a relatively early stage, the lawsuit challenged the idea that the district was environmentally responsible. Also, by initiating litigation without informing the district, the suit was an affront to Wodraska's personal commitment to dispute resolution and the district's successful experience with it. Jim Garner, chair of the district board, expressed the feelings of many district officials when he said publicly that the suit was an attack on the personal integrity of the board members and the district staff.

Of course environmentalists and park staff saw it differently. As they remember, there was good reason for skepticism about whether SWIM would lead to significant efforts to stop the sugar industry from sending polluted water into the Everglades. In the last year, newly elected Governor Martinez, a Republican, had appointed five new board members, including several conservatives and individuals with close ties to the sugar industry and vegetable growers. Four new members were about to be added, including a new chair. Some of the outgoing members, who had been appointed by the previous Democratic governor, were regarded as sympathetic to environmental values.

Although the new board had been cordial to federal officials, it did not seem like a group that would use the Everglades SWIM to create major change. SWIM plans are only plans; by themselves, they do not force any specific action. So the Everglades SWIM might well have resulted in little or nothing. Although the district staff had prepared a thorough analysis of the effects of phosphorus on the WCAs, the refuge, and the park, the environmentalists felt that the district was not committed to following through; the district's early drafts of the SWIM plan included no numerical standards for phosphorus and no timetable for improving water quality.

Furthermore, federal officials and environmentalists took little comfort from the steps that the state and the district were taking to reduce the flow of nitrates and phosphorus from dairy farms into Lake Okeechobee. The district had drafted regulations covering the farms, but the state had decided it would issue them and had weakened them. The final regulations did not include numerical standards for how much cleanup would be required. The district did plan to buy out some farms and pay others to install best management practices, such as special drains to carry water from areas where cows stood and dropped manure. The buyout cost was $600 per cow.[22] Although this might have been enough to induce dairy farmers to act, it would have been vastly expensive to buy out the $1.5 billion sugar industry. It was also clear that the sugar industry would resist efforts to regulate its operations.

It is hard to judge whether the SWIM process would have resulted in action as effective as the eventual settlement of the lawsuit was. Several key district officials insist that the SWIM process would have been effective. Perhaps the most balanced judgment is that of Timer Powers, a highly respected businessman and former member of the district board, who later played a key role in settling the lawsuit. Powers says that the district was "drifting" on the issue of water quality in 1988 and was not giving it adequate attention.

If the district was irritated and angered by the lawsuit, the response of the state was somewhat different. Governor Martinez had been elected with strong support from the sugar industry. His appointed director of the Department of Environmental Regulation stated publicly, early in his term, that he thought the department's job was to serve developers, a statement that had been widely criticized.

However, the state of Florida has been on record since 1983 as favoring restoration of the Everglades. Martinez and his predecessor had published annual "Save the Everglades" reports, which listed specific steps the state had taken to change the flow of water and restore populations of key species of birds and animals. Thus Martinez was not insensitive to environmental values and issues. Two months after the lawsuit was filed, he supported a proposal that the state should not renew a lease for 3,742 acres in the EAA that was being farmed for sugar.[23] He supported a proposal to construct an experimental artificial wetland on this tract. The wetland would take drainage from the cane fields and alter the vegetation, by growing cattails and by other measures, in order to remove phosphorus from the water before it was discharged to the WCA.

Martinez was unwilling to take a strong stand against the lawsuit. However, the director of his Department of Environmental Regulation had been sued. So the governor tried to undercut Lehtinen. He made front-page news hand-delivering a letter to U.S. Attorney General Thornburgh (visiting Florida at the time) asking that the Justice Department intervene to settle the suit. Martinez wrote that it would be a waste of money to proceed with litigation and would slow down the state's current efforts to protect the Everglades.[24]

This gave Lehtinen the high ground. He responded that he was happy to settle the lawsuit as long as there was proper protection for the park and the refuge. Thornburgh took no action until after the presidential election. Then an assistant attorney general called Lehtinen to Washington to explain. After this meeting, there were long and intensive discussions about the legal issues raised by the lawsuit. However, the assistant attorney general left office with the Reagan administration, a career official took over until the Bush administration filled the position in August 1989, and Thornburgh stayed aloof. Martinez took no further action to press for either dropping or settling the suit.

Meanwhile, the sugar industry was outraged. To its adversaries, the industry seems "unattractive, unresponsive, and arrogant, with a terrible reputation for its labor practices," in the words of one federal official. "They are an unregulated industry and always have been. Even after our victory in the litigation, they just don't get it."

There is a long history of government support for the sugar industry. Government support for the industry goes much deeper than its investment of millions of dollars in draining the EAA. As the director of the Florida Sugar Cane League is quick to say, even before the U.S. Constitution was written, the colonies agreed to provide financial support to domestic sugar producers. This tradition is still alive. The federal government imposes quotas on the import of sugar and has embargoed Cuban sugar. As a result of quotas and the embargo, the price of sugar in the United States is more than twice the price of sugar on world markets (as of August 1993).

The Florida sugar industry is controlled by a relatively small number of individuals, many of whom are quite conservative politically. Although some sugar is grown on a number of small farms in the EAA, the vast majority of the land is owned by four organizations that also operate mills to process sugar cane. Independent farmers have long-term contracts with these mills.

The largest landholder and owner of two mills is the U.S. Sugar Company. It was organized in the 1930s by the Mott family, which held a major interest in General Motors. Currently, U.S. Sugar is controlled by the Mott Foundation, and the employees of the company own a 49 percent minority interest. The second largest landowner and operator of three mills is also privately held. It is the Flo-Sun company, which is owned by the Fanjul family. Alexandro Fanjul, Sr., owned sugar mills in Cuba, lost them all after the revolution, came to the United States, and rebuilt his fortune. A Cuban flag still flies in front of his mill alongside the flags of the United States and Florida. The third owner is Talisman Sugar, which is owned by the St. Joe Paper Company, a large, multinational paper, transportation, and real estate firm. Talisman owns one mill. Its land is along the south border of the EAA, is less productive than the holdings of the other producers, and is currently for sale. The fourth major interest is the Sugar Cane Cooperative of Florida, an association of about thirty farms. The cooperative owns one mill.

U.S. Sugar was long the leader of the sugar family. But in 1988, when the lawsuit was filed, the chair of the environmental committee of the Florida Sugar Cane League was George Wedgworth, president of the Sugar Cane Cooperative. Wedgworth's rhetoric is flamboyant and provocative, but his views on environmental issues are not uncommon in the industry. Wedgworth says that over the past fifty years, the sugar industry has been confronted with a number of "arsonists, who go around setting fires just to see things burn." One of the first arsonists, he says, was Eleanor Roosevelt, who criticized sugar in the 1940s for its labor practices. He believes that today's attacks by environmentalists are just more of the same, and just as unfounded as Roosevelt's.[25]

In the 1930s and 1940s, the industry recruited black field laborers from around the South, equipped field foremen with guns, and, it was alleged, treated workers as little better than slaves. When federal agencies took the industry to court, and when labor was short during the Second World War, the industry began bringing in temporary laborers from Jamaica and other Caribbean islands to cut cane during the harvest season.[26]

Jamaicans are still cutting cane in the EAA. Critics of the sugar cane industry allege that the Jamaicans work for very low wages—less than the minimum wage—and have little protection against serious injury in the cane fields. The workers have no guarantee against immediate dismissal and live in substandard housing. Spokesmen for the industry respond that the workers return voluntarily year after year because they earn far more in Florida than they could in Jamaica. Recently, however, the industry has reduced its employment of temporary workers from the Caribbean. It is shifting toward harvesting with machines, although the machines tear at the roots of the sugar plants and make it necessary to replant the field a year or two sooner than if the cane is cut by hand.

POLARIZATION AND DEADLOCK

Looking back, Nathaniel Reed, a nationally prominent Republican environmentalist and a member of the district board before and again after the lawsuit, regrets that the district did not open quiet discussions with Lehtinen in the fall of 1988 to work out a settlement. Nothing like this took place. Lehtinen and Finley accompanied the lawsuit with dramatic attacks on the state, the district, and the sugar industry. Finley spoke of phosphorus as a cancer spreading throughout the south. Lehtinen added, "When the question is asked, 'Should the [sugar] industry be stopped or the Everglades saved?' the answer is, 'The Everglades should be saved.' " He charged that the state and the district had "breached the public trust." [27] The district and the sugar industry responded with rhetoric that was milder but equally firm. The district insisted that the lawsuit was flawed and that the Surface Water Improvement and Management process would address the problem satisfactorily. This verbal standoff set a pattern of deadlock that persisted until January 1991.

Escalation

The battle became increasingly bitter. When he first met Suzan Ponzoli, the lead attorney in Lehtinen's office, a top lawyer at Skadden Arps told her he would not be lectured to by a "schoolmarm." Meanwhile, Ponzoli requested voluminous documentation from the district and began to schedule depositions with many district staffers. The district decided not to allow federal attorneys to search the files themselves but to have district staff photocopy the records. The sugar industry and national environmental groups also requested copies. Work at the district headquarters slowed as files were turned inside out, copying machines hummed, and lawyers filled nearby hotel rooms, waiting for documents.

On December 23, one day before the deadline for filing the district's response to the complaint, Lehtinen amended the complaint, dropping several central features from the original. The district's lawyers at Skadden Arps protested that this proved that the original complaint had been frivolous. They alleged that Lehtinen had engaged in unprofessional conduct and asked that the federal government reimburse the district for the cost of preparing its response to the original complaint.

Several months later, the conflict escalated again when, acting on a tip, Lehtinen sent FBI agents protected with bulletproof vests into a mill owned by U.S. Sugar. The tipster had said toxic wastes were being stored in drums labeled "used oil," which turned out not to be true. However, the agents did find records showing evidence that toxic wastes had been dumped illegally for several years. There was extensive publicity, and eventually U.S. Sugar paid a $3.75 million fine.

Thus the lawsuit quickly developed into what a lawyer for the Sugar Cane League called World War III. In Wodraska's words, "I have never seen an issue get out of control so fast." The air filled with motions, countermotions, petitions, and stipulations. As one federal prosecutor said, "We fought over everything—the cause of action, permission to take action, every word of the complaint, bringing the corps of engineers into the suit, dismissal, discovery, every rule of civil procedure, the day, hour, time, and location of every deposition. It was unbelievable."

What Was Really at Issue?

On its surface, the lawsuit was a classic example of environmental litigation. The central legal and factual issues in the litigation were regulatory issues—whether permits should be obtained for the pumps at the southern edge of the Everglades Agricultural Area and, if so, the proper standard for phosphorus in the water passing through the pumps. Furthermore, the lawsuit seemed to be a vivid illustration of the principle that the federal government must take a leadership role in environmental policy if environmental values are to be protected.

One side was the federal government, backed by environmentalists. (Ten national environmental groups intervened, and both the Sierra Club Legal Defense Fund and the Environmental Defense Fund assigned attorneys to the case.) On the other side were the state and a local governmental agency that had long been closely allied with a powerful economic interest. Technically, the sugar industry was not a party to the litigation. The Florida Sugar Cane League requested status as intervenors, but the presiding judge refused. However, he did allow two small towns in the EAA to intervene because the effluent from their municipal sewage treatment plant contained phosphorus. The towns wanted to become involved because they were dependent on the sugar industry; one of them calls itself the "Sweetest town in the U.S." The sugar industry paid the costs of the cities' attorneys.

There were, however, three elements that were not typical. For one thing, the immediate legal issue was one of state rather than federal law: whether the pumps needed a state permit. Lehtinen did not contend that the district had violated the Clean Water Act; instead he argued that the state and the district were violating state water quality laws. The lawsuit was litigated in federal court because the parties damaged by the state's alleged negligence were a national park and a national wildlife refuge. The Constitution provides that cases to which federal agencies are a party may be tried in federal court.

It was highly unusual for the Department of Justice to litigate questions of state law or to ask whether a permitting action (in this case, the failure to require a permit) by a state agency was violating state law. Recently, the Department of Justice and federal courts have become deeply enmeshed in such state issues as funding for state prisons, the operation of state institutions for mentally retarded people, boundaries of legislative districts, and the racial balance of public schools. However, in these cases, federal action is predicated on federal law or on constitutional requirements. Assistant Attorney General Richard Stewart, who took office in August 1989, can think of no Department of Justice case that involves the federal government in litigating state regulatory practices in the same fashion as the Everglades case did. The closest example involves adjudication of water rights for national parks and wildernesses in the West. For many of these cases, Congress took steps to waive the federal government's "sovereign immunity" to suits in state courts, so that Department of Justice attorneys could pursue federal claims through state processes, administrative or judicial.

The second distinctive feature of the Everglades case was that although the legal issues were regulatory, the public debate during 1989 and 1990 was not only about permits and regulations but also about public works—the construction of artificial wetlands. The Everglades SWIM plan, issued in draft in 1989, proposed that 40,000 acres of land be leveed off and converted to artificial marshes, like the experimental wetland that had been approved in late 1988, just after the lawsuit was filed.

There was acrimonious debate about which land should be used and who would pay. Environmentalists insisted that no public lands should be used to clean sugar's dirty water. The sugar industry said that if this much land were taken out of production, a sugar mill would have to close. Furthermore, the industry insisted that it was not responsible for paying for the wetlands. At one point U.S. Sugar's attorney, Robert Buker, told a meeting that the sugar industry would support a cleanup if the federal government "writes us a check for $350 million." [28]

Environmentalists responded that other industries were expected to pay to clean up after themselves and that the sugar industry should not be an exception. The Wilderness Society engaged a team of university economists and scientists to estimate the total public subsidies that were already being given to the sugar industry. Lehtinen said publicly that although the lawsuit did not raise the question of who would pay for cleanup, the plan for financing wetlands should be specific and realistic, and as a Floridian he thought the sugar industry should pay.

The third distinctive feature of the litigation was the lack of clarity about the objectives of the litigation. The district raised this point from the outset. It claimed that the complaint did not ask for anything that the SWIM process was not already doing. Jim Garner, a lawyer who was chair of the district board, said that he had fought many lawsuits, but "this is the only time in my life that I had no idea what the other side was after." Doran Jason, another board member, said, "We don't have a responsible party on the other side. The only way to get rid of the lawsuit is to elect Dexter Lehtinen to Congress in a few years." [29]

In court, federal attorneys argued that the complaint was quite specific. But in interviews afterward, they were more candid. The fact was, says Stewart, that "Lehtinen had not thought through what he wanted." Furthermore, it was not easy to define specific remedies. If the SWIM set standards and timetables for reducing the level of phosphorus, this would be an improvement. But "agricultural pollution was clearly only the opening wedge in a much larger issue," Stewart says. "It was really a question of changing the culture of the district, the state, and the industry.... The federal government could not impose a solution because that would involve structural reform. What we had to do was like playing judo on the system." Eventually, in November 1990, in order to detour around the problems of complexity and vagueness of federal goals, federal attorneys decided to try to separate the case into two parts. They requested a summary judgment on the narrower question of the liability of the state and district, which would allow the litigants to turn to the second issue of what remedies might be required.

Efforts to Break the Deadlock

In 1989 and 1990 there were several efforts to break the deadlock. In court and behind the scenes, the district sought to split the federal agencies. In 1990 the sugar industry tried to remove the grounds for the litigation by amending state law, and Governor Martinez tried to broker a settlement. All of these efforts failed.

Questions about whether all federal agencies supported the lawsuit arose from the very first day. As explained above, the Department of Justice's support for Lehtinen's action was uncertain at first. Justice was disturbed by the lawsuit's assertion that the federal government could protect national parks from pollution because the pollution was a nuisance that harmed federal lands. Justice attorneys felt that this would set a precedent that might apply to state water laws in the West and stir up tremendous political controversy.

Lehtinen agreed to retreat from this legal argument, and the lawsuit was amended in December. As Lehtinen said later, it was someone else's job to protect other national parks; his main interest was in saving the Everglades.[30] In the amended complaint, the cause of action was narrowed. The lawsuit argued only that the Florida Department of Environmental Regulation and the South Florida Water Management District were failing to enforce state laws that allegedly required permits for the pumps that moved water in the wet season from the EAA to the Water Conservation Areas, and eventually to the park.

This approach brought the Department of Justice into the case on Lehtinen's side, but the position of other federal agencies was still uncertain. When Richard Stewart took office as an assistant attorney general in August 1989, he decided that his main job was to "get the federal family together." He convened a meeting of assistant secretaries from the Department of the Interior (representing the National Park Service and the Fish and Wildlife Service), the U.S. Army (representing the corps of engineers), and the Department of Agriculture (representing the Soil Conservation Service). To unify these various agencies, each with its own perspective on the Everglades, it was decided that the federal government would submit a single package of comments on the Everglades SWIM plan. Negotiating the agreement to do this and executing it took over six months; the comments were submitted in March 1990.

Stewart says that the matter was handled at his level—that of assistant secretary—with no interference from the White House. There were occasional questions and "grousing," but no concerted effort to shape the federal position. The only overt sign of political interference in the case occurred when Interior Secretary Manuel Lujan delayed the filing of the federal motion for summary judgment during Martinez's reelection campaign.

There were five or six meetings at the assistant secretary level in Washington, and assistant secretaries made a trip together to the park. Meanwhile, a multiagency team of scientists and other career employees drafted joint comments on the SWIM plan. The federal team also commissioned research studies about the scientific issues in the case; over $1 million of Justice's funds were spent on consultants and experts. Justice asked the Interior Department to contribute, but no funds were forthcoming. At one point, the sugar industry asked the court for access to the minutes of what it called the "remedy committee" of federal officials. The court refused.

The Environmental Protection Agency was not an active participant in most of this federal activity. EPA had already taken the position that its statutes did not apply to the pumps. However, EPA was being asked to approve nondegradation standards for Outstanding Natural Resource Water in Florida, submitted by the state under the Clean Water Act. The park and the refuge had been designated by the state as Outstanding Florida Waters, but the standards for this designation were weak, especially on agricultural runoff. Justice was concerned that if EPA accepted the standards for Outstanding Florida Waters, this would undercut the litigation. Stewart worked with the Atlanta regional office to forestall this step.

While federal agencies were slowly coalescing into a united front, the sugar industry was exploring ways to undercut the lawsuit. In 1989, it persuaded the legislature to create the Everglades Agricultural Area Environmental Protection District, in House Bill 1502. This body would be controlled by landowners in the EAA, who would have one vote for each acre of farmland they owned. The group had the power to build structures and conduct studies and other activities addressing environmental issues in the EAA. This district was empowered to tax landowners up to $5 per acre per year, which would amount to about $2 million annually. In 1990, the figure was raised to $10. Implicitly, this figure was the sugar industry's offer of funding to build artificial wetlands or to take other remedial action. Since the draft SWIM projected the cost of artificial wetlands in the range of $200 million or more, the industry's offer was not viewed as particularly generous.

In addition, the industry mobilized scientific and public relations efforts to fight the federal lawsuit. The EAA Environmental Protection District entered a multiyear contract with Curtis Richardson, a Duke University professor who is an expert on wetlands. The Florida Sugar Cane League hired a respected Florida scientist who had worked for the phosphate industry and held a position on the board of the Florida Wildlife Federation. Citing Richardson's expertise, the industry argued that sugar is a benign crop from an environmental point of view. In the muck of the EAA, cane requires very little fertilizer, unlike the vegetables grown on other parts of the EAA. Therefore, drainage from cane fields is cleaner than that from other fields. Also, since cane is a perennial grass, it does not have to be replanted more than once every three or four years, thus reducing erosion. It grows very thickly, which discourages pests, and the industry uses biological controls rather than large amounts of pesticide.

Indeed, the water pumped off cane fields is quite low in phosphorus by many standards. It runs between 75 and 120 parts of phosphorus per billion (ppb), whereas effluent from the municipal sewage treatment plant in Jacksonville, Florida, contains 100 ppb, the drinking water in the state capital contains 80 ppb, and rain over the Everglades may contain 60 to 70 ppb. (Water in the WCAs and the park contains much less phosphorus. The park's scientists say the normal level in the park is 7 to 14 ppb.)[31]

In addition to contesting the science that formed the basis for the lawsuit, the industry sought to remove the legal underpinnings for the case. In 1990, the industry pushed for legislation that would require the district to establish a large area of artificial wetlands but would also exempt the district from obtaining permits for the pumps on the southern edge of the EAA. This latter provision would have removed the major point of the federal complaint against the district. On a close vote, the state legislature killed the bill. This is said to have been the first important loss for the sugar industry in the legislature.

Although most of the activity in 1989 and 1990 was devoted to building up the strength of the two sides, there were several discussions among key players about ways to settle the lawsuit. Most of these discussions got nowhere. Environmentalists contend that when they asked for a private meeting with the sugar industry, industry representatives brought along a court reporter. District officials say that when they opened quiet talks with Lehtinen, he would reveal the details in press statements the following day.

One effort to settle the case did result in a specific proposal. It was organized by Nat Reed and Charles Lee of the Florida Audubon Society. Key parts were played by Jim Garner, chair of the district board, and Flo-Sun. Reed saw the problem as a land use conflict. He approached Talisman Sugar and Flo-Sun with the concept that the state and the district might obtain Talisman's lands and convert some of them to wetlands. Flo-Sun would purchase the Talisman lands and then sell them to or exchange them with the state for state-owned tracts that were highly productive cane fields. In addition, the sugar industry would contribute $41 million to the cost of building the wetlands.[32] Three meetings were held to discuss the sale-and-swap option, as well as the idea of converting parts of a WCA into an artificial wetland.

Both Reed and Lee are Republicans. Governor Martinez, also a Republican, was facing reelection in November 1990, and the environmentalists argued that he needed to resolve the lawsuit to avoid being linked with polluters. After Martinez's 1988 appeal to Washington, the state had taken a back seat to the district, letting the district work through the SWIM process on its own. The state filed short briefs as litigation progressed, generally supporting the district's arguments but adding little. In the spring of 1990, after the first draft SWIM plan was issued, staff in the Department of Environmental Regulation worked closely with district staff to prepare a letter of comment. But the director of the Department of Environmental Regulation rejected it and wrote his own highly critical comments, which infuriated the district. In short, Martinez seemed to be content to keep his distance from the district without siding openly with the environmentalists or against the powerful sugar industry.

In September, Martinez tried to take a leadership role but was unsuccessful. In a highly publicized meeting of sugar executives, Florida environmentalists, and district officials, the governor endorsed the proposal that Lee and Reed had developed. But several key parties had not been consulted or had not signed on to the compromise. Not only were Lehtinen, the park, and the refuge not part of the negotiations, but staff of the national environmental organizations and the Department of Justice were also left out, and Florida environmentalists were divided. Lehtinen denounced the proposal as not providing enough reliable funding to build artificial wetlands of adequate size. The district said it had not taken a formal position on the proposal, and support quickly melted away.

SETTLEMENT OF THE LAWSUIT

Governor Martinez stood for reelection in November 1990. After his proposed compromise fell flat in September 1990, his opponent, former U.S. senator Lawton Chiles, began making an issue of the lawsuit. Chiles did not endorse one side or the other; he simply said that spending millions of dollars on Washington attorneys was an outrageous waste of money. Newspapers uncovered the fact that Skadden Arps attorneys had billed the district $33.60 for coffee, juice, and danish for four lawyers when they held a meeting in their conference room in Washington one morning to discuss the suit. *The American Lawyer* later deplored Skadden Arps's billing practices in an article entitled "Skaddenomics: The Ludicrous World of Law Firm Billing," while noting that other large law firms had similar billing practices.[33] The issue of the district's legal fees was one of several that carried Chiles to victory.

By the end of 1990, the district's legal position was looking weak. A year earlier, its motion to dismiss the federal complaint had been promptly rejected in an oral ruling from the bench as soon as the lawyers had finished their arguments. The federal coalition seemed to be holding firm, and a date had been set to hear the federal motion for a summary judgment. Nonetheless, the district had a hard time accepting

ing the fact that it could not deal with the lawsuit as a state issue by negotiating with Florida environmentalists and pushing ahead with the SWIM plan. At one point the district hired a retired justice of the Florida Supreme Court to ask whether it would be possible somehow to set the suit aside. Predictably, he said it was not. Skadden, Arps, Meagher, and Flom recommended that the district seek to settle the suit by inviting the park, the refuge, and the corps of engineers to participate in redrafting the suit.[34] The district board agonized over whether to settle and voted narrowly instead to appropriate more money to pay for attorneys.

From his first day in office, Chiles made it clear that, unlike Governor Martinez, he would take charge of the issue and bring it to a settlement. His first speech after the inauguration was to the annual meeting of the Everglades Coalition, a consortium of environmental groups. He told them that he was commander-in-chief of the state's environmental programs and that he would settle the case within six months.

Chiles's first effort to settle was, like Martinez's, an effort to start a discussion among the key players in state politics. He called a summit of state environmentalists, state and district officials, and the sugar industry. Sugar trucked dozens of farm laborers to the room where the summit was being held and paid employees to hold signs protesting that they would lose their jobs. After a few hours, Chiles walked out.[35]

Although the summit led nowhere, other lines of action were more promising. To settle the case, Chiles mobilized all available tools, including his command of the executive branch (specifically the Department of Environmental Regulation), his influence with the legislature, his ability to appoint members of the district board, and, ultimately, his own ability to pull a rabbit out of the hat.

The State Enters Negotiations

Even before his inauguration, the governor had talked with the superintendents of the park and the refuge. After Chiles took office, Carol Browner, a longtime aide who became his secretary of the Department of Environmental Regulation, contacted Steve Herman, the career attorney managing the case in the Washington office of the Department of Justice. Hearing that Herman would be willing to discuss settlement terms, she flew to Washington the following day.

These initial conversations soon developed into serious negotiations. The governor's strategy was to avoid embracing any substantive position on the issues raised in the suit. Instead, he asked that both sides designate their chief scientists, who would then be asked to resolve the dispute.

The negotiation process soon evolved into a three-ring circus. In one ring were the scientists. This group included three federal employees: Mike Soukup, director of a research center at the Everglades National Park; Dan Scheidt, a staff scientist at the center; and Mark Maffei, a biologist at the Loxahatchee National Wildlife Refuge. The top-ranking member from the district was Tom MacVicar, deputy executive director responsible for water resource activities. The state Department of Environmental Regulation was represented by Richard Harvey, a career program manager. From time to time, additional staffers and consultants were brought into the group, so that it sometimes got as large as two dozen people. When the negotiations bogged down, a state agency that mediated environmental disputes managed the process for a time.

In the second ring were the lawyers. Federal interests were represented by Suzan Ponzoli and others from Lehtinen's office, and by Steve Herman and other attorneys from the Department of Justice in Washington. In the third ring were the principals, including Lehtinen, Assistant Attorney General Richard Stewart, Browner, and Timer Powers of the district. Powers was a highly respected independent businessman and civic leader. Soon after Chiles made it clear that he wished to see a settlement, Wodraska, the district's executive director, asked Powers to join the district staff to help out. Powers soon became the senior person from the district working on the case.

Many of the participants in the negotiations say that Powers was the key to the process. During his earlier tenure with the district board, he had played the central role in negotiating two of the district's greatest environmental achievements—the settlement of Indian water rights claims and the design of the Kissimmee restoration. Powers was deeply committed to open and participatory processes. He was not identified with the Surface Water Improvement and Management plan and made it a point not to take sides on substantive issues facing the negotiators. However, he did insist that negotiating sessions not be allowed to end without agreement to meet again. Powers's role was to monitor the negotiations closely and to soothe people so that they would return to the negotiating table after the most bitter disagreements. Steve Herman of the Department of Justice said later, "Timer brought about the settlement by an act of will. . . . He assumed that everyone had good intentions and insisted that the negotiations not break down." [36]

The scientists were first asked to address the technical question of what level of phosphorus was harmful to the Everglades. As one participant in these discussions recalled: "This was a relatively straightforward technical issue, and we were able to come to agreement fairly quickly. But then we were told to answer a more difficult question: how big an artificial wetland would be required to bring Everglades Agricultural Area waters down to an acceptable standard. This was tough." The scientists struggled with this issue, handicapped by the fact that their lawyers did not want to reveal the parameters of the mathematical models used to estimate how phosphorus would behave in the wetlands and downstream.

Neither the sugar industry nor the environmentalists were at the table for the negotiations. Supposedly, discussions were conducted secretly, but in fact information leaked out, and both the sugar industry and the environmentalists looked for ways to tell the negotiators what they felt about the emerging agreements. The sugar industry may have had more difficulty finding out what was being discussed because their traditional relationships with the district were under severe strain. But the environmentalists had been working closely with Lehtinen's office, the park, and the refuge from the start. At an early point in the litigation, Paul Parks of the environmental organization FOREVERGLADES had been a paid consultant to the Department of Justice.

Browner Lobbies the Legislature

Although sugar and the environmentalists were not directly involved in the negotiations, they were quite active in the state legislature. As the scientists struggled to estimate the proper size of artificial wetlands, the focus of activity shifted to the legislature. Several legislators who were favorable to environmental values, together with Florida-based environmental leaders, had drafted legislation that would concede the original point of Lehtinen's suit by requiring the district to apply to the Department of Environmental Regulation for permits for the EAA pumps. The bill would also require the district to promulgate rules for permitting farmlands to pump phosphorus-laden waters into drainage canals and to construct artificial wetlands (called stormwater treatment areas). In addition, the bill would grant the district power to condemn farmlands for use as wetlands and to raise funds to construct the wetlands.

The sugar industry was able to insert several provisions in the legislation that safeguarded its interests. One important provision required that if the district assessed farmers for cleanup costs, the assessment on each farm must be based on the amount of phosphorus that the farm contributed to the total. (Some environmentalists feel this might eventually become a serious problem, because underwriters for state bonds to build the wetlands might be uncomfortable about determining how much farmers should pay.)

The legislation moved through the House before Chiles and Browner became deeply involved. The sugar industry also held back, calculating perhaps that its strength lay in the Senate. After the bill passed the House, the governor threw his strength behind it, and Browner lobbied actively in the Senate, working closely with environmental lobbyists and environmentally inclined legislators. As it became clear that the bill would pass, U.S. Sugar and Flo-Sun took a neutral position, and the legislation passed both houses unanimously. It was named the Marjory Stoneman Douglas Everglades Protection Act, in honor of the author of *The Everglades: River of Grass,* who at the age of 101 was still an active environmentalist. Chiles signed the bill at a ceremony in her home.[37]

A New Team at the District

In addition to using the Department of Environmental Regulation to open negotiations with the Department of Justice and lobbying the state legislature, Chiles used his power to appoint the members of the district board. In the end, appointment power was perhaps Chiles's most important tool. Chiles had the authority to appoint five new members to the district board, and he asked Browner to recruit people who would be committed to settling the lawsuit—one way or another. Jim Garner, who as chair of the board had strong influence on the district's conduct of the litigation, quickly became a lame duck, and he left the board when his term expired in late March 1991. Chiles also let it be known that he was not particularly supportive of John Wodraska, and Wodraska resigned in June. Powers became interim executive director and did not hesitate to use his authority to move the negotiations ahead. Skadden Arps's role with the district had also come to an end, so by late spring all of the top decision makers at the district had been replaced.

The Surrender and the Agreement

Early in spring, soon after Chiles made a public commitment to try to settle the case, Lehtinen had agreed to a sixty-day stay to allow for negotiations. When the sixty days had expired, scientists were still struggling to agree on the appropriate size for an artificial wetland, new members had been named to the board, Wodraska had resigned, and the Douglas Act had passed the legislature. Chiles decided to go to court himself, as a lawyer for the state, to ask the judge for a year's stay to continue the negotiations.

Lehtinen opposed the delay. Lehtinen told the judge that he should not be influenced by the Douglas Act or other steps that Governor Chiles had taken. "This lawsuit is not about permits," Lehtinen said. "It is not about plans, either. . . . What we did was sue over the quality of the water." He lifted a glass of water, which, he said, had been taken from the Everglades over the weekend, asserting, "I haven't heard any-thing in court today saying that the water is any better than it was six months ago. . . . Why won't they stand at this podium and say that the water is dirty?" [38]

At this point, Chiles made his offer of surrender. He said he would be happy to stipulate that the water was dirty, thus conceding a key point that the district's lawyers had been resisting for over two years. As Lt. Gov. Buddy MacKay said later, "Lawton [Chiles] astounded all the lawyers, most of all his own." The judge called a recess, and the lawyers gathered in excited groups to talk about what to do next.

The hearing ended with agreement on a two-month stay. Over this period, the negotiations moved ahead rapidly. Yet there were many dif-ficulties in coming to a final agreement, which had to be signed by five federal agencies as well as by the state and the district. One difficult issue was the size of the artificial wetlands. The scientists were able to agree on a range of acreage, and the principals finally selected the spe-cific number. Some observers feel changes in the acreage became the measure of who was winning the negotiations.

All parties agreed that it would be helpful to have a technical oversight committee of scientists to monitor further planning, research, and implementation of the settlement.[39] However, the EPA objected at first because it had not been on the committee.

The final issue was whether the federal court would retain jurisdiction over the agreement so that federal lawyers could request a trial if the district and state did not implement the agreement as planned. Negotiations broke down late one night when federal attorneys insisted on this point, and the district and the state said they lacked the authority to agree. The next morning, the district and the state conceded the point.

On July 8, six months after he took office, Chiles announced that Lehtinen, the federal agencies, and the district had agreed to a thirty-page settlement. The document was submitted to the district board and then to the federal court for approval.

BARRIERS TO RESOLUTION

The settlement dramatically changed the legal situation as well as political alignments. The Marjory Stoneman Douglas Act had directed that the pumps be subject to permitting and that the district require farmers in the EAA to obtain permits for water drained from their lands. The settlement added specific interim numerical standards for the quality of the water passing through the pumps. The act had also committed the district to build artificial wetlands. To this, the settlement added a specific acreage of at least 34,700 effective acres. The settlement also established a schedule for issuance of the permits and construction of the wetlands, and it provided that if this schedule was not met, the U.S. attorney could petition the court to reopen the case.[40]

In addition to these legal provisions, the settlement made a fundamental change in the political situation. When the district, the state, and federal agencies signed the settlement, this act put them all on the same side of the table. Thus the iron triangle of district-sugar-corps was broken, and a new alliance of district-state-corps-environmentalists-park-refuge emerged. In Bob Dreher's words, "It is getting very crowded on our side of the table." [41] The only parties on the other side of the table were the sugar industry and the towns in the EAA.

Although the settlement did constitute substantial movement toward cleaning up the water in the Everglades, it did not put all of the pieces in place to reduce the phosphorus in the EAA outflow. It did not provide funds to build artificial wetlands or to convince everyone that the wetlands were a good idea. Also, the new coalition faced continued legal resistance from the sugar industry. Thus, no action was yet possible to clean the water. To remove phosphorus and improve water management in the Everglades, the district and several other key parties had to take additional steps toward a new set of policies and a new style of politics.

The Missing Funds

The cost of building the artificial wetlands described in the settlement was usually estimated at around $400 million.[42] The district had the statutory authority to raise its millage by enough to cover this amount. In addition, the sugar industry had already made a public commitment to Governor Martinez in 1990 to provide $40 million. The local electrical utility had committed $17.5 million as a mitigation payment for putting power lines through the Water Conservation Areas. About $5 million of state funds were already earmarked to help.

However, $400 million was only part of the potential burden that the district and its allies were facing. The district was also proposing to restore the Kissimmee, also at an estimated cost of $400 million. And the federal government had agreed to expand the Everglades National Park to the east if the state and the district would help purchase the lands. Furthermore, if the artificial wetlands did not solve the Everglades problem, perhaps other costly changes would be required. Thus, the total bill could exceed $1 billion.

Are Wetlands the Answer?

To get the money, the district and its allies had to obtain agreement about how it would be spent. At this time many of the key players were uneasy about the proposed artificial wetlands. The wetlands would rely on advanced technology in two respects: they would be much larger than any existing constructed wetlands, and they would be expected to lower the phosphorus to a much lower level than had been achieved by most other artificial wetlands. Key staff in the district said quite openly that the settlement did not resolve large unanswered questions about the design. According to Tom MacVicar, the district's top engineer, the people in the negotiation team (which included himself) "were technically unqualified to design the wetlands. . . . It would have been better if we had gone through the normal public works process, with plenty of opportunity for public review and comment."

The pilot wetland that was approved by Governor Martinez in 1988 will eventually provide some clues about how well the technology works. However, deadlines in the settlement left little time to learn anything from operating the pilot wetland before finalizing the design of the larger wetlands.

The technical design of the wetlands is a relatively small issue compared with the question of whether they are a good investment. The sugar industry had been saying for years that the phosphorus coming off its lands was not a significant problem compared with the disruption of the hydroperiod in the Everglades. Sugar, industry said, had been made the scapegoat for a much bigger problem. The real problem was that over half of the Everglades had been drained for urban uses and farming, and the traditional flow of water had been disrupted.

Although the district no longer denied that water coming off cane fields was dirty, virtually everyone involved with the issue recognized that fixing the phosphorus was only a prelude to addressing the much more complex and difficult problem of adjusting the hydroperiod. By themselves, the wetlands will do nothing to restore the flow of water in the Everglades. In fact, the wetlands could damage the hydroperiod, because if the wetlands are located on land that used to be dry farmland, they may lose water by evaporation and discharge less water into the WCAs and the park. Scientists at the park and district agree that the wetlands will not be enough to solve the environmental problems of the Everglades. In the words of Mike Soukup, research director for the park, "Removing the phosphorus is a necessary step but will not be sufficient to save the Everglades." [43]

This leads to two very difficult questions. First, what steps can be taken to restore—or at least move toward a restoration of—the hydroperiod? And second, is the continued presence of the sugar industry in the EAA a barrier to restoring the hydroperiod?

The Marjory Stoneman Douglas Act and the settlement both touched on the issue of the hydroperiod but did not offer specific proposals. The Douglas Act required the district to prepare a SWIM plan "to bring facilities into compliance with applicable water quality standards and *restore the Everglades hydroperiod*" (emphasis added).[44] The settlement went a step further with a clear statement of purpose about the park and refuge but made no reference to the remainder of the Everglades. It required that "the parties commit themselves to guarantee water quality and water quantity needed to preserve and restore the unique flora and fauna of the park and the refuge." [45]

No specific proposals were on the table in 1991 about how the hydroperiod might be changed. There was talk of restoring the sheet flow, which would involve breaching some of the existing levees. Another option was building an aquatic flowway, which would reestablish the connection between Lake Okeechobee and the southern Everglades. No one had suggested a specific design, but a flowway could involve new structures and canals.

In addition to new facilities, restoring the hydroperiod would involve changes in the distribution of water. Thus, restoration raises the question of how much water is needed for the urban areas along the South Florida coast and the sugar industry, as well as for the Everglades. Work has begun on building the scientific base that would answer these questions. The district has built a "natural systems model" to quantify water levels and flows in the primeval Everglades as well as in the current system. In 1990, Congress appropriated funds for the park to develop a detailed plan for restoring a more natural flow of water to and through the Everglades. The park is adding information about wildlife and vegetation to the natural systems model.

Legal Stalemate

The third barrier to a settlement was yet more concrete and overwhelming. The sugar industry did not accept the settlement as final. Instead, they continued to file appeals, requests under the Freedom of Information Act to see documents that were exchanged between the participants in negotiations, and motions demanding delays for various reasons, such as preparation of an environmental impact statement on the settlement agreement.

Sugar fought back in public as well as in court. In the spring of 1992, almost a year after the settlement had been announced, U.S. Sugar

placed a series of ads denouncing Hoeveler's decision in Florida newspapers and magazines. The ads said that the settlement had produced
an unreasonable standard for the quality of water flowing off the cane
fields; at 50 parts per billion, the standard called for water "cleaner than
rain." The ads also denounced the fact that sugar was excluded from
the discussions that led to the settlement. "Florida abandoned good
government in the Everglades controversy," the ads said. In the words
of Andy Rackley, general manager of the Florida Sugar Cane League,
"We've never had our day in court."

So the settlement did not reduce the workload of the attorneys or
ease the climate of tension and conflict. Months passed with motions
and countermotions, and the chances of meeting the deadlines in the
settlement dwindled.

TOWARD AN AGREEMENT WITH THE SUGAR INDUSTRY

Nine months after the June 1991 settlement, Judge Hoeveler gave it
his final approval, after considering and rejecting numerous objections
by the sugar industry. This opened a phase that was focused not on the
lawsuit but on crafting a new mediated agreement.

The Beginnings of a Truce with Sugar

Publicly, the sugar industry took a long time to retreat from its position that phosphorus was not a serious problem and that sugar was not
the culprit. However, behind the scenes, both Flo-Sun and U.S. Sugar
began putting out feelers for compromise. As early as January 1992,
some industry executives said privately that the real issue was not
whether there was a problem with phosphorus, but simply how much
money the sugar industry would have to pay to clean it up. As one
executive said, "We recognize that we must clean up the water coming
off our fields, but we must be sure that we can tell the banks how much
it will cost. And it must be a reasonable amount."

In April 1992, the sugar industry shifted its public position significantly. For the first time, the industry publicly proposed alternatives to
SWIM's artificial wetlands, thus implicitly recognizing the need to cut
the flow of phosphorus from its lands into the Everglades. At a meeting
of the district board, the Sugar Cane League promised that farmers

would adjust their pumping schedules, fine-tune their use of fertilizer, and help towns in the EAA remove water from sewage effluent or pump the effluent into deep aquifers. The league said that it was testing alternative ways to remove phosphorus, including lining irrigation canals with limestone, using algae to "scrub" phosphorus from drainage water, and storing water in deep aquifers during the rainy season, rather than draining the water into the Everglades. The league also proposed a system of credits, or transferable rights for emissions of phosphorus, modeled after the acid rain provisions of the 1990 Clean Air Act.[46]

In making their proposals, industry officials said they were trying to "de-escalate the litigation." But within two days of announcing its alternatives, sugar also filed a series of appeals of the SWIM plan. Bob Buker, a vice president of U.S. Sugar, protested that the settlement and the final SWIM "appears to be the work of environmental absolutists for whom eliminating farming is as important as addressing Everglades problems. . . . We are at fault for not presenting alternatives earlier, but the regulators are equally at fault." [47]

The sugar industry's plan was so sketchy, and came so close to its new legal action, that it was easy to reject. Tom MacVicar said (or key staff in the district said confidentially) that many of sugar's proposals were "smoke and mirrors that were never much more than a distraction." But there were good political reasons not to reject sugar's overtures out of hand. The district board still had a minority of members who had been appointed by Governor Martinez, and many of these members were not comfortable with the settlement. The board adopted the SWIM plan in early March 1992 by only a 5-3 vote, and one board member released his own plan for solving the phosphorus problem at much lower cost.

A public agency cannot shut itself off from an important stakeholder, even if the stakeholder has filed suits, so the district opened its doors to sugar. The district invited scientists from other agencies and from the sugar industry to comment on preliminary plans for artificial wetlands. The district also organized the Scientific Advisory Group for the Everglades (SAGE) to share information about research and to discuss district plans. All interested agencies were invited to participate.

In addition to these practical reasons for working with sugar, there was considerable willingness among district staff to try to rebuild working relationships with the sugar industry. One reason was that the new allies were not entirely comfortable with each other on a personal level. The two and a 'half years of costly litigation left a legacy of bitterness and disillusionment. As one top district executive said, "The litigation was very painful for us. We were used to being the good guys, and it told us we were not. I sometimes wonder if the district will survive." On a more personal level, some of the scientists who worked for federal and local agencies felt that they had been ill-used during the litigation. As one federal scientist said, "Lots of people took things personally during the lawsuit, and I have found it difficult to set these feelings aside. I do not trust people at the district any more. It is difficult to work with them. I have lost friendships."

The most poignant statement was made by Timer Powers. He learned during the settlement negotiations that he had incurable throat cancer. Sometimes he equated the cancer in his throat with the bitterness felt by those who did not have a chance to speak their mind during the negotiations. If people do not have a chance to say their piece, he said, this exclusion will eventually be lethal to the settlement and to the district itself.

So as the sugar industry slowly and awkwardly moved to soften its position, state and district officials also reached out to sugar. At the January 1992 meeting of the Everglades Coalition, Alan Milledge, the new chair of the board, publicly called for bringing sugar into the circle of agreement. The governor met quietly with sugar executives, and Nat Reed organized an informal two-day meeting for top executives from U.S. Sugar and Flo-Sun to exchange views with leaders of Florida environmental groups.

When the Sugar Cane League offered its way of solving the phosphorus problem in April 1992, the reaction was guardedly positive. Responding to sugar's plan, Alan Milledge said, "What we are beginning to do today is to put our swords down." [48] The U.S. attorney's office "cautioned against trusting Big Sugar completely," according to the *Miami Herald,* but said the office would support the league's plan if it were shown to be scientifically sound. [49]

The environmental community was divided about how to respond to the sugar industry's overtures. It was easy to criticize the industry's plan as lacking in sufficient detail and based on unsound science. But in addition to making public statements asking sugar to withdraw its law-suits, should environmentalists try to reach an agreement with sugar interests by entering into private conversations with them?

The mere presence of private lands in the middle of the Everglades makes it harder to manage the system to approximate the original flow of water. For decades, many environmentalists had sought to rid the Everglades of all private lands. Their goal now seems to be within reach. Even among those environmentalists who did not expect that the EAA could ever be returned entirely to wetlands, many thought that they could build an effective coalition for restoration without accommo-dating sugar. They were persuaded that the settlement would commit federal agencies to supporting restoration, and they were convinced that they could defeat sugar again in the Florida legislature if they had to.

Paul Parks of FOREVERGLADES expressed this feeling in telling an audience of environmentalists, state and local politicians, and agency offi-cials at the 1992 Everglades Coalition conference that the settlement had created a "new unity" against the "common enemy": the sugar industry. His organization distributed bumper stickers that said "Just Say No to Sugar." Joe Podgor of Friends of the Everglades, an organization that counts Marjory Stoneman Douglas as its most illustrious member, was even more explicit. His goal is simply to get agriculture out of the EAA. In contrast, Nat Reed told the 1992 Everglades Coalition conference that "the EAA should stay prime agricultural area, as long as it can be eco-nomically successful without adverse environmental impacts."

There are reasons an environmentalist might prefer sugar to other "evils." As noted above, of the crops that can be grown in the EAA, sugar is relatively benign. Water coming off cane fields is much cleaner than flows off vegetable fields, and far cleaner than runoff from urban areas. Over the next few years, it is possible that farmers in the EAA will turn away from sugar to land uses that are more harmful to the Everglades. Although the sugar industry is quite profitable, it is politi-cally vulnerable, not only on environmental issues but also on issues linked more directly to the industry's bottom line, such as trade. A free trade agreement between the United States and Mexico, or changes in the General Agreement on Tariffs and Trade, might allow cheap Mexi-can or Caribbean sugar into the United States. And if Fidel Castro fell, the United States might allow imports of Cuban sugar.

It is not clear how the Florida sugar industry would respond to increased competition from imported sugar. Perhaps some lands are so productive that their sugar could match the price of imported sugar. But perhaps not. U.S. Sugar raises vegetables as well as cane and might shift acreage away from sugar. Or the company might try to purchase other land in Florida or elsewhere if the economics of growing sugar in the EAA change dramatically. Fanjul interests already raise sugar in the Dominican Republic and might try to return to Cuba if Castro falls. The Talisman properties are already for sale; their lands have the shallowest muck and are the least productive cane fields in the EAA. Many of the smaller farmers who belong to the co-op have rich land and might be unwilling or unable to move.

Some concerned environmentalists, like Charles Lee of the Florida Audubon Society, fear that if the sugar industry did become unprofitable, the alternative might eventually be suburbanization of the EAA, as it is less than forty-five minutes from rapidly growing suburban areas. Everyone agrees that from the standpoint of the health of the Everglades ecosystem, paving the EAA would be the worst of all possible alternatives.

Designing a Mediation Process

As had been mandated in the settlement and in the SWIM, the district wrote a regulation for on-farm best management practices (BMPs) for phosphorus and other pollutants. The most effective BMP, it said, would be to let stormwater stand in fields longer, so that the soil would not dry out and oxidize, leaving the phosphorus behind to be absorbed by the next rainfall. A second BMP would be to fertilize more carefully—for example, by applying chemicals in bands along the roots of crops rather than across the whole field. The sugar industry announced that it would not object to these BMPs and, indeed, would comply with them immediately.

By the end of 1992, data showed remarkable drops in concentrations of phosphorus flowing through the canals and pumps at the southern edge of the Everglades Agricultural Area—a reduction of as much as 35 to 40 percent. No data were available from individual fields, so it was impossible to know whether the cleaner water was coming from farms that were using BMPs. Some environmentalists dismissed the data as a random fluctuation, but the sugar industry and the district were impressed.

There was little controversy about the BMP rules and they were approved without appeal. But the SWIM, with its plan for expensive artificial wetlands, was another matter. Over the spring, both sides prepared for appeals and litigation. Initially, many state and district officials were confident that they could defeat sugar's objections to the SWIM in court. But the industry made it clear that it would spend millions of dollars to fight. As Lt. Gov. Buddy MacKay remembers, "When someone says we can beat you in court, the first instinct is to get ready to fight. But after four or five months, we came down to earth. It became clear that the industry could tie us up in court for five to ten years and postpone the day when we got started on cleaning up the Everglades."

Even if the district and the state were successful in defeating legal challenges to the settlement in federal court and to state approval of the SWIM, other legal battles loomed ahead. The district would have to condemn private land to build the artificial wetlands. After that, the Douglas Act required that in order to assess farmers for the cost of building the wetlands, the district would have to determine how much phosphorus each farm was contributing. This would be both a technical challenge and another opportunity for litigation.

So the district, the state, and the Department of Justice decided to explore the possibility of a mediated agreement with the sugar industry. The district organized a half-day meeting of the principals in Orlando. It was to be a closed meeting, but at the last minute, the press were allowed to attend. This was the first time that all of the key players had been in the room together. The discussion was civil but did not get far beyond a statement of different positions.

This meeting convinced the district that it needed a professional mediator, who could orchestrate a series of less public conversations. After discussions with the various parties, the district hired Gerald Cormick of the University of Washington as a mediator.

Cormick conducted a series of meetings with the different parties in December 1991 and January 1992. He then proposed that he organize a technical group and a policy group, using a format similar to the one used in the 1991 negotiations, which had led to settlement of the lawsuit. However, these new negotiations would be more open; the sugar industry would participate actively, along with the state, the district, federal officials, environmentalists, tribes, and any local governments that were interested.

The Technical Agreement

As in the 1991 negotiations, most of the progress that was made early resulted from agreement on technical issues. The technical group met far more often than the policy group. Cormick spent hours shuttling between the participants, and there were long conversations over the phone. The atmosphere was much more open than it had been in 1991. For example, there were no lawyers to keep scientists from sharing their ideas about the effects of phosphorus on wetlands. Both the sugar industry and the federal-state-district team had experts on hand who would calculate what adding a new tract would achieve, while other participants watched them tap away on their laptop computers.

As the process unfolded, the technical group moved away from a debate about the SWIM. Tom MacVicar remembers that "no one really liked the plan in the SWIM." The primary objection was that the SWIM would not do much to improve the hydroperiod. So the technical group began looking for water that could be diverted to the Everglades. This additional water would make up for water that would be lost to evaporation when farmers kept water longer on their fields, to comply with BMPs.

The technical group found ways to bring 270,000 acre feet into the Everglades—about 10 percent of the fresh water that is currently flushed into the Gulf of Mexico or the Atlantic without passing through the Everglades. Some of the water came from a tract east of the EAA with farms, wetlands, and some housing. The residents and farmers there had long complained that they wanted more drainage. Other water was being drained north from the EAA into Lake Okeechobee, and from there to the coast via rivers.

Although there had been active debate in 1991 about whether the artificial wetlands would really work, the technical group did not cut back on the acreage of the wetlands. There were two reasons for this. One was that there was more information suggesting that the wetlands would effectively remove phosphorus. Since the July 1991 settlement, scientists had gathered more information about phosphorus in the

WCAs. For example, two new transects were plotted south of discharge structures in WCA-2, and information from one transect suggested that the wetlands would work more efficiently than had been assumed in 1991. A national panel of experts had reviewed the original plans for the wetlands and suggested that the district find ways to prevent short-circuiting during periods of high flow. But they did seem optimistic that the wetlands would work.

Also during 1991 and 1992, the district had examined the sugar industry's proposals for other ways of removing phosphorus, such as treating waters with chemicals or running them over limestone. With the possible exception of on-farm techniques, these proposals seemed to be as costly as and no more effective than artificial wetlands.

The second reason for not reducing the acreage of wetlands was that if more water were to be moved into the Everglades, it would have to be cleaned up somehow. The wetlands could do this job, too. In addition, a representative of the Miccosukee tribe participating in the technical group suggested that water from west of the EAA, which was now draining through the reservation, might be treated in the wetlands also. So yet more acreage was added, bringing the total to 40,000 acres.

The result was a technical plan that addressed far more than the polluted waters passing through pumps at the southern edge of the EAA, which had been the focus of Lehtinen's lawsuit. The plan attempted to help native Americans, improve the hydroperiod, and reduce unwanted discharges of fresh water into saline estuaries. As well as helping the Everglades, the plan even offered some relief to Florida Bay, the portion of the Gulf of Mexico just south of the Everglades. The bay had become increasingly saline because it was receiving less fresh water. In the last half dozen years, the bay had experienced sharp drops in fish, shrimp, lobsters, and sea grasses, and there had been massive blooms of algae. The technical plan would not begin to solve the problems in Florida Bay, but by making a little more fresh water available, it might improve the situation somewhat.

The Changing Political Climate

As the technical group worked, the political tide in Washington and in West Palm Beach began to turn against sugar. Several people in the

Clinton administration were strong advocates for restoration of the Everglades. Carol Browner became administrator of the Environmental Protection Agency. She recused herself from decisions that might involve a review of her earlier activities as a state official, but she did make several public statements about the importance of restoring the Everglades and about EPA's role in such endeavors. She also put in a phone call to Bruce Babbitt, the new secretary of the interior, and encouraged him to take a personal interest in the Everglades.

Babbitt had hired George Frampton, former president of the Wilderness Society, as assistant secretary for fish, wildlife, and parks. Frampton knew the Everglades well from Jim Webb's work. Brooks Yeager became the Interior Department's director of policy and planning; he had been legislative director of the National Audubon Society, which had just made a major commitment of resources by opening an Everglades campaign office in West Palm Beach. In Congress, George Miller took over chairmanship of the House Committee on Interior and Insular Affairs, and although he is from California, he took a special interest in the Everglades. Two new members of Congress from South Florida were named to the House Committee on Appropriations, and they became advocates for investing in Everglades research and restoration.

The first practical signs of the changing political climate appeared at the 1993 meeting of the Everglades Coalition in February. Governor Chiles, who attended the meeting, said, "I'm the captain of the ship" for Everglades restoration. If nothing happens, he said, "blame me." George Miller also attended, along with several other current and retired members of Congress.

U.S. Sugar and Flo-Sun released new plans at the conference to resolve the Everglades litigation. U.S. Sugar offered to drop its lawsuits, to support 35,000 acres of artificial wetlands, and to remove every pound of phosphorus that entered the water on its lands. Flo-Sun proposed spending $110 million for treating effluents chemically and earmarking 80,000 acres of public lands as a storage area for water that could be released to restore the hydroperiod.

Babbitt won the biggest headlines. He had previously announced that one of his major initiatives as secretary would be an ecosystem approach to solving environmental problems. On taking office, he faced a bitter controversy about whether to reduce timber harvests on federal land in the Pacific Northwest in order to protect endangered species like the spotted owl. And he faced a tough fight in Congress over reauthorization of the Endangered Species Act.

Babbitt's new approach expressed the central themes of civic environmentalism: prevention, sustainable development, ecosystems, and collaborative action by multiple agencies and multiple levels of government. For example, Babbitt organized a National Biological Survey to provide better information about ecosystems in trouble and about species in danger of extinction. Rather than waiting for an ecological "train wreck" to occur before invoking the Endangered Species Act, government officials would try to stop problems before they started and would coordinate their preventive efforts across agencies. These efforts would include looking both at potential environmental problems and at the economic dimension, such as the future needs of agriculture, timber, and urban areas.

Babbitt said he had made the Everglades the location of one of his first public appearances because the Everglades would be the model for his new approach. The Everglades would be "the prototype that proves across this country that we have the capacity to deal with these issues. . . . We're all going to be coming back to the Everglades as the test case for all park systems, for all states, for the entire country." [50]

To make the Everglades the model, Babbitt announced that George Frampton would lead a new interagency task force on the Everglades. Environmentalists and agency officials in the audience were very pleased. They were guaranteed to get attention and action in Washington.

Soon after the coalition meeting, Governor Chiles appointed three new members to the district board: an environmental educator, a community leader who quickly showed herself to be sensitive to environmental perspectives, and Nat Reed, who had long been a leading advocate for restoring the Everglades. Chiles also designated Lt. Gov. Buddy MacKay as point person to ensure that the mediation process was successful. The climate was changing in West Palm Beach and Tallahassee as well as in Washington.

Negotiations in Washington

This new political climate and the report from the technical group set the stage for cutting a deal about money. How much would the sugar industry pay to build artificial wetlands? Would they really drop their lawsuits? It was time to find out.

As long ago as 1990, the sugar industry had expressed willingness to be taxed to finance some kind of recovery plan, supporting state legislation to create a special taxing district in the Everglades. Slowly the amount that sugar was prepared to pay had risen. Buddy MacKay and district officials met quietly with sugar executives and pushed for a higher figure. By June 1993, there were signs that U.S. Sugar and Flo-Sun would agree to a plan requiring the industry to pay about $6 million per year; then the U.S. Sugar board met, and the offer became $10 million.

But time was beginning to run out. The state had twice postponed hearings on sugar's appeal of the SWIM plan to allow the mediation process to continue, and a third postponement would be necessary. If the third postponement was not obtained, soon district and state officials would have to take time out from the mediation process to give depositions for the hearing on the SWIM. Because of the complexity of the litigation, these depositions would take a great deal of time. Buddy MacKay recalls seeing a plan that would have required key staff members to prepare for the hearings six hours a day, five days a week, for nine months.

The Department of Justice was not willing to go along with another postponement in the absence of a written agreement showing that the SWIM appeal might be settled. Feeling he could get no more money from the sugar industry, MacKay suggested that Babbitt become directly involved.

Top sugar officials came to Washington to meet with George Frampton, Bonnie Cohen (another Interior Department assistant secretary), and Brooks Yeager. What had been a fairly open and fluid process in Florida now became a tough two-party negotiation. Frampton cleared his calendar to meet with the sugar executives. Buddy MacKay also came to Washington and attended some of the meetings. And Frampton's former colleague, Jim Webb, flew north and prowled the halls of the Interior Department, tracking rumors of how the negotiations were going. But the final deal was struck between federal officials and executives of the two sugar companies. When it was done, Frampton called MacKay, who assented to the agreement.

On July 13, 1993, two years after Governor Chiles had announced the settlement of Lehtinen's lawsuit, Secretary Babbitt appeared at a press conference with the heads of Flo-Sun and U.S. Sugar to announce agreement on a "statement of principles." The statement said that the sugar industry would pay up to $322 million over twenty years to help build a somewhat larger system of wetlands than had been called for by the July 1991 settlement. Sugar agreed to withdraw its lawsuits after a 90-day period, during which the details could be worked out. The statement included a schedule for building the wetlands but pushed back deadlines for meeting water quality standards five years beyond the deadlines in the 1991 settlement.

Babbitt was exultant about the agreement. "The River of Grass has been given a new lease on life. This is a tremendous step toward the restoration of a unique and beautiful ecosystem. We have chosen to spend money where it is needed most, in the Everglades, not the courtroom. With this action we expect to head off what could have been another decade of litigation." [51] As Brooks Yeager explained later,

> The federal government has no direct influence over the sugar industry; we were in court over the state's failure to enforce state water standards. The sugar industry had clearly indicated that it could tie up the state's efforts to meet interim standards for phosphorus for years with litigation. Our lawyers told us that when we won, we would probably not get as much as the technical plan offered. We want to get action not only on interim standards but also on final standards, which would be lower and would provide more protection for the park and the refuge. But there is no way to get to final standards as long as we are in court about interim standards.
>
> In addition, we face other problems in the Everglades: restoration of the Kissimmee River, removing pollution from the EAA, and protecting Florida Bay. There is work to be done on the C-111 basin and in the Taylor and Shark River Slough [just northeast of the park, south of the EAA]. It would be difficult to make progress on these problems as long as we were in court. Meanwhile, phosphorus was pouring into the Loxahatchee refuge every day, and the problem was getting worse. We did not have all the time in the world to settle the lawsuit.[52]

After Babbitt's announcement, Nelson Fairbanks of U.S. Sugar and Alfred Fanjul of Flo-Sun thanked Babbitt and MacKay. Americans had cast their votes in November 1992 for change, Fanjul said, and "today, the Clinton administration delivers." Fanjul hailed the agreement as "the end of gridlock in the Everglades." Sugar was "making common cause with the administration and environmentalists to achieve a common purpose—to save jobs and protect the environment." [53]

Fanjul's reference to a "common purpose" with environmentalists was an overstatement. It was not clear that environmentalists were ready to sign on. Paul Parks of FOREVERGLADES (a project of the Florida Wildlife Association) and Tom Bancroft of the new National Audubon Society Everglades office had participated actively in the technical group, and Parks had endorsed the technical plan as acceptable, if not perfect. But no environmentalist had been asked to approve the agreement in Washington. The negotiations had been among parties that would pay to build the wetlands—the federal government, the state, the district, and the sugar industry—and the federal government had not invited environmentalists to the table.

However, the secretary did invite environmentalists to participate in the press conference. Jim Webb of the Wilderness Society spoke after Babbitt and the sugar executives, carefully spelling out the concerns that he and his colleagues in Florida had. These concerns, he said, must be addressed during the 90-day period. The statement was vague on many points. For example, how would the statement of principles dovetail with the 1991 settlement? Would environmentalists and other intervenors in the lawsuit retain the right to intervene and take the case back to court if implementation of the statement of principles was slow? If the wetlands cost more than expected, who would pay additional costs? Also, the technical plan had called for only as many acres of wetland as necessary to reduce the concentration of phosphorus to 50 parts per billion, whereas the settlement of the litigation called for a second phase target that would be much lower. The statement of principles gave no assurances about a second phase and might have been read to say that the sugar industry would pay nothing more to meet these standards. Environmentalists must be involved in answering these and other questions during the 90-day period for working out details, Webb said.

After a question-and-answer session on the statement of principles, Joe Browder stood and denounced the agreement. "It is an absolute betrayal of the Everglades, and it will not stand," he said. When the press conference was over, Browder spoke directly to Babbitt. With a

Miami Herald reporter listening, Browder said, "I cannot understand why you would agree to this." Babbitt answered, "That's my job, Joe, to find compromise." [54]

Searching for a compromise, Browder said later, was precisely the problem. The secretary of the interior has a legal responsibility to prevent degradation of Everglades National Park, but "[this] is very different from his responsibility to make balanced management decisions for BLM [Bureau of Land Management] or national forest lands, where it is his job to reconcile conflicting uses. Bruce decided to be a mediator, and that was the fatal flaw." [55]

Moving to a Second Settlement?

When this book was completed in early August 1993, a controversy was raging in Florida over the statement of principles. Misgivings fell into two broad categories.

First, there were some who did not support the technical plan. On one side, the Sugar Growers' Cooperative, which represents small growers, remained unconvinced that it should pay to build wetlands before there was better evidence that they would remove phosphorus effectively. On the other side, Joe Podgor of Friends of the Everglades said, "[The technical plan] is a fraud. It turns the headwaters of the Everglades into a sewage treatment plant." [56] Browder said it was a bad idea to divert small amounts of water to the Everglades without looking at the broader questions of water allocation. Once initial diversions were made, it might be more difficult to get more water. Furthermore, Browder thought it inappropriate for the public to pay to clean up this water, especially when diverting water from east of the EAA might only encourage suburban sprawl in the areas.

Nineteen national and Florida organizations, including the major environmental groups, wrote a letter to Secretary Babbitt expressing their dissatisfaction with the statement of principles and asking that between 70,000 and 120,000 acres of EAA lands be set aside for wetlands, which they said was the only acceptable treatment system. They asked for additional treatment areas for any water below quality standards that was brought into the Everglades to restore the hydroperiod.[57] The letter objected to the fact that the statement of principles would not meet the deadlines that had been established in the July 1991 settlement. These deadlines had been very ambitious, and almost two years had already passed with little to show. It was clear to most insiders that a collapse of the mediation and a return to the courts would postpone action for at least five more years, beyond the deadlines in either settlement. But to endorse the new settlement seemed to some the equivalent of accepting delay.

In the public press, the issue of money overshadowed these concerns. Was it true that, in the words of the headline of an article by *Miami Herald* columnist Carl Hiaasen, "Big Sugar Gets a Sweet Deal in Plan for Glades Cleanup"?[58] Before the negotiations had begun in Washington, the sugar industry had offered to pay about $10 million a year while the wetlands were being built. The statement of principles committed the industry to pay at least $11.625 million, and up to $18.5 million if it was not able to remove 45 percent of the phosphorus from its own lands. The agreement said that sugar would pay at least 47.9 percent of the total cost. Sugar would eventually pay at least $233 million and as much as $322 million if BMPs turned out to be less successful in reducing phosphorus.

Since sugar's $233 to $322 million contribution would be made over twenty years, its present value was clearly less than that amount. Was it enough? Furthermore, sugar would pay between $11.6 and $12.5 million in the first year, whereas the district would increase taxes by about 18 percent to raise $21.6 million for the years when the wetlands were being built. For these first years, taxpayers would pay much more than sugar. Was this fair? In addition, sugar's contributions were to be made over twenty years; how firm were these commitments?

Defending the agreement, Tom MacVicar of the district replied that industry's fair share might be the cost of building and operating the wetlands needed to clean water from the cane fields. This was somewhere between $150 and $250 million, slightly less than industry's share of $233 to $322 million. The rest of the total bill of $465 million was for improving the hydroperiod, building wetlands to treat the waters diverted to the Everglades, and doing additional research. It is reasonable, said MacVicar, for taxpayers, the state, and the federal government to share these costs.[59]

Although the tax increase would be only $10 per year for a $100,000 house, the political climate in South Florida makes it difficult to raise taxes. Several local officials have also protested that taxpayers are being asked to pay too much. Even before the settlement, the Broward County commissioners had demanded that sugar pay the full costs of cleanup. After the settlement, local officials from areas far downstream from the EAA and in the Keys denounced the agreement as "taxation without representation" and threatened to sue.[60] Their citizens were not polluting the Everglades, they said, so why should they be taxed?

Clean Water Action roundly denounced the agreement. It is a canvassing organization that sends teams of young workers into neighborhoods to talk with citizens, distribute leaflets, circulate petitions, and raise funds. It had not been a party to the litigation and had generally avoided "insider" activism, opting not to participate in the mediation process. Instead, it organized citizen protests and conducted letter writing campaigns. Clean Water Action's position in the controversy has been straightforward: polluters must pay, and sugar is not paying enough. It helped bring 50 senior citizens to a district board meeting soon after the announcement. One told a reporter, "We're bailing out the sugar industry; this is unfair."

The Sleeping Giant Begins to Wake

In July 1991, environmentalists found themselves united with federal, state, and district officials against sugar. The July 1993 statement of principles united government officials and the sugar industry, with the environmentalists outside the tent. But this new alliance may not be stable. Political decision makers seem very conscious of the risks they are taking in imposing additional taxes, siding with sugar, and possibly breaking with environmentalists. Furthermore, there is the tricky legal problem of getting Judge Hoeveler to amend the 1991 settlement to accommodate a 1993 agreement. Environmental groups are a party to the litigation and could challenge an attempt to rewrite the 1991 settlement.

To complicate even further the political and legal risks posed by the 1993 agreement, Dexter Lehtinen has reemerged as a player. This time he is part-time counsel to the Miccosuke Indians. Still a colorful populist, Lehtinen denounced the July 1993 settlement: "It has the potential to be the Munich of the Everglades, in which government buys peace in our time with Big Sugar, leaving to others at a later date the difficult task of actually saving the Everglades." [61]

The story is clearly not over. If the 1993 settlement falls apart, the result could be a return to federal and state courts. Even if Gerald Cormick is able to finish the mediation successfully, with detailed agreements to supplement the statement of principles, the debate about the Everglades will not be over. The technical plan probably will not improve the hydroperiod enough to save Everglades National Park or to restore Florida Bay. The district may shift its attention to Florida Bay and craft a plan to fill in some canals, restore sheet flow, and divert fresh waters so they flow into the bay.

Three things are clear about the future. One is that money will be the central issue in restoration of the Everglades. The district and the U.S. Army Corps of Engineers are already committed to restoring the Kissimmee River in the north at a cost of $400 million, to reducing phosphorus in Lake Okeechobee by buying out dairies, and to spending $465 million on the EAA. The total bill for restoring the Everglades and Florida Bay could be in the billions, not counting the unknown cost of providing clean water to and disposing of waste water from settled areas.

The second thing that clearly lies ahead is an awakened, active interest in the Everglades on the part of residents of the urban coast. When restoration of the Kissimmee River and the Everglades was in the planning stages, urban areas expressed little interest in the project. For the first several years after Lehtinen's lawsuit, urban voters and politicians were not visible in the Everglades debate. Broward County Commissioner Lori Parrish told the 1992 meeting of the Everglades Coalition: "When I go to the district meetings, I see the environmentalists and I see the sugar industry, but I do not see the urban point of view. . . . Preserving the Everglades has been a lot of talk up until now; we never saw real action. Now perhaps it is time to decide, and urban interests will want to know what percentage of the water is going to the Everglades, what to urban areas, and what to agriculture. And then we can decide who will pay." [62]

These are questions that make district managers nervous. Tom MacVicar calls the urban voters the sleeping giant. Although they rarely pay much attention to the relatively small portion of their tax bill that supports the district, when aroused, they are a potent political force. He recalls what happened when the district roused the sleeping giant by imposing water conservation restrictions during the drought of the late 1980s. The district restricted lawn watering and car washing. "We got 925 phone calls before 8:30 a.m. the next morning, and our phones were tied up for two days. The phone system went out, and we had to install a trailer in the parking lot to handle all of the phone calls for the next six months." [63] In 1993, the sleeping giant began to stir. When the technical group suggested using waters from east of the EAA to restore the hydroperiod in the Everglades, managers of urban water systems all along the east coast began to pay attention and filled empty chairs at the technical group's meetings.

How strong is public support in South Florida for protecting and restoring the Everglades? Jim Webb's answer in 1992 was that no Florida politician could afford to be against protecting the Everglades, but that support was just as wide and just as shallow as the Everglades system itself. This raises an important point about the politics of the litigation and settlement of the lawsuit. During the four years after the lawsuit had been filed, the Everglades battle included only a few insiders. More than one person told me that I could learn the whole story by talking to fewer than twenty people. It was an insiders' game of a few federal officials and environmentalists tussling with a few state officials and large sugar producers.

But now the Everglades issue is attracting the attention of urban voters. As of mid-1993, the urban voice is speaking mostly about money and is demanding that the sugar industry pay more. The rhetoric of some opponents of the statement of principles sounds very much like anti-tax populism. But eventually restoration of the Everglades will involve much more than the EAA and phosphorus. When this happens, will urban activists encourage spending public dollars on restoration?

The Kissimmee experience suggests how the politics of restoration might evolve as urban residents learn how much it will cost to restore the Everglades. Even after the district's careful sounding out of local interests in the Kissimmee valley, some residents of trailer parks that were to be partly flooded and some farmers opposed the restoration. In the tradition of not-in-my-backyard protesters, they formed a group called ROAR (Residents Opposing the Alleged Restoration) and hired lawyers. The rhetoric the residents use is instructive. "Why are public dollars being spent on this project," one woman asked the district board, "when children in our schools do not have enough textbooks? Taxpayers will pay for this project; the birds won't pay for it." [64]

The Kissimmee valley is not a heavily settled area, and the trailer courts are small. The Kissimmee restoration can be redesigned to avoid flooding the trailer courts without losing many environmental benefits. South of Lake Okeechobee, conflicts between proponents of environmental restoration and other interests will be sharper. Who will speak for the birds south of the lake?

Several environmentalists recognize that they must find allies in urban Florida to have any hope of paying the bill for restoration. Jim Webb is working to convince urban interests that the cheapest way to provide water for growing urban areas is to keep water in the Everglades, where it would replenish the Biscayne aquifer and feed the wells from which urban areas get their water. If it is not clear that restoration will deliver some practical benefits to the urban coast, like resolving some of their water problems, then restoration plans may never be fully implemented, Webb says. [65]

Joe Browder suggests that there may be more support from developers for restoration of the Everglades than one might expect. He cites the case of the Big Cypress Swamp. During the 1960s, when a jetport was proposed for the area, large landholders and area developers initially favored the jetport and hoped to profit from growth around it. However, when environmentalists protested, developers took a second look at the tremendous costs of draining water and installing public infrastructure in the area. They decided that they would rather see limited public funds spent along the coast, where they also held land, than develop the Big Cypress. A roughly similar story might unfold in the EAA. Browder predicts: "It is not necessary or desirable to get sugar out of the EAA to solve water quality problems or to restore the natural Everglades system. When agriculture inevitably becomes a diseconomic use of the land, there will be pressure for urbanization. But when developers see the tremendous costs of building desalinization plants to provide water along the coast, combined with the costs of public infrastructure in an urbanized EAA, they would rather see public funds spent to manage the water supply in the EAA." [66]

One of the weakest links in the alliance for Everglades restoration has been the absence of a strong base in the large Cuban and African-

American communities of South Florida. As in most other states, the major environmental organizations in Florida are overwhelmingly white and affluent. South Florida environmentalists are making a major effort to increase the diversity of their movement, reaching out, for example, to the Cuban community in Miami, a powerful economic and political force. A Cuban-American businessman who once served on the Water Management District Board has joined the national board of the Wilderness Society, and Joe Browder, who moved to Washington after helping to defeat the Everglades jetport in the 1960s and is still active in Everglades issues, has built ties with Cuban-American businesses. In 1991, the Everglades Coalition held its annual meeting in Miami and emphasized that urban areas share the same concerns as environmental interests: both want a plentiful supply of water for the Everglades, both to replenish the Biscayne aquifer and to protect the park.

Building a strong political base in urban South Florida for restoration of the Everglades will take time. Only a handful of African Americans and Hispanics attended the meeting of the Everglades Coalition in 1992. But several Cuban-American and African-American elected officials spoke out against the statement of principles when the Dade County Commissioners voted against it, and in opinion surveys Clean Water Action has conducted, it finds consistently higher support for anti-sugar, pro-Everglades positions in Hispanic households than in non-Hispanic households.[67]

A third thing is clear about the future. Because restoration of the Everglades is tied to providing and financing water for settled areas, restoration is more than a purely environmental task; it is a matter of charting a course of sustainable development for South Florida. It is therefore clear that many of the key decisions will be made at the state and local levels. The federal government can prod and contribute to state and local decision-making processes, but it cannot command or control them.

The federal government is beginning to take steps that could lead to a major commitment of its resources for restoration. In 1992, the Everglades Coalition called for an ambitious step—rewriting the congressional statute that authorizes the Central and South Florida Flood Control Project. A reauthorization might expand the statutory language about protecting fish and wildlife and call for restoring water quality and quantity in federally owned lands or in a broader area.[68] At its annual conference in January 1992, the Everglades Coalition released a thirty-page agenda for restoration.[69] In June 1993, shortly before the announcement of the statement of principles, the coalition released a second, more detailed plan.

As well as releasing its own plan, the coalition has successfully lobbied Congress to authorize and appropriate funds for a study by the U.S. Army Corps of Engineers of the water management system in South Florida. This could be a first step to rewriting the statute for the project. One of the first things that Bruce Babbitt did after returning from the Everglades Coalition meeting in February 1993 was to call the acting assistant secretary of the Army who supervises the corps' civil works and encourage him to find funds immediately to begin work on this study. At Babbitt's urging, the corps extended an invitation to both the park and the refuge to send staff to the corps' Jacksonville office, so that the study could incorporate environmental considerations into the decision-making process from the outset. This degree of close cooperation is new.

The corps' plan could well lead to a major commitment of federal dollars to restoration. However, it is important to remember that the Everglades is not the only ecosystem of interest to Congress and to the Office of Management and Budget. The Everglades is perhaps second in line, after the old growth forests of the Pacific Northwest. Already lining up for money are the Chesapeake Bay, San Francisco Delta, Columbia River, coastal scrub "eco-regions" in Southern California, and possibly Narragansett Bay. Eventually the Everglades will have to compete for federal dollars in a climate of tight budgets. It is highly unlikely that substantial federal resources will be forthcoming unless state and local governments pay, too.

The district has a second planning process, which might help build public support for a major investment of state and local dollars in the replumbing of the Everglades. State legislation requires the district to prepare a water supply plan by fall 1994. The plan would specify where and how developed areas along the east coast will get water. Since these areas now get their water from the Biscayne aquifer, which is replenished by surface flows through the Everglades, this study will link restoration of water flows through the Everglades to the issue of municipal water supply. In addition, Lieutenant Governor MacKay is pushing for a state commission that would map a policy for sustainable development in South Florida. "We have exceeded the carrying capacity of the ecosystem in South Florida," he says, "yet we continue to bring in new people, and the costs of handling them are very high. People are led to believe that South Florida is a cheap place to live, but the costs of serving them keep rising. It is grossly unfair to encourage retirees on fixed incomes to move to Florida and then raise the taxes. It is almost a bait and switch. We do not have a framework in place to assure sustainability, and we need one." [70]

Environmentally inclined federal officials like Babbitt, Browner, and Frampton can continue to use their considerable power to push the state and the district to restore the Everglades ecosystem. But as Suzan Ponzoli warned at the 1992 Everglades Coalition meeting, as a matter of political reality, the window of opportunity will not be open forever. When it comes to making the investments that will be necessary to restore the Everglades, the key decisions will be made in Florida, by Floridians.

CONCLUSION

The crux of the Everglades lawsuit was a regulatory issue—the question of whether the district should obtain a permit for pumps on the southern edge of the Everglades Agricultural Area. However, as the story of the lawsuit and the settlement shows, restoring the Everglades will take much more than federal pressure to force Florida to be a tough regulator. South Florida and Iowa face very similar questions. Although the headlines in Florida focused on litigation and permits, the real question facing the state is where to invest scarce public dollars to achieve both economic and environmental goals.

The central theme of the story of Lehtinen's lawsuit is how politics, and especially the roles of state and federal agencies, change as the problems facing endangered ecosystems are identified and governments respond. There are several steps in this process, beginning with identifying the threats to an ecosystem and bringing them to public notice. Next, agencies must agree that they are responsible for contributing to a solution, and then specific measures must be designed and implemented. The story of the Everglades suggests that as these changes take place, politics moves from the regime of confrontation, federal leadership, and focus on regulation that was described in Chapter 1, toward a more collaborative, state-centered regime that makes extensive use of nonregulatory tools—in other words, toward a regime of civic environmentalism.

The first lesson of the story of the Everglades is that federal officials can help push the threats to an ecosystem into the public arena for discussion. This is certainly an essential step. A regime that relies on superior federal legal power—on a federal gorilla in the closet—can raise the visibility of threats to an ecosystem and force state and local agencies to make some kind of response. But power in ecosystems is fragmented. The Everglades story is not one in which a single federal agency insisted that a state administer federal environmental statutes aggressively. Indeed, the crux of the lawsuit concerned state water quality regulations, not federal law. EPA was a bystander through most of the three years of litigation and still is not a member of the technical operating committee that oversees implementation of the settlement. The lawsuit was not so much a question of exerting superior federal legal authority as of the independent initiatives of three federal officials—a U.S. attorney, a park superintendent, and a wildlife refuge manager—who took advantage of a fragmented governmental system.

The lawsuit also made clear to the public that there was another form of fragmentation, which is often recognized only by insiders. Within each agency, power is so dispersed that there are opportunities for officials to act as independent policy entrepreneurs. In the Everglades lawsuit, a park superintendent, a federal attorney, and a refuge manager took advantage of this fragmentation and proceeded to sue the state of Florida without informing their superiors in Washington about their intent. It was almost a year before Assistant U.S. Attorney General Stewart took a public position of unified federal support for the lawsuit and unified opposition to the district's SWIM plans for the Everglades. Even then, it took a great deal of scrambling to maintain this public unity, and at the last minute the EPA threatened not to support the settlement.

The second lesson is that federal officials have limited ability, even when united, to make state and local agencies agree that they share the responsibility for solving the problems facing an endangered ecosystem.

Even when the federal government had overcome its own internal fragmentation to the point where it could file unified comments on the district's SWIM plan for the Everglades, the district still was not forced to submit to the federal will. The deadlock between the district and the sugar industry on one side and the federal agencies and the environmentalists on the other was broken only when the governor of Florida became personally involved. Governor Chiles's "surrender" was anything but that; his admission that the water in the Everglades was dirty and his declaration that public agencies must find a way to make it clean are what broke the deadlock. As Chiles said, he was trying to get the armies to lay down their swords and start building a solution.

It is possible to conceive of an end to the litigation without leadership by Governor Chiles, Carol Browner, and Timer Powers. Perhaps if the case had gone to trial, a federal judge would have rendered a clear, substantive decision. (It is also possible that the judge would have ruled on narrow technical grounds, or that an appeals court would have found a way to turn the issue back to the state, as the district's lawyers had tried to do for two years.) But a substantive ruling would almost certainly have centered on phosphorus and artificial wetlands. The settlement engineered by the governor opens the door to solutions to larger and more important environmental problems, including disruption of the flow of water through the Everglades.

The third lesson of the lawsuit concerns the varied resources that Governor Chiles was able to bring to the job of crafting a governmental response to the problems in the Everglades. The governor added his own authority to the alliance, including his ability to appoint the members of the district board, to influence the legislative process, and to direct Carol Browner and other top state officials to make settlement of the litigation their top priority. The governor also found a way to mobilize the loose community of scientists who had been working on environmental issues in the Everglades for many years. When lawyers were included in the scientists' discussions, communication and some personal relationships among scientists broke down. The governor's insistence that scientists set standards for water and design artificial wetlands reopened communication and led to a new union of technical agreement and political purpose.

The governor also mobilized a larger, more diffuse community, that of South Florida itself. During the election campaign of 1990, he took advantage of a widespread feeling that the litigation was not good for South Florida and that Governor Martinez had failed in his responsibilities by not finding a way to end it. Chiles put his finger on this feeling when he criticized the spending of millions of dollars on Washington lawyers. Chiles's intervention also created an opportunity for Timer Powers to play a key role. This highly respected civic leader worked with great patience and at substantial personal cost to rebuild channels of communication and personal relationships that the lawsuit had damaged or destroyed, and to end the litigation. None of these resources— the governor's own powers, a unified scientific community, or civic support—could have been mobilized by the federal government.

In short, the experience of the Everglades litigation suggests that although federal agencies can raise issues, the process of forging an agreement to face these issues requires leadership by top state officials, dialogue and agreement among the local scientific community, and local civic leadership.

The fourth lesson of the story of Lehtinen's lawsuit and the settlement concerns the differences between the politics of identifying the problem and the politics of solving it. In the terms used in Chapter 2, the politics of restoration will involve extensive use of nonregulatory tools like subsidies and improved public services, rely on a politics of coalition building and cooperation rather than confrontation, and focus on bargaining at the state and local levels.

The lawsuit and the 1991 settlement accomplished the task of putting restoration of the Everglades on the public agenda. Federal and state agencies and the district have agreed they must accept part of the responsibility for changing the water management practices in South Florida that are threatening the Everglades.

The 1993 mediation and statement of principles took civic consensus one step further. The two dominant firms in the sugar industry have now committed their resources to reducing the phosphorus coming from their fields. The next step, getting formal agreements about specific plans to protect the Everglades, has just started. Even if the agreement of July 1993 collapses, it has suggested how the politics of restoring the Everglades might work.

The first feature of the politics of restoration will be a new kind of federal participation in decision making at the state and local levels. In this process, federal agencies are beginning to work with state and local agencies on a very different basis. The emerging federal role is far larger than the oversight envisioned in the settlement's provisions for returning to federal court. Federal officials are participating in state and local decision-making processes. As they share information that helps shape state and local decisions, federal participants will ensure that federal interests are addressed and will implicitly concede that these processes, which are matters of state law and not of federal regulation, are legitimate and effective.

Federal officials talk a lot about participating in state and local decision making. For example, federal land managers in the West are often active participants in local community activities, and federal land management decisions often take into consideration state and local concerns. However, if the Everglades ecosystem is to be restored, a much more intensive form of federal participation in state and local decisions about the Everglades will be required. Replumbing the water management system in South Florida will be a matter of extensive change and repeated fine tuning. For this process to work, federal officials must bring their expertise and information to the district's water supply planning processes and to discussions about the management of canals and pumps, which are far removed from the EAA and the problem of phosphorus. As this happens, the federal role will shift from being a gorilla in the closet to being an equal at the table.

A second feature of the politics of restoring ecosystems is that from time to time, the center of action will move from state and local processes to Washington, D.C. The June 1993 negotiations among Babbitt, Frampton, and the sugar industry are an example. But it is not always easy to get all of the diverse parties to participate in a negotiation led by busy federal officials, far from the threatened ecosystem. So the trick will be to link action on the federal stage successfully with action on the state and local levels. If the statement of principles that federal officials negotiated is to be implemented, the lead may have to shift back to the district's mediation process.

In the long run, it may be most efficient to consolidate federal and state-level planning to support this multilevel decision-making process. For example, if the statement of principles stands, then it might be a good idea to link the district's water supply plan or Lieutenant Governor MacKay's commission on a sustainable future for South Florida to the plan for reconfiguring the Central and South Florida Water Management Project, which the U.S. Army Corps of Engineers has begun to prepare in cooperation with the Fish and Wildlife Service and the National Park Service.

A third feature of the emerging politics of restoration is participation by new players. There are many more people at the table in South Florida now than before the lawsuit, and more are arriving. Some essential participants have not yet come to the table. The major developers along the urban east coast have been quiet, as has most of the African-American and Cuban-American leadership in South Florida.

If urban interests do arrive, they will transform the process. By the sheer number and variety of their interests, they will dilute the black hat-white hat cleavage between environmental and industry forces, and their presence will move the process toward multifaceted collaboration and bargaining. A successful politics of restoration will look quite different from the battles of 1988-1991. It will have some of the same elements as the politics of public works; there will be sometimes friendly, sometimes wary cooperation, interspersed with tussles over dollars.

Although the politics of restoration and the politics of public works projects are similar, there is a critical difference between them. With the politics of restoration there can be no iron triangle, because there is not likely to be the same concentrated package of benefits that can be appropriated for private gain. For example, farmers will not be able to irrigate new lands. This does not mean that self-interest will be absent. Indeed, a successful politics of restoration may well depend on discovering new self-interested motives for protecting the Everglades. Jim Webb and Joe Browder believe urban developers will prefer that scarce public dollars for infrastructure be spent in urban areas rather than on developing lands in the Everglades; keeping the Everglades alive will replenish aquifers in urban areas and thus keep down the cost of providing water to urban residents. However, there is an important difference between these self-interested motives and the motives of farmers and municipalities that promoted water projects in the past. Instead of putting their hands out for a federal subsidy, as the farmers did, urban developers would be asking that government *not* spend money to tame the wilderness; they would be asking that government spend its limited resources on meeting public needs in settled areas.

A fourth feature of the politics of restoration will be the role that tight budgets and anti-tax politics play. In Iowa, tight budgets have made it difficult for the state to maintain a strong commitment to sustainable agriculture. In Florida, those who oppose tax increases are joining forces with environmentalists, who demand that the sugar industry pay more. But eventually Florida taxpayers will have to dig deep into their pockets for some of the costs of restoration.

A successful politics of restoration will rest on a cultural change that was dramatized on Earth Day—the widespread acceptance of the notion that government, business, and individual citizens must adjust their behavior to take environmental values into account. Specifically, it will require acceptance of the notion that public agencies that manage sensitive lands, such as the National Park Service, should invest funds and effort beyond their jurisdiction in order to protect federal lands. At the local level, the politics of restoration will rest on the willingness of urban residents to pay higher taxes to the South Florida Water Management District in order to protect birds, alligators, and saw grass, as well as the aquifer that supplies their water.

It remains to be seen whether these ideas and these emerging relationships between traditional and new players in water politics in South Florida will take firm hold. As Suzan Ponzoli has cautioned, the political will to implement the settlement agreement will not last forever unless there is significant progress. Pressure from the outside has created opportunities for local civic environmentalism to work out a sustainable future for South Florida. If local leaders can grasp this opportunity, they can save both the Everglades and their economic future.

NOTES

1. Frank Cerabino and Randy Loftis, "U.S. Files Suit to Halt Everglades Pollution," *Miami Herald,* October 13, 1981, 1A.
2. Heather Dewar, "World War III? Volleys Fired in Pollution Fight," *Miami Herald,* April 12, 1989, 1B, 4B.
3. Heather Dewar, "Chiles on Glades Water: Just Clean It," *Miami Herald,* May 21, 1991, 1A, 21A.

4. James Webb, "Managing Nature in the Everglades," *EPA Journal* (November-December 1990): 50.

5. Ibid., 49.

6. Luther J. Carter, *The Florida Experience: Land and Water Policy in a Growth State* (Baltimore: Johns Hopkins University Press, 1974), 1-40.

7. South Florida Water Management District, "Surface Water Improvement and Management Plan for the Everglades: Draft" (West Palm Beach, January 2, 1992), 5.

8. Richard Stewart, interview with author, Washington, D.C., March 31, 1992.

9. Marjory Douglas, *The Everglades: River of Grass*, rev. ed. (Sarasota, Fla.: Pineapple Press, 1988).

10. Carter, *The Florida Experience*, 113.

11. See "Report of the District Engineer," in "Comprehensive Report on Central and Southern Florida for Flood Control and Other Purposes," U.S. House of Representatives, Document No. 643, May 6, 1948, 13-14.

12. Blair T. Bauer and Betsy A. Lyons, *Keeping Florida Afloat: A Case Study of Governmental Responses to Increasing Demands on a Finite Resource* (Washington, D.C.: Conservation Foundation, 1989).

13. Craig Diamond, *An Analysis of Public Subsidies and Externalities Affecting Water Use in South Florida*, submitted to the Wilderness Society (Fort Lauderdale: Florida Atlantic University and Florida International University, Joint Center for Environmental and Urban Problems, 1990), 30-31.

14. Surface Water Improvement and Management Act, F.S. 1989, 373.4595(2)(a)(1).

15. Robert Cahn and Patricia Cahn, "Florida's Threatened Sanctuaries: Will Agricultural Pollution Ruin a Famous National Park and a Major Wildlife Refuge?" *Defenders*, May-June 1990, 12.

16. See Robert Gottlieb, *A Life of Its Own: The Politics and Power of Water* (San Diego, Calif.: Harcourt Brace Jovanovich, 1988), 199-239; and Helen Ingram, *Water Politics: Continuity and Change* (Albuquerque: University of New Mexico Press, 1990), 130-132.

17. "Tough on Crime, But ...," *Miami Herald*, January 14, 1992, editorial page.

18. Return flows from agriculture are clearly exempted from the Clean Water Act; however, the waters passing through the pumps at the southern border of the Everglades Agricultural Area were mostly drainage, so they might have been subject to the law. Author's interview with Bob Dreher, Washington, D.C., February 19, 1992.

19. Bauer and Lyons, *Keeping Florida Afloat*, 49-67.

20. See Stephen S. Light, John R. Wodraska, and Joe Sabrina, "The Southern Everglades: The Evolution of Water Management," *National Forum: Phi Kappa Phi Journal* 69, no. 1 (Winter 1989).

21. Author's interviews with Nancy Roen, Key Largo, January 9, 1992; and with John Wodraska, Fort Lauderdale, January 15, 1992.

22. "Water Managers Want Delay in Federal Protection Effort," *Miami Herald,* March 10, 1989, 3B.

23. "Push Nutrient Removal," *Miami Herald,* December 6, 1990, 34A.

24. Paul Anderson, "Martinez Seeks to Settle U.S. Suit on Water Quality," *Miami Herald,* November 2, 1988, 1A, 7A.

25. George Wedgworth, interview with author, Belle Glade, January 14, 1992.

26. See Alex Wilkinson, *Big Sugar: Seasons in the Cane Fields of Florida* (New York: Vintage Books, 1989).

27. Frank Cerabino and Randy Loftis, "U.S. Files Suit," 1A, 19A.

28. Heather Dewar, "Political Battle Drives Glades Suit," *Miami Herald,* February 19, 1990, 1B, 2B.

29. Michael Crook, "Water Board to Spend Millions to Fight U.S.," *Miami Herald,* February 15, 1990, 2B.

30. Cahn and Cahn, "Florida's Threatened Sanctuaries," 14.

31. Andy Rackley, Florida Sugar Cane League, interview with author, Clewiston, January 14, 1992.

32. Sean Holton, "Progress on Trial in the Everglades: We Have Tamed the Wilderness, but Can We Keep It from Dying?" *Orlando Sentinel,* September 16, 1990, A1.

33. Susan Beck and Michael Orey, "Skaddenomics: The Ludicrous World of Law Firm Billing," *American Lawyer* (September 1991): 92-97.

34. Jeffrey Kleinman, "Water Managers Will Ask Judge to Settle Glades Suit," *Miami Herald,* May 10, 1991, 4B.

35. Heather Dewar and Michael Crook, "Glades Summit 'Disappointing,'" *Miami Herald,* February 9, 1991, 5B.

36. Steve Herman, interview with author, Washington, D.C., February 21, 1992.

37. David Gluckman, "The Marjory Stoneman Douglas Everglades Protection Act," *Environmental and Urban Issues* (Fall 1991): 17-27.

38. *U.S. v. South Florida Water Management District et al.,* transcript of hearing proceedings, May 21, 1991, 40, 43, 54; and Heather Dewar, "Chiles on Glades Water: Just Clean It," *Miami Herald,* May 21, 1991, 1A, 21A.

39. U.S. District Court, Southern District of Florida, *U.S. v. South Florida Water Management District et al.*, Case 88-1886-CIV-Hoeveler, Agreement, July 11, 1991.

40. Ibid., 14.

41. Bob Dreher, interview with author, Washington, D.C., February 21, 1992.

42. Kirk Brown, "Board Will Hear Sugar's Cleanup Bid," *Palm Beach Post,* April 10, 1992, 1B.

43. Mike Soukup, interview with author, Key Largo, January 10, 1992.

44. Marjory Stoneman Douglas, Everglades Protection Act, HBS 2157 sect. 1871, 373.4592(3)(a)1.

45. U.S. District Court, Southern District of Florida, Agreement, July 11, 1991.

46. Florida Sugar Cane League, "A Strategy to Revitalize the Everglades and Preserve Farming" (Presentation to the South Florida Water Management District Board, April 7, 1992).

47. Robert H. Buker, Jr., "Let's Work on Plan Better Than SWIM," letter to the *Miami Herald,* March 21, 1992.

48. Dan Carson, executive vice president of Flo-Sun, Inc., quoted in Kirk Brown, "Board Will Hear Sugar's Cleanup Bid," *Palm Beach Post,* April 10, 1992, 3B.

49. Michael Crook, "Sugar Industry Offers New Glades Program," *Miami Herald,* April 10, 1992.

50. Kirk Brown, "Babbitt to Form Task Force to Help Save Everglades," *Miami Herald,* February 23, 1993, 1A, 12A.

51. Press release, U.S. Department of the Interior, "Historic Everglades Agreement Is Announced: Federal, State, and Industry Partnership to Begin Massive Effort to Restore and Protect Everglades Ecosystem," July 13, 1993.

52. Brooks Yeager, interview with author, Washington, D.C., August 12, 1993.

53. Statement by Flo-Sun, Inc.

54. Paul Anderson and Lori Rozsa, "Glades Pact Is Hailed, Reviled," *Miami Herald,* July 14, 1993, 1A, 6A. Browder recalls that Babbitt said only, "That's my job," not adding the phrase about compromise.

55. Joe Browder, interviews with author, Washington, D.C., July 23 and August 10, 1993.

56. Carl Hiaasen, "Big Sugar Gets a Sweet Deal in Plan for Glades Cleanup," *Miami Herald,* July 15, 1993.

57. Letter to Bruce Babbitt from the Everglades Coalition, July 30, 1993.

58. Carl Hiaasen, "Big Sugar Gets a Sweet Deal."

59. Tom MacVicar, telephone interview with author, August 3, 1993.

60. Dan Keating, "Keys Protest Tax for Glades Cleanup," *Miami Herald,* July 18, 1993, B1; and Emma Ross, "Lawsuits Loom: Panel Initially OKs Glades-Plan Tax Hike," *Naples Daily News,* July 16, 1993.
61. Karl Vick, "Agreement Would Clean Up the Everglades," *St. Petersburg Times,* July 14, 1993, 1.
62. Lori Parrish (Speech delivered at the Annual Meeting of the Everglades Coalition, Key Largo, Fla., January 11, 1992).
63. Tom MacVicar, interview with author, Key Largo, January 11, 1992.
64. Hearing before the South Florida Water Management District Board, January 16, 1992.
65. Jim Webb, interview with author, Washington, D.C., July 22, 1993.
66. Joe Browder, interview with author, Washington, D.C., March 5, 1992.
67. Joe Browder, written communication, August 10, 1993. Browder adds that "things are changing down there, in ways that neither the Fanjuls nor Tallahasee and Washington officials have figured out."
68. The report notes: "The extensive changes wrought in the Everglades areas will result in the loss of certain unique wildlife habitats. The Fish and Wildlife Service decries this loss even though it may be overshadowed by benefit to the fishery." From "Comprehensive Report on Central and Southern Florida for Flood Control and Other Purposes" (Chief of Engineers, U.S. Army), Washington, D.C., U.S. House of Representatives, May 6, 1948, H. Doc. 646.
69. Everglades Coalition, *Everglades in the 21st Century: The Water Management Future* (Washington, D.C.: Everglades Coalition, 1992).
70. Buddy MacKay, interview with author, Tallahassee, August 3, 1993.

CHAPTER SIX

Conserving Electricity in Colorado:
Negotiating in the Shadow of the Law

E nergy efficiency is both an economic and an environmental issue. The energy industry accounts for about 10 percent of the U.S. economy; public utilities, which provide electricity and gas to homes and businesses, account for about half of this total. If Americans could spend less on energy and still get the cold beer and hot showers they want, the economy would be stronger and more productive.

Conserving energy is also an effective way to prevent many kinds of pollution. For example, consider the generation of electricity, which accounts for over one-third of all energy consumption in the United States today and is expected to account for over two-fifths of all energy consumption twenty years from now.[1] Coal-fired electrical power plants, the source of most electricity, produce carbon dioxide and other greenhouse gasses, acid rain, and local air pollution; furthermore, environmental problems are associated with the mining of coal and the transmission of electricity. These problems can be very large; for example, 11 percent of all of the greenhouse gasses produced in the world are byproducts of burning fossil fuel to generate electricity in the United States.[2] Ralph Cavanagh, a lawyer who works on electricity issues for the Natural Resources Defense Council, sums it up as follows: "Energy efficiency is quite simply the most powerful engine of environmental protection ever devised."[3]

This chapter analyzes efforts in Colorado and other states to encourage the conservation of electrical energy. The story revolves around three technical terms: demand-side management (DSM), inte-

TABLE 6-1

TECHNICAL TERMS IN THE POWER DEBATE

Demand-Side Management (DSM)	Measures taken to use less electricity. These can include using more efficient lighting, heating, or air conditioning; changing manufacturing processes; and using electronic energy control systems. Utilities encourage and finance DSM through free or subsidized energy-saving equipment, rebates, educational campaigns, and technical assistance. In contrast, supply-side management includes measures to increase the supply of energy, for example, by building new generating facilities.
Integrated Resource Planning (IRP)	Comprehensive planning of future demand for electricity and of alternative measures, including both DSM and supply-side measures, to meet this demand.
Decoupling	Measures to remove the link between the total sales of a utility and profits, so that a utility's profits are not reduced when customers are persuaded to use less electricity.

grated resource planning (IRP), and decoupling of profits from sales (Table 6-1). At its core, this jargon boils down to two simple things—an increased reliance on information and collaboration.

The utility industry is moving away from relying exclusively on using commodities like coal to create electricity and moving toward relying on information about how to meet consumers' needs for heating, lighting, cooling, and power. Demand-side management includes hundreds of things that people can do to use less electricity, such as installing fluorescent lighting, insulating homes, redesigning industrial production processes, auditing the use of electricity, and using electronic control systems to use energy more efficiently. Each of these activities requires the application of information and expertise. Rather than just flipping the switch, users of electricity must find someone who has the expertise to analyze their needs and to design a way to meet the needs with less electricity.

Collaboration is an inevitable consequence of the shift from commodities to information. To design a DSM activity to meet the needs of an individual customer, it is often necessary to tap information and expertise from widely dispersed sources. Also, if a governmental agency or a utility decides to encourage DSM, it must use the knowledge and expertise of a wide variety of organizations that are familiar with the needs and circumstances of many different kinds of customers. The vehicle for engaging organizations is a design process called integrated resource planning. IRP includes a series of public meetings, roundtables, studies, and other activities that result in an integrated resource plan. The plan quantifies consumer demand, says how much of demand will be met by conservation and how much will be met by generating electricity, and specifies both the demand-side programs that will encourage conservation and the supply-side activities that will generate electricity.

Decoupling is an important prerequisite to collaboration. As will be explained in more detail later, most utilities have a good reason to prefer generating electricity to encouraging conservation. The reason is simple—utility profits are regulated by state governments, and the level of profits is tied to sales of electricity, not to meeting consumer demands for cold beer and hot showers. Decoupling is the term for breaking the link between profits and sales by finding another way to calculate allowable profits. Unless the link can be broken by decoupling, utilities are likely to be skeptical of DSM and to resist collaboration that results in DSM.

The story of adopting DSM, IRP, and decoupling—or to avoid the jargon, the story of redesigning the electricity industry around the concepts of information and collaboration—is similar to the stories told in the two previous chapters. In all three chapters, the question is whether there is a path that allows economic growth and development while reducing environmental risks. But the Colorado story is different in three ways.

First, there was no dramatic turning point in Colorado, like Governor Chiles's appearance in federal court. The Colorado story is a slow ratcheting of state policy, step by step, toward new objectives. The focus of the story is the Colorado Public Utilities Commission, which, like other states' commissions, regulates the operations of electrical utilities. The issue of energy conservation first came to the Colorado commission's attention formally in 1979, but neither this effort, nor efforts in 1981 and 1984, had much impact on commission policy or on public utilities. In 1988 and 1989, there were renewed efforts to encourage energy conservation, and marginal changes occurred in the performance of public utilities' activities. A sixth effort, in 1991-1993, finally led to commission policies that required energy conservation efforts by the largest public utility in Colorado. The battles over energy conservation are not over, but this sixth effort does appear to have brought fundamental change to the policy and politics of energy conservation in the state.

Second, there was no confrontation between federal and state authority in Colorado. State public utility commissions regulate electrical utilities; until late 1992, Congress had not enacted preemptive statutes that required state commissions to consider energy conservation. However, as in the Iowa case, independent policy entrepreneurs within the federal government, and also national private foundations, have used other means to influence events in Colorado and other states. This influence was exerted indirectly, by providing information about energy conservation strategies to state public utility commissions and by financing state-level advocates for these strategies. The federal role was to nourish the growth of the informal network of energy conservation experts that has developed around the country over the past decade.

Third, Colorado's battles were fought not in the legislature (as in Iowa) or in federal court (as in Florida) but in a state regulatory process. Public utility commissions are regulatory agencies charged with ensuring that utilities do not charge excessive rates. In 1991-1993, the decisions to encourage energy conservation resulted in new regulations that govern how electrical utilities in Colorado must submit applications for changes in rates and how rates are determined.

The story of efforts in Colorado to promote the conservation of electrical energy illustrates the ideas presented in Chapter 1 about bottom-up, civic environmentalism. Although the commission did adopt new regulations, the tools that are being used to promote conservation are nonregulatory tools, such as subsidies and technical assistance for consumers of electricity, public education, and incentives for utilities.

In addition, as suggested in Chapter 1, the shift to nonregulatory tools resulted in a somewhat less confrontational politics. In the 1970s, when the cost of electricity was rising rapidly, the regulation of electrical utilities was a highly charged adversarial process. As public utility commissions have turned their attention to energy conservation, many states have developed formal collaborative processes and have experimented with ways to make the regulatory process itself less formal and confrontational. In Colorado, the movement from adversarial to collaborative styles of decision making has been highly controversial at times, with bitter resistance by some and occasional public charges of unethical behavior by decision makers. But the decisions made in 1992 do seem to have put utility politics in Colorado on a new track. Although final decisions are still made in a hearing room, as a result of arguments between lawyers and expert witnesses, new processes are developing that include formal collaboration, as well as extensive public participation, in a multisided give-and-take.

The subtitle of this chapter reflects the tension between adversarial and collaborative styles. It comes from an article that Robert Mnookin and Lewis Kornhauser, two distinguished law professors, wrote in 1979. "We see the primary function of contemporary divorce law not as imposing order from above, but rather as providing a framework within which divorcing couples can themselves determine their postdissolution rights and possibilities." [4] Specifically, Mnookin and Kornhauser note that parties in divorce cases often come to private agreements and use the courts as a rubber stamp to give these agreements the force of law. They argue that courts should support this process, for example, by encouraging the use of alternative dispute resolution procedures.

Many of the advocates of energy conservation take a similar position. They argue that the best way to attain energy conservation is to change procedures by using collaborative mechanisms to sort out the issues before taking questions into the regulatory process. This chapter explains why collaboration does seem to be the best way to approach energy conservation. It also shows that the road to collaboration about energy conservation in the shadow of the public utility commission's regulatory process can be rocky.

TRADITIONAL UTILITY TECHNOLOGY AND POLITICS

The electric power industry is big business in every sense of the word. Its physical facilities are massive and impressively engineered; its financial resources are equal to those of the largest industries in the country; and its concentrated political and economic powers dwarf the clout of almost all of its customers.

The Clout of the Electric Power Industry

Physical installations built by the electricity industry are technological marvels. Most electricity is generated at large power stations that produce hundreds of megawatts. A 600-megawatt facility would generate enough electricity for the state of Vermont and cost over a billion dollars. The generating facilities that are owned by individual utilities, or consortia of utilities, are linked by vast regional grids of transmission lines. Power is "wheeled" from one area to another to meet seasonal fluctuations as well as emergency needs when individual units or lines fail. The western grid, which stretches from North Dakota to New Mexico to California to British Columbia, is the largest connected manmade physical structure on earth. The electricity industry is also a powerful force in the world of business. On a list of the 1,000 largest investor-owned firms, there are 88 electrical utilities, with a market value of $218 billion, about 22 percent more than the market value of the 83 largest banks.[5] Individually, most privately owned utilities are large corporations and important presences in their communities. For example, the Public Service Company of Colorado, which serves over 60 percent of Colorado's population, including Denver and most of its suburbs, employs 6,600 workers.[6]

The sheer size of most utilities gives them the clout to be important players in state and local politics, and most utilities have important reasons to be concerned about state and local policies. In this day of multinational corporations, utilities are among the few corporations that cannot pick up and move to another location. As long as they are in the business of delivering electricity to customers in their service area, the financial strength of public utilities and the returns to their shareholders depend not only on the performance of the firm but also on the health of the local economy. Utilities have long recognized this fact. Many offer low rates to attract new businesses to their service areas. Most utilities are strong supporters of local chambers of commerce and other organizations that seek to create what they feel is a favorable political and cultural climate for economic growth.

Utilities as Monopolies

However, there is a dark side to the relationship between utilities and their service area. Electrical utilities are natural monopolies—or at least they have been so since the days of Samuel Insull. Insull, an aide to Thomas Edison, organized one of the first large electrical utilities, Commonwealth Edison of Chicago. When electricity was first produced and sold commercially, it quickly became apparent that it was most efficient to have only one set of power lines running down each street. Insull demonstrated that high voltage transmission lines could link small local monopolies at low cost, so that they could be consolidated into large firms serving whole metropolitan areas and outlying rural areas. Insull also proved that regional utilities could take advantage of significant economies of scale in the generation of electricity. These organizational innovations made electrical utilities powerful monopolies.[7]

The monopolistic position of electric power companies may be eroding, but it has shaped the political institutions that have been used to govern the industry. The governance system for the electricity industry has three major parts. All three parts seek to limit the economic and political power of potential monopolists and protect the consumer.

The first and most important part of the system of governance for the electricity industry is state law, which establishes public utility commissions. The central responsibility of these commissions is to regulate the prices (or "rates") that utilities charge their customers and thus "[en]sure that [citizens] receive utility services at affordable prices and in a safe manner."[8] In most states, rates are established on the basis of the costs of providing service, plus a rate of return (or profit) equal to perhaps 10 to 14 percent. The difficulties of determining the cost of capital and appropriate rate of return, and of allocating costs among different classes of service, and thus setting appropriate rates for different groups of customers, create a vast area for potential disagreement and litigation. In addition to setting rates, state commissions issue certificates of "public convenience and necessity" for new generating facilities and transmission lines and assess whether utility investments are "prudent" expenditures.

These commissions assumed responsibility for regulating the electric power industry during the Progressive Era. In the fashion of that time, they are organized to conduct impartial rational assessments, far removed from the hurly-burly of narrow political considerations. They function almost like courts, with strict rules of procedure and evidence. The commissions are not completely immune from political influence; indeed, in eleven states the members of the commission are elected.[9] However, all states insulate commissions from political pressures by strict rules governing ex parte communication (outside formal channels) to ensure that commission decision-making processes are open, fair, and based on evidence presented during a formal process.

The second part of the system of governance for the electrical industry includes federal statutes that regulate private producers of electricity. The Federal Energy Regulatory Commission regulates the sale of bulk power among utilities. The Public Utility Holding Company Act was enacted in 1935 to break up three large holding companies that controlled 49 percent of the nation's investor-owned electrical utilities.[10] The Public Utilities Regulatory Policies Act, passed in 1978 as part of President Carter's energy plan, requires utilities to pay fair prices for electricity offered for distribution over a utility's grid by independent power producers. These independent producers include firms that own small dams, firms that cogenerate both electricity for the grid and heat for a manufacturing process, and others.

The third leg of the governance system is public power. The rationale for public ownership is that rates will be lower if there are no stockholders because ratepayers own the utility. Public power comes in three forms. Municipally owned utilities, such as those in Los Angeles, Sacramento, and Colorado Springs, provide 14.7 percent of all electricity, 80 percent of which they generate themselves. Another 7.4 percent is provided by rural electrical cooperatives (62 percent of which they generate).[11] Rural electrical cooperatives were created by the federal government during the 1930s and continue to receive subsidized federal financing because it is often unprofitable for privately owned firms to extend electrical lines into sparsely populated areas. Local co-ops have formed regional generation and transmission co-ops to act as wholesalers of power. There were two such co-ops in Colorado until recently: Colorado-Ute Electric Association in western Colorado and Tri-State, north and east of Denver. Finally, five federal agencies generate power at large dams along the Columbia, Colorado, Tennessee, and other rivers. Four of these, including the Bonneville Power Administration in the Pacific Northwest and the Western Area Power Administration in the Rockies and Southwest, sell the electricity to utilities that in turn sell to customers. The Tennessee Valley Authority (TVA) sells its electricity directly to consumers.

Traditional Utility Politics

The politics of electrical utility regulation in the states has often been adversarial, setting defenders of the public against monopolists. The populist spirit of utility regulation is captured in the florid language of a poem, "The Quest of the NARUC," which is prominently displayed in the current policy statement of the National Association of Regulatory Utility Commissioners, whose members include all the state commissions as well as Canadian regulatory agencies and several federal agencies.

> There are across this great land of ours,
> Tribunes who labor through the hours . . .
> To impose your will on mighty utilities . . .
> To stamp out excessive rates,
> And end discrimination among people and States
> They have fought your fight
> To make all things right
> Their trumpets will never sound retreat
> As long as the public needs relief.[12]

In the 1950s and 1960s, state commissions faced the undemanding task of reducing electricity rates periodically. The reason was that demand for electricity was growing rapidly, and new, larger generating facilities were invariably cheaper. Thus, as new capacity came on line, the average cost of electricity fell. In these circumstances, it was not hard to reconcile the divergent interests of ratepayers and monopolists. Rates could fall while profits remained healthy.

In the 1970s, the climate shifted abruptly as commissions were faced with regular requests for higher rates to cover rising costs. There were three reasons for higher costs. First, the price of oil and other fossil fuels jumped, raising operating costs. Second, interest rates rose, making large-scale, multiyear construction projects more expensive. Third, the cost of building new generating facilities increased as economies of scale began to peter out. "Rate shock" created a new climate of hostility and bitterness at state commissions. Customers protested that they could not pay their electricity bills. Confrontations between utilities and customers even turned violent in a few cases, with scattered physical attacks on executives' cars and on utility employees.[13] During the 1970s, many states established offices of consumer counsel or consumer advocates to bolster safeguards against monopolistic rates. Many states now have these independent offices, which participate in commission hearings as adversaries of the utilities. The Colorado Office of Consumer Counsel is part of the attorney general's office. It was organized in the early 1980s and was established by law in 1984.

THE EVOLUTION OF POLICY AND POLITICS IN THE 1980s

Writing about the late 1970s, William Gormley described public utility regulation as "complex and conflictual. Solutions are seldom obvious, and decisions are seldom consensual." However, Gormley predicted that energy conservation issues might change the nature of public utility politics. "The emergence of energy conservation as a consensual policy could at least limit the scope of the conflict." [14] It is beginning to appear that Gormley's instincts were right. The politics of regulating the electricity industry are still changing, but the story of how conservation has been handled in Colorado and other states suggests that collaborative processes, and a search for formulas that give utilities a stake in conservation, may become as important as confrontation.

The story of how energy conservation became part of the agenda of the Colorado Public Utilities Commission illustrates both how conservation has been included on the public policy agendas in states and how collaboration has increased. The tale is more complicated than those of the two previous chapters, largely because events in Colorado are so closely intertwined with events in other states. The story is organized in three phases. The first phase includes efforts to get conservation on the policy agenda in 1979-1984 in several states; advocates for energy conservation made little headway in Colorado at this point. In 1988-1991, in the second phase, there were efforts to build mechanisms for collaboration about energy conservation in several states, with great success in some states and some progress in Colorado. In the third phase, 1991-1993, the Colorado Public Utilities Commission made a commitment to energy conservation. A chronology of events in Colorado and other states appears in Table 6-2, and a list of key players appears in Table 6-3 (p. 217).

PHASE ONE: GETTING CONSERVATION ON THE AGENDA

In 1976, a young environmentalist named Amory Lovins published an article in *Foreign Affairs* arguing for a "soft energy path." The soft path would consist of conservation, reliance on renewable energy resources, and small-scale generation of electricity. Lovins deplored the "hard" path of centralized, large-scale generation of energy using fossil fuels and nuclear power as unnecessarily expensive.[15] The electricity industry, along with other energy industries, responded with scorn. Utilities were strongly committed to the concept of large central generating stations. Gormley quotes one utility executive as saying:

> Electric utilities are run by engineers, and they're like kids with erector sets. And if you give them the money, they'll buy the biggest doggone erector set that you ever saw. . . . If you give an electric utility manager who is an engineer the money, he'll take it and he'll build something with it, and then you're gonna pay on it for thirty years.[16]

Zach Willey's Model

The story of the change in the willingness of the electric power industry to consider alternatives to the hard path of large central generating stations begins in California in the 1970s. There the battle was especially fierce because environmentalists were strong locally, while the Pacific Gas and Electric Company (PG&E), Southern California Edison (SCE), and municipally owned utilities were planning to build nuclear plants as well as large coal-fired plants that would use coal from new mines near national parks in Utah.

TABLE 6-2

CHRONOLOGY OF EVENTS IN THE COLORADO CASE

1. Getting Energy Conservation on the Agenda
Events in Colorado

1978 Friends of the Earth intervenes in a Public Service Company of Colorado (PSCo) rate case.

1981 Legislation is passed allowing the Colorado Public Utilities Commission (PUC) to take energy conservation into account.

1984 Ron Lehr is appointed to the PUC.

Lehr proposes Rule 34, which would have required integrated resource planning (IRP).

The legislature, led by the house majority leader, passes a bill to deregulate transmission lines below 115 kv; Gov. Richard D. Lamm vetoes the bill. The legislature cuts 5 positions from the PUC staff.

Events Outside Colorado

1976 Amory Lovins publishes article on the "hard path" and the "soft path."

1977 The Environmental Defense Fund first intervenes in rate cases in California.

1979 The California Public Utilities Commission fines Pacific Gas and Electric for inattention to energy conservation and renewables.

1980 Southern California Edison announces a conservation program.

1984 Formation of the National Association of Regulatory Utility Commissioners (NARUC) Committee on Energy Conservation.

2. Demand-Side Management and Collaboration
Events in Colorado

1988 Special open meetings begin.

1989 Gary Nakarado joins the Public Utility Commission.

PSCo announces a pilot demand-side management (DSM) program.

1990 Draft generic policy statement.

Events Outside Colorado

1981 Early conservation programs in the Northwest and New England begin.

1988 Start of first collaborative process in Connecticut.

NARUC Committee on Energy Conservation meeting in Aspen: David Moskovitz proposes decoupling.

(Continued on next page)

TABLE 6-2 *(CONTINUED)*

1989 Formation of the Association of Demand-Side Professionals.

1990 California collaborative process begins.

3. Toward a Decision in Colorado

1990 In December PSCo files rate case; PUC responds with a request for refunds.

1991 In January Land and Water Fund receives grant and intervenes in rate case. In June PSCo and the Office of Consumer Counsel (OCC) propose a settlement, postponing consideration of DSM and IRP.

In July settlement agreement made, with schedule for consideration of DSM and IRP.

1992 In June PSCo supports decoupling, then changes its position.

In July Nakarado withdraws his support for decoupling temporarily. Commissioner Augie Cook leaves the PUC.

In August commissioners announce draft IRP regulation.

In September PUC, PSCo, the Office of Consumer Counsel, and major business interests propose a settlement without decoupling.

In October coal companies, coal-mining counties, PSCo, and the OCC seek to postpone action on IRP.

In December PUC adopts regulations for IRP.

1993 In January PUC decision on decoupling made.

In 1976, PG&E filed for a rate increase, informing the state public utility commission that it planned to quadruple its budget for capital construction over the next decade and would have to increase its rate of return from 9 percent to 14 percent to raise the $13 billion that it planned to spend on large coal and nuclear power stations. Meanwhile, PG&E was not planning to spend anything on energy conservation.[17] The Berkeley office of the Environmental Defense Fund (EDF) decided to intervene in the rate case.

EDF could have attacked PG&E solely on environmental grounds, as many other environmental groups were doing. However, EDF's niche in the environmental movement was bringing scientific expertise to bear on environmental issues. The EDF team also included an economist named Zach Willey. His work shaped a different strategy. Willey built a mathematical model to conduct an economic evaluation of the alternatives open to PG&E. It accepted much of PG&E's own information but was also fueled by studies of renewable energy and energy conservation technologies. Many of these studies had been performed with federal dollars at Stanford Research Institute, Lawrence Berkeley Laboratory, and the Jet Propulsion Laboratory, all in California. Authors of some of these studies helped Willey convert their generic findings to specific numbers that would quantify alternatives available to the reluctant PG&E. Essentially, Willey's model was a practical test of Amory Lovins's contention that a soft path is cheaper.

At first, PG&E dismissed Willey's model as irrelevant and unsound. However, EDF achieved some notable successes. When challenged to provide better estimates, the utility was forced to concede that Willey's model appeared to provide realistic figures and that their own estimates were flawed. In 1979, the state commission fined PG&E $14 million for its inattention to energy conservation and other alternatives suggested by the EDF model. In 1980, EDF presented testimony that conservation and renewables would be a cheaper alternative than building the Allen-Warner Valley coal-fired plant near Bryce Canyon National Park in Utah. Faced with Willey's figures, as well as attacks on the environmental impacts of the plant, PG&E and its partner, Southern California Edison, canceled the project. SCE announced "a major change in corporate policy regarding the sources of future electricity for its customers." SCE planned to develop almost 2,000 megawatts of power through the kinds of alternatives that EDF's model had found to be economical.[18]

News of Willey's model spread to other states even before EDF had scored major successes in California. In 1978, Attorney General Bill Clinton of Arkansas invited Willey to visit the state and toyed with the idea of asking Arkansas Power and Light to consider energy conservation. However, after being elected governor, Clinton decided that taking on the

TABLE 6-3

KEY PARTICIPANTS IN THE COLORADO CASE

In Colorado	Public Utilities Commission commissioners: Ron Lehr (1984-1990), Augie Cook (1988-1992), Gary Nakarado (1988-1993), Christine Alvarez (1990-1992), Bob Temmer (1992-present); Morey Wolfson, assistant to the commissioners (1985-present)
	Office of Consumer Counsel: Ron Binz (1984-present)
	Office of Energy Conservation: Ron Lehr (1977-1981), Jay Brizie (1983-present)
	Public Service Company of Colorado: Del Hock, president (1985-present)
	Colorado-Ute Electric Association
	Tri-State Generation and Transmission Cooperative
	Environmentalists: Amory Lovins; Kelley Green, Land and Water (LAW) Fund; Bruce Driver, LAW Fund
Outside Colorado	Zach Willey, Environmental Defense Fund, Berkeley, Calif.
	Ralph Cavanagh, Natural Resources Defense Council, San Francisco
	Conservation Law Foundation, Boston
	David Moskovitz, public utility commissioner and then independent consultant, Maine
	Southern California Edison, Los Angeles
	Pacific Gas and Electric, San Francisco
	Pacific Power and Light, later named Pacificorp, Portland, Ore.
	Bonneville Power Administration, Portland, Ore.
	New England Electrical System

utility would be a major political battle and was not as important as his other objectives.[19] The same year, a young environmentalist named Kevin Markey was running a one-man office in Colorado for Friends of the Earth. He had a mathematical bent and was intrigued by Willey's model. Markey arranged for Willey to visit Colorado as an expert witness for environmental groups intervening in a request by the Public Service Company of Colorado that electricity rates be raised to pay for a new coal-fired power plant. Willey testified that his model showed there were often cheaper sources of power than coal-fired plants. The environmentalists did not have the resources to hire Willey to build a model to evaluate the specific choices in Colorado, but the public utility commission nonetheless seemed to be impressed by Willey's arguments and approved a smaller rate hike than the service company had proposed.

Although neither Clinton nor Markey got Willey to build a model for his state, others did. And several consulting firms built their own mathematical models for utilities and utility commissions to use in comparing soft path conservation and renewables with hard path power plants. In addition, Willey's model, ELFIN, has been improved, and in its most recent form is still widely used. What Willey was part of, and Colorado and Arkansas missed, was the beginning of a revolution in the technology of utility decision making. As powerful personal computers became available, it was possible for small teams to analyze vast arrays of data about how utilities might choose to generate electricity. As a PG&E economist told EDF after the battles were over, EDF's model had helped to catalyze "a major informational revolution inside the company." This revolution transformed the company by allowing professionals who were not construction engineers to become knowledgeable about the details of utility planning.

> There needs to be a lot of quantitative analysis in planning, and everybody in the company had his own little model to do his piece of it; but there was no bridge, no connection between them. So it was a major assignment to bring all these models into a system, and in essence do what [EDF was] already doing, in a simple way, on the outside—and very able to do it. The company was incapable of doing that on the inside. Just now, this year for the first time, we're finally able to link all the models up.[20]

As EDF perfected ELFIN, and others built their models, the idea spread that utilities should be forced to give full and fair consideration to sources of energy besides the central generation stations they owned. Markey and other environmentalists helped a liberal Democratic state senator to write legislation that said the public utility commission "may consider . . . energy conservation" in setting rates. The senator found a

Republican cosponsor, and the bill passed. But the commission took no concrete steps to ensure that utilities would incorporate conservation into their plans or to build the commission's own capacity to evaluate conservation. In the same year, the Office of Energy Conservation—part of the office of Gov. Richard D. Lamm, staffed by a number of active environmentalists and federally funded—made two efforts to raise energy conservation issues with the commission. The office intervened in a generic docket on interstate sales of electricity, questioning whether conservation would reduce the need for additional coal-fired plants. Also, it offered to help the commission write regulations for energy audits of residential facilities, as required by federal legislation. The commission ignored the office's comments on the intervention and refused to cooperate with the regulations, saying that cooperation would constitute ex parte communication and thus be illegal.

Least-Cost Planning and IRP

The idea of requiring utilities to consider alternative ways of satisfying the demand for electricity and the technology of models like ELFIN coalesced in the early 1980s into the concept of "least-cost" planning, now often called integrated resource planning (IRP). Environmentalists strongly favor it as a way of putting energy conservation and renewable energy on an equal analytical footing with conventional sources of electricity. Independent power producers also favor it as a device to ensure that their projects receive attention. More recently, the gas industry has become supportive of least-cost planning, at least in states where an impartial analysis of the options might suggest that switching from electricity to gas would lower the costs of meeting consumers' demands for space heating and hot water. However, many executives in the electric power industry have been skeptical, seeing least-cost planning as a useful management tool but as an intrusion into their business when mandated and overseen by state public utility commissions.

In 1984, the concept of IRP arrived in Colorado. Once again, the proposal was to copy an idea from another western state, and once again, the proposal failed. The episode began when a seat became vacant on the three-member state commission. Governor Lamm, a Democrat, decided to make a serious effort to introduce an environmental perspective into the agency. His first nomination was Steve Pomerance, who was—and still is—very interested in electrical utilities. Pomerance is the younger brother of a Washington, D.C., environmentalist who was at the time president of Friends of the Earth. The state senate refused to confirm him. Lamm then appointed Ron Binz; when the senate turned him down as well, the Republican attorney general appointed Binz as head of the newly created Office of Consumer Counsel. Lamm's third nomination was Ron Lehr, deputy director of the Office of Energy Conservation. At this point, the senate backed down and accepted Lehr's nomination.

After Lehr took office, he took two steps that began a slow transformation of the way the commission functioned. First, Lehr led an effort to promulgate formal rules defining impermissible ex parte conduct. These rules made it easier for commissioners and staff to open informal discussions with other state agencies as well as with the service company, other utilities, and interest groups. Second, Morey Wolfson was added to the commission staff. Wolfson was familiar with energy conservation from his work in the state Division of Housing and had once been an active environmentalist. At the commission, Wolfson filled a new role. He was not an economist and would not be involved in reviewing details of proposed rate structures. Instead, he worked directly for the public utility commissioners as a multipurpose aide and policy adviser. Over the years, Wolfson worked quietly with Lehr and other commissioners, responding to their interests in conservation, renewable energy, and other policy areas, and helping them design independent initiatives to push these causes, rather than waiting for the service company and others to file rate cases. Together, these two steps equipped the commission to become a proactive force for utility reform.

Lehr's first proactive proposal was for the commission to adopt a procedure for integrated resource planning that was modeled on IRP in Nevada. This would have involved hiring an independent consultant to help in preparing plans describing how utilities would meet the rising demand for electricity. The service company objected vociferously to letting any outsider plan for their system under the guidance of the commission, and Lehr could not get either of the two other commissioners to support his proposal. Rather than turn Lehr down flat, the service company offered to prepare an annual *Gold Book* outlining its long-range plans and to hold an annual meeting at which interested parties could ask questions about it. This allowed the service company to say that it was conducting a formal least-cost planning process, but that it was doing so as a matter of good business practice and would not reveal the details to the public or to the commission. For three years commission staff and others attended these briefings, but no one claimed that the format allowed for much discussion.

The *Gold Book* presented the service company's view that coal-fired generating stations, not conservation, were the best way to meet Colorado's demand for energy. The service company and its customers are blessed with relatively cheap electricity. Rates in Colorado are currently about half those of customers on the two coasts (where there has been the greatest interest in conservation). Most service company electricity is generated by plants that burn inexpensive coal that is strip mined in Wyoming and brought by train to power plants near Denver. There are also strip mines and underground mines in Colorado that produce more expensive coal. Most Colorado mines lie across the Continental Divide from the population centers of Denver, Colorado Springs, and Pueblo. Because it is more expensive and must be moved over the mountains to serve the urban customers, most Colorado coal is burned in generating stations on the Western Slope. The service company buys some Colorado coal as a way to diversify its sources of supply and to support the Colorado economy.

While Lehr was pushing for IRP, the Republican-controlled legislature was working on its own public utility commission agenda. The previous year, the legislature had passed a bill that allowed rural electric cooperatives to remove themselves from commission jurisdiction if they wished to do so. Lamm had not objected. During the year that Lehr joined the commission, the Republicans pursued the goal of deregulation further, pushing through a bill that would deregulate all transmission lines below 115 kilovolts and all operations of Colorado-Ute, an association that generated and distributed electricity to its fourteen members, which are all rural cooperatives. Colorado-Ute was the second biggest utility in the state. Lamm vetoed this bill. Then, the house majority leader, an electrical contractor who did a great deal of work for the service company, persuaded the Republican caucus to eliminate five staff positions that had been added recently at the commission. With the IRP proposal lacking support and the legislature clearly unhappy, Lehr and Lamm faced political realities. Lehr did continue to raise the topic of energy conservation and renewables when the opportunity arose, but without IRP, and with the service company not asking for major rate increases, there were few chances to do so. From 1984 to 1988 the major focus of attention at the commission was on the break-up of AT&T and on telecommunications issues.

Although Lehr was not successful in placing energy conservation on the agendas of the service company and the commission in 1984, the idea continued to make progress in other states and at the federal level. In 1983, a group of state public utility commissioners proposed a committee on energy conservation within the National Association of Regulatory Utility Commissioners (NARUC). Members of the NARUC electricity committee objected that they could handle this issue adequately, and the executive committee concurred. In an unusual display of aggressiveness, the issue was raised on the floor at the annual meeting, and the membership overruled the executive committee. Lehr became an active member of the committee.

From the perspective of public utility commission officials in a state like Colorado, the NARUC Committee on Energy Conservation was an important source of intellectual and emotional nourishment. It soon formed links with individual federal officials who were pushing for a stronger stance on energy conservation. In 1986, Rep. Claudine Schneider of Rhode Island, a Republican who had once been state director of Friends of the Earth, sponsored legislation that created a program of research and public education on IRP within the Department of Energy (DOE). Although the administration opposed the proposal and did not request an appropriation for the program when it was created, Schneider and others ensured that it was established and received a small appropriation of $1 million per year, starting in 1988. As Wolfson later wrote, now DOE had some "innovators and transformers in its midst.... They formed a partnership. The partners recognized that success in innovation diffusion required creating new avenues for action. The first avenue decided upon was DOE support for [the NARUC Committee on Energy Conservation's] educational activities." [21]

One of the first things that the new DOE program did was make a grant to NARUC, and in April 1988, the NARUC Committee on Energy Conservation held its first national conference on energy conservation and utilities, in Aspen, Colorado, home of Amory Lovins. The

DOE program also supported expanded work at national laboratories such as the Lawrence Berkeley Laboratory in California and the Oak Ridge Laboratory in Tennessee, and scientists became frequent attendees at NARUC meetings and conferences.

By the end of the 1980s, the energy conservation committee was flourishing, and IRP was spreading. A 1990 study prepared by the consulting firm of Barakat and Chamberlin for the Electric Power Research Institute found that twenty-three states had functioning least-cost planning processes, and all but eight were considering or developing least-cost strategies.[22] A more cautious study using a comprehensive definition of IRP and relying on interviews and a more detailed questionnaire found that only eleven states had adopted IRP in 1991 and that fifteen state commissions were not even considering IRP.[23] Both studies showed that Colorado had not adopted IRP. Phase 1 was ending with changes in other states, but there had been very little progress toward policies to encourage energy conservation by electrical utilities in Colorado.

PHASE TWO: DEMAND-SIDE MANAGEMENT AND COLLABORATION

The next effort to raise the issue of energy conservation at the Colorado Public Utilities Commission came in 1988. It focused not on planning but on implementation—including what came to be called demand-side management (DSM). As the phrase indicates, DSM seeks to satisfy customers' needs not by increasing the supply of electricity but by influencing the demand for electricity—for example, by encouraging conservation measures that would allow beer to be cooled with less electricity.*

Demand-Side Management

It is not new for utilities to work on the demand side, but it is new for them to try to reduce the demand for electricity. In addition to pioneering supply-side technologies like high-voltage power lines, Samuel Insull had been a pioneer on the demand side. One of his greatest successes was persuading millions of Americans to purchase electric refrigerators in the 1920s and 1930s, thus increasing the demand for elec-

---

*Some writers define DSM to include any effort by utilities to influence demand, including those that might increase the use of electricity.

tricity. In the 1960s, most utilities had active marketing departments that encouraged customers to adopt all-electric heating and to use more "labor-saving" electric appliances. Utilities also offered free technical assistance to their commercial and industrial customers to help design lighting and heating systems, as well as consulting on industrial processes.[24]

When the energy crisis hit in the early 1970s, most utilities stopped trying to increase the demand for electricity. The Public Service Company of Colorado disbanded its marketing department and removed the electric refrigerators and freezers from the lobby of its headquarters in downtown Denver. Other utilities stopped their marketing efforts or changed the focus to helping large customers cut back their use of electricity in times of short supply. In the 1980s, utilities again expanded their activities on the demand side, but this time, they sought to reduce demand rather than increase it.

Amory Lovins and other proponents of the soft path argue that it is cheaper to conserve energy than to build conventional power generating facilities. However, they argue that customers will often fail to invest in conservation measures, even if doing so would reduce their use of electricity and save them money. There are several barriers that may keep energy conservation below optimal levels. Barriers include customers' desire that up-front investments in conservation be recouped by quick paybacks in the form of lower electricity bills (usually in three years or less), a lack of reliable information on energy conservation technologies, and a lack of qualified contractors and DSM professionals. Also, the person who faces the decision about whether to invest in energy conservation is often different from the person who pays monthly utility bills. For example, landlords pay for insulation, furnaces, and sometimes large appliances, and developers and architects decide how much energy efficiency to design into new buildings. However, monthly utility bills are paid by renters or homeowners who may not be involved in these decisions. Economic theory suggests that landlords and developers who invest in conservation should be able to raise their prices, but this may not work out in practice.

To overcome barriers to the adoption of energy conservation measures, utilities can provide information, finance customer investments in conservation, and provide direct subsidies. In some cases, utilities have given away fluorescent light bulbs or offered to wrap customers' water heaters with insulation. Proponents of DSM argue that utilities should be just as willing to invest their dollars in these programs as in increasing the supply of electricity. In Amory Lovins's phrase, utilities should invest in "negawatts" as well as in megawatts.

DSM is controversial partly because it is difficult to measure its effectiveness. The desired effect is that something *not* happen. Critics sometimes argue that studies of DSM are flawed because they give DSM credit for reductions in electricity use when the cause is actually an economic slowdown. Other skeptics argue that reductions in the actual use of electricity are exaggerated because studies ignore the "snapback" that occurs when high-efficiency light bulbs and other devices fail and customers replace them with inefficient conventional devices. When experts on DSM meet, the discussion often turns to the need to develop more sophisticated measurement tools.

Collaborative Processes

In the early 1980s, a few utilities began to take DSM seriously. Following EDF's successes in California in 1979 and 1980, PG&E's investments in conservation and efficiency rose to $138 million in 1985, and Southern California Edison spent $64 million in 1984.[25] Without being pushed by environmentalists, the New England Electrical System announced in 1979 that it would invest in energy conservation.[26]

The failure of the gigantic Washington Public Power System, aptly called WPPS, or "whoops," also stimulated energy conservation efforts. WPPS was organized by the Bonneville Power Administration with the assistance of several rural electrical cooperatives in the Pacific Northwest. It experienced major cost overruns on a giant nuclear facility in conjunction with shortfalls in demand. WPPS was unable to meet payments on its bonds and declared bankruptcy, dragging several small rural cooperatives down with it. As these events unfolded, in 1981 Congress mandated in the Pacific Northwest Power Conservation Act that "conservation should be treated as a generating resource" by the Bonneville Power Administration. This statute created the Northwest Power Planning Council, which included representatives of state governments as well as the Bonneville Power Administration, and charged the council with preparing a balanced energy plan. Local managers for the Bonneville Power Administration organized conservation programs to meet the different needs and opportunities of local industries and communities. There were also conservation efforts among private utilities in the region. Pressured by Ralph Cavanagh of the Natural Resources Defense Council's office in San Francisco, Pacific Power and Light experimented with conservation, most notably with a $20 million, five-year model program in Hood River, Oregon. The Hood River project was carefully evaluated. Program managers found results encouraging, although electricity savings were only 15 percent (at a higher cost than had been expected) because prior use of electricity in the community had already been quite low.[27]

Although only a few utilities were seriously experimenting with conservation, these experiments were important. Slowly, a new field of knowledge and expertise emerged. The California Energy Commission published a handbook for evaluating the costs and likely payoffs of different conservation programs. The Association of Demand-Side Management Professionals was formed in December 1989. Bill LeBlanc, then with the Electric Power Research Institute, was encouraged to help organize the group and later became its president. In less than two years, its membership rose to more than 1,300 people, about half of whom worked for utilities and another third of whom worked for consulting firms that serve the industry.[28]

Since 1988, the spread of DSM has been strongly associated with the use of collaborative processes. Informal collaborative negotiations are not new, but their use in designing energy conservation programs is. When EDF took on PG&E, and when Governor Clinton considered the prospects for energy conservation in Arkansas, there had been no examples of collaborative discussions between electrical utilities and environmentalists about something as important as how utilities satisfied their customers' demands for electricity. The climate was adversarial, not cooperative.

Until the late 1980s, utilities were on the defensive. Many had failed to foresee that rate increases of the 1970s would lead customers to cut back on their use of electricity. Also, many of the large generating stations started during the 1970s, especially nuclear plants, experienced major cost overruns. High interest rates and tighter environmental controls on air emissions, on coal mining, and on operation of nuclear power plants helped to increase costs. When a major recession hit in 1982, many utilities found they were overextended.

In New England, as in most other parts of the country, the political climate in the early 1980s was one of bitter confrontation. Environmentalists attacked the Seabrook nuclear project in southern New Hampshire, a hydroelectric project on the Penobscot River in Maine, and transmission lines bringing hydroelectric power south from Quebec. In these fights, environmentalists always argued that conservation would reduce the need for new projects, and utilities rebutted these claims. When the Conservation Law Foundation intervened in several states to fight Seabrook, the Public Service Company of New Hampshire (the largest shareholder in Seabrook) dismissed its claims as "informational terrorism." [29]

By 1986, Seabrook was dragging its owners toward the same fate as that of WPPS. However, despite large cost overruns, Seabrook owners faced not shortfalls in demand but a booming economy and the possibility of shortfalls in power supply. (Scattered brownouts did occur in 1987.) In late 1986, faced with this mix of financial, political, and other impending problems, New England governors called for a regional effort of least-cost planning. The Conservation Law Foundation responded with a report entitled *Power to Share*, which argued that conservation could meet the region's entire need for electrical power over the next twenty years without any expansion in supply.

At this point, in December 1987, the Connecticut Light and Power Company asked its public utility commission for a rate increase and a decrease in spending on conservation. The utility argued that since it had facilities to produce more power than it could sell, it was unwise to invest in conservation. The Conservation Law Foundation intervened and tapped an informal network of experts and experience that had been building slowly. They brought in Arthur Rosenfeld, whose work at Lawrence Berkeley Laboratory had been used by Zach Willey; Tom Foley, who managed resource planning for the Northwest Power Planning Council; and Gil Peach, who managed the Hood River project and other conservation activities of Pacific Power and Light.

Foley testified that it was possible to find opportunities to invest in conservation during periods of surplus capacity. And he argued that it was prudent to do so because these periods would not last forever, and the experience would be helpful when any surplus disappeared. The commission was convinced. It ordered a doubling of expenditure on conservation and told the utility to cooperate with the Conservation Law Foundation in designing ways to spend the additional funds. Then William Ellis, chair and chief executive officer of Northeast Utilities, the parent of Connecticut Light and Power, stepped across the line of antagonism that divided environmentalists from utilities. He offered the foundation $250,000 to pay the expenses of experts who would help the utility redesign its conservation program. Soon after, the Massachusetts public utility commission ordered five utilities to meet with intervenors and other interested parties to respond to conservation and load management issues. The utilities signed an agreement creating a collaborative process in Massachusetts. Both states' collaborative processes were successful. They resulted in expanded conservation programs that were endorsed by the foundation and the utilities and accepted by the state commissions. Amory Lovins commented that the foundation "is now even exploiting inter-service rivalry between some of the utilities over who can get the most credit for the best efficiency program." [30]

California was not willing to be left behind. The California Energy Commission issued a report pointing out that utility spending on conservation had declined since the mid-1980s. Ralph Cavanagh of the Natural Resources Defense Council organized and led a collaborative process that resulted in January 1990 in *An Energy Efficiency Blueprint for California*. This report committed four major utilities in the state to increasing their annual conservation spending in 1991 by 96 percent over 1988 levels.[31]

Giving Incentives to Utilities

Although the New England and California collaboratives have led to expansions of DSM programs, these programs still take a small part of most utility budgets. Since 1989, there has been an active discussion about whether traditional rate-making procedures create disincentives for utility spending on DSM. This interest was sparked partly by a speech by David Moskovitz, who was then public utility commissioner in Maine, to the first NARUC Conservation Committee conference in

Aspen in 1988. As Lehr remembers the event: "We had heard several fine speeches about conservation, and then David stood up and electrified the audience. He said that our talk was empty words, that there would be few investments of significant size in DSM until commissions broke the link between sales and profits." [32]

The speech led to a resolution, sponsored by the Committee on Energy Conservation and passed by NARUC later that year, encouraging public utility commissions to make least-cost conservation alternatives the "most profitable component" of utility plans.[33] Moskovitz argued in the speech, and later in a widely distributed paper published by NARUC, that utilities lost money when they invested in DSM. The link between sales and profits is buried in the formulas that commissions use to calculate rates.[34] Decoupling sales and profits requires finding another base for setting rates. One option, which has been adopted in Washington, New York, and Maine, is to set rates on the basis of an estimated cost per customer, using historical data to set the figures. In this situation, when utilities can induce customers to use less electricity, fuel costs will drop, and profits will increase. Another option is to give utilities incentives for investing in conservation, perhaps on the basis of an estimate of kilowatt hours to be saved by conservation measures.

Both options suffer from the problem that is inherent in DSM—the difficulty of estimation. Traditional regulators and utility executives are understandably uneasy about adopting rate-setting formulas that are based on negawatt estimates of how much electricity consumers *might* have used. Hundreds of millions of dollars are on the table in rate setting, and it is not unreasonable to want to see hard, measurable data on costs, investments, and payoff. In this sense, DSM is inherently "smoke and mirrors," even if conservation really is cheaper.* If Moskovitz is correct (which most experts now agree is the case), and if a public utility commission does not decouple sales and profits or give utilities financial incentives to invest in conservation, the only way to encourage DSM is to mandate it, given that profits will drop if a utility submits to the dictates of the commission.

---

*Some experts suggest that public utility commissions might step in and try to act as bankers, finding ways to assure that utilities can borrow on their investments in DSM.

Initial Discussion of DSM in Colorado

News of successful collaboration in New England spread very quickly to Colorado. By this time, Ron Lehr had gained an ally on the state commission. In 1987, newly elected Gov. Roy Romer, a Democrat, had the opportunity to fill a position in the commission. The incumbent, Edie Miller, was an economist who was primarily concerned with the traditional commission issues of rates and monopoly profits, not with conservation. Although Miller was interested in being reappointed, Romer decided instead to find someone who was more in tune with his top priority of economic development. (At the time, the Colorado economy was quite depressed, because of low energy prices and a sharp downturn in the western energy industry, as well as the end of a speculative boom that had been fueled by energy-related growth.)

Romer's first choice for the commission position was a developer who said that the commission should encourage economic development. This was too dramatic a break with orthodox commission policies for many people, so Romer instead chose Augie Cook, a businessman who had been in the heating and plumbing industry. Cook's style was much less dramatic than Lehr's, but he became a firm supporter of the energy conservation issues that Lehr had pioneered at the commission.

In 1988, while the Conservation Law Foundation was showing how collaborative processes could be used to advance the cause of conservation, Lehr and Cook raised the issue again. A professor from the Harvard Business School was invited to visit Colorado to explore the potential for a collaborative process. His assessment was enthusiastic, but local experts were more cautious. So, rather than launch a full-scale collaborative negotiation process, the commission sponsored a series of twenty special open meetings to discuss various issues facing it and the electricity industry. The meetings covered a broad range of topics, including DSM, least-cost planning, acid rain, global warming, solar energy, the electricity needs for Denver's new international airport, and special needs of low-income families.

Ron Lehr had been laying the groundwork for this step for years. To the meetings he invited many people whom he had met with informally over the years. More than twenty groups participated in the meetings, including several that were only peripheral players in traditional utility regulation.

The list included an economist from the federally supported National Renewable Energy Laboratory, a utility executive from Florida who was knowledgeable about energy service companies, the president of an association of managers of downtown buildings, a specialist in conservation from a city-owned utility on the west coast, and many others. Using funds obtained from the federal Department of Energy, the state Office of Energy Conservation paid for national experts to fly in for several of the meetings. As commission chair, Augie Cook ran most of the meetings, but they were informal discussions rather than adjudicatory hearings.

The special open meetings did not lead to any formal action, but Lehr feels that they were successful. He remembers one meeting as a critical turning point. Lehr had asked Public Service Company of Colorado's representatives whether they were planning for a transition from an electromechanical path to an electronic future, one in which users could monitor and adjust their electricity use continuously. "The service company said their strategy was to invest in coal-fired plants. But then an engineer from Climax Mining [a large molybdenum mine owned by Amax] raised his hand and said that his firm had invested $200,000 in computer controls and had been able to save 10 megawatts of power. I sat quietly and then called a recess to let the lesson sink in." [35] Apparently Climax had saved power at the cost of $20 per kilowatt—about 1 percent of the projected cost of the service company's next coal-fired plant.

In the spring of 1989, after a year of special meetings, there was a first sign that the service company's position might be shifting. The company got a new chairman, Del Hock. The previous chairman was an engineer who had made his name building the service company's Fort St. Vrain plant. This plant used a unique technology but had the same financial problems as WPPS and Seabrook. It never operated at full capacity; in 1984, the public utility commission refused to allow the service company to include its full costs in the rate base. Instead, the company spun off Fort St. Vrain as a subsidiary independent power producer, and company stockholders were forced to cover cost overruns.

Del Hock is an accountant, trained to watch the bottom line of profits more closely than the top line of kilowatt hours produced. He sent a letter to the commission saying that he was too busy to attend the special open meetings but that the company was "fully committed" to energy conservation.[36]

Later that summer, the service company followed up on this rhetorical signal. The utility issued a request for proposals that would conserve 2 megawatts of power (of their 3,800-megawatt load, which was growing at 70 megawatts per year). There were bids for 6 megawatts, and the service company eventually accepted bids for 4 megawatts. Prices were above the Climax figure, but the price of $196 per kilowatt was far below the cost for new coal-fired capacity of over $1,500 per kilowatt. Eventually the company organized six DSM pilot projects and began to build a staff of experts in demand-side management.

The Generic Inquiry into DSM in Colorado

Another important change in 1989 was the arrival of a new public utility commissioner, Gary Nakarado. To everyone's surprise, Nakarado became a strong partisan of conservation, vice chair of the NARUC Committee on Energy Conservation, and the third member of the commission firmly in favor of conservation.

Nakarado is a lawyer and a Republican, who was looking in 1989 for new challenges. He had not been active politically and had never heard of demand-side management or integrated resource planning. However, he had heard of Amory Lovins and telephoned him. Lovins told him that public utility commissioners were the most important energy officials in the country. This sounded interesting, so Nakarado put his name forward. The governor and service company executives interviewed him during the confirmation process. Neither in these meetings nor at legislative hearings was Nakarado asked about his views on environmental issues, energy efficiency, or collaborative processes.

Nakarado brought to the commission a strong interest in team building and cooperation. This landed him in hot water almost immediately and was a signal of how sharply the commission's modus operandi was to change. The flareup also illustrated how traditional regulators might respond to collaborative processes.

Taking his lead from Romer, Nakarado's first move was to build informal relationships with the service company and USWest (the regional Bell telephone company). He met the top officers over breakfast and invited the treasurer of the company and the CEO of USWest to attend an annual conference that Lovins sponsored at a Colorado mountain resort. To be friendly, Nakarado accepted an invitation to go up early with the USWest executive for a morning of trout fishing, and to save money, Nakarado shared a condominium with the executive. Nakarado also met USWest executives socially—more than thirty-two times over a period of eighteen months. Also, as Colorado-Ute began to face financial difficulties, Nakarado reached out to its executives informally, trying to understand the scope of its problems and possible implications for public policy.[37]

To traditionalists, this sounded sleazy—like a violation of the spirit of the rule against ex parte communication, if not the law. As Ron Binz later told a reporter, "I think utility commissioners can be friends with three million people in Colorado, but there are 150 people who are off limits. I don't believe the public wants the commission to socialize with utilities." [38] Denver newspapers printed articles that included critical comments by Binz and Miller as well as Nakarado's denial that anything was amiss. A Democratic legislator introduced a bill prohibiting conversations between commission staff or commissioners and regulated businesses. It passed the House and died. Nakarado recused himself from one decision involving Colorado-Ute, after a protest by Ron Binz, and met with the editorial boards of both papers to explain his conduct. The governor's office investigated the affair, finding nothing wrong.

In the spring of 1990, when the brouhaha had subsided, the commission decided to move ahead with energy conservation. The commission opened a generic inquiry about DSM, and Nakarado became the hearing officer. In August, he issued an interim decision announcing a series of five hearings in the fall, which would culminate in a generic policy statement. Everything that an environmentalist would want was to be on the table, including the following "influences and considerations":

1. An international, interdependent, and competitive global economy with increasing income disparities within and among nations.
2. A global physical environment at risk.
3. An opportunity for society to reduce present and future risk and discontinuities by pursuing diversity of energy supply sources, developing renewable energy resources, and investing in efficiency.
4. Improvement of the political and regulatory process by integrating

the strengths of democracy, markets, and technology toward a sustainable culture.[39]

The generic policy statement was to address everything, from environmental issues to the very nature of the regulatory process. Once again, the Office of Energy Conservation supported the process by bringing in national experts to speak at the hearings and to consult informally with itself, the service company, and others.

Nakarado recalls the hearings on this generic inquiry as being especially useful in "speaking to the staff of the commission in a way they cannot ignore." They were accustomed to a much more clearly defined set of issues—rates and monopoly profits. "Deep within, the staff feels that the rate of return to the company is the most important issue, more important even than whether the customers get good service and low rates. The generic inquiry was to get at the question of what it meant for the job of the staff when demand was a variable and not a fixed quantity." [40]

The generic inquiry resulted in a radical draft policy statement. It said that the commission would be guided by the "influences and considerations" that Nakarado had raised in July, endorsed an article in *Scientific American* by Amory Lovins and two employees of the Electric Power Research Institute (which is supported by investor-owned utilities), and announced that the commission would adopt integrated resource planning, encourage utilities to invest in DSM, consider environmental costs in evaluating utility alternatives, and move toward a more collaborative approach to decision making.

The draft policy statement was approved unanimously by the commission in December 1990. But Governor Romer decided not to reappoint Ron Lehr, and the policy statement stalled. Romer appointed Christine Alvarez to the commission. Alvarez is a lawyer and an expert in administrative law. She refused to sign a final version of the policy statement, saying that the document had not been through the proper rule-making procedures. Not wanting to create tension with Alvarez just after her arrival, Nakarado and Cook postponed final action on the draft policy statement and eventually set it aside. In retrospect, Wolfson says, the statement had "served its purpose" in sending signals of the commission's position, and was superseded by a new development.[41]

PHASE THREE: TOWARD A DECISION IN COLORADO

Within a few weeks after Alvarez joined the commission, a new DSM/IRP episode began. The service company filed its first rate case in eight years. This precipitated a formal agreement among the company, the commission, and many other parties to participate in a process of collaboration and adjudicatory hearings that would lead to a formal commission decision about IRP, DSM, and decoupling. By mutual agreement, events were moving to a moment of truth. For years, Ron Lehr (and later Augie Cook, Morey Wolfson, Gary Nakarado, and others outside the commission) had tried to engage the company and others in a discussion of how Amory Lovins's vision of a soft path might be implemented in Colorado. Now the company signed a formal agreement to put these ideas on the commission's agenda and implicitly promised that some kind of agreement might be reached. This was to be a test of whether the stakeholders in Colorado would embrace the new tools of DSM and a new, more collaborative style of politics.

The Legal and Political Situations
On the Eve of the Rate Case

From the legal point of view, very little had changed in Colorado since 1978. The rules that guided the service company's presentation of the rate case and the commission's decision had not changed significantly. Although the commission had approved the company's pilot DSM program in 1989 and allowed the company to include the costs of the program in its rate base as expenses, it had not adopted IRP or decoupled profits from sales. The draft generic policy statement had no legal force. Thus, if the commission wanted to raise energy conservation issues during the rate case, it would be starting almost from scratch. There was very little policy on the books to guide a discussion and a decision.

However, from a political point of view, several important milestones had passed. The commission had sent clear signals that it was embarked on a course of radical change, and neither the legislature nor the service company had yet openly objected. Indeed, the company had sent signals back that it was willing to proceed with some amount of DSM by announcing not only its first 2-megawatt pilot program but also eleven additional small pilots and a two-step DSM bidding program for 100 megawatts.

The Office of Energy Conservation (OEC) was prepared for the rate case. Before the case was filed, it had checked with the governor's office and obtained clearance to hire a nationally known firm to help explore strategies for getting DSM and decoupling on the commission's agenda for a decision. The rate case provided an excellent opportunity, albeit an unexpected one, to push the OEC agenda.

In addition, OEC now had a new ally—the Land and Water (LAW) Fund of the Rockies. The alliance was born during the winter of 1989 when Kelley Green went cross-country skiing with Ron Lehr and Bruce Driver. The three were old friends. Green is a lawyer who has spent her career in the environmental movement. She had just established the LAW Fund as a public-interest law firm to serve environmental groups in Colorado and adjoining states. Driver had worked on utility issues for the Department of Energy and the U.S. House Committee on Energy and Commerce before moving to Denver to work on water conservation at the Western Governors' Association. He was currently practicing law in Denver.

The three discussed whether the commission could take on the service company without outside help. After the trip, Green heard that the Pew Charitable Trusts, a large national foundation, was interested in building capacity in different parts of the country to raise conservation issues in public utility commission hearings. Also, the Pew Trusts, the MacArthur Foundation, and the Rockefeller Foundation had established the Energy Foundation with a fund of $20 million to make grants over three years for various activities that would encourage conservation and the use of renewable energy, including advocacy on behalf of energy conservation in state utility commissions.[42] Green decided to apply for a Pew grant and asked Driver to manage the project. The grant arrived just in time for the service company rate case. The LAW Fund and OEC both intervened and, in the words of Jay Brizie of OEC, "were joined at the hip" as partners for the two years. OEC hired consultants to work on decoupling and DSM, whereas the LAW Fund obtained help on environmental issues and IRP.

The Public Service Company Rate Case Takes Shape

For eight years, there had been no service company rate case. The last public utility commission decision had allowed the company to make small adjustments in its rates when its costs changed. But in January 1991, the company asked for a 4 percent increase in gas rates and a 1.3 percent reduction in electric rates. Two months later, the commission staff and Ron Binz's Office of Consumer Counsel (OCC) filed responses. Both argued that the service company had earned more than the allowed rate of return over the past several years because of technical flukes in the formulas for annual rate readjustments. The staff recommended that the company refund more than $150 million to its customers. OCC concurred.

This created a major problem for the company. By itself, $150 million would be a significant slice of the company's annual revenues of $1.7 billion. In addition, the company was facing a decision about how to pay for decommissioning the Fort St. Vrain nuclear plant. It was not clear how much this would cost, or whether the commission would permit the company to include a portion of the cost in the rate base.

These financial uncertainties came at a critical time for the company. One year earlier, Colorado-Ute had declared bankruptcy, and the company was negotiating to purchase half of Colorado-Ute's customer base and 25 percent of its generating capacity. If the company did not convince the bankruptcy judge that it could finance this purchase, it might not be able to purchase Colorado-Ute. Then it was highly likely that Pacificorp, an investor-owned utility based in Oregon, would step in. Pacificorp was originally Pacific Power and Light (PP&L), the utility that pioneered DSM in Hood River, Oregon. When the energy boom in the West collapsed, leaving Colorado-Ute, Utah Power and Light, and many other utilities in debt with new plants that were no longer needed, PP&L decided to expand. It earned the nickname "Pac Man" for its quick gobbling up of bankrupt companies at bargain prices. It had purchased Utah Power and Light, and if it could gain a foothold in Colorado, then it might expand south toward New Mexico. Pacificorp had offered to purchase 25 percent of Colorado-Ute's generating capacity and was eager to buy more.

Unless the service company was willing to let Pacificorp into Colorado, it had to settle the rate case quickly. So it met with the OCC and, in June, announced a settlement. The company would return $22 million to electric customers, reduce electricity rates, raise gas rates slightly, and accept a lower rate of return pending the next rate case. The agreement said that decoupling profits from sales and DSM were "ancillary issues" that would be handled in the next rate case. This case would not be heard until after the expiration of Cook's and Nakarado's appointments to the commission. Perhaps they would be reappointed; perhaps not. Apparently, neither OCC nor the service company was eager to have the current members of the commission rule on IRP and DSM.

The proposal to postpone a decision on energy conservation upset Nakarado and Cook. But the bottom line in traditional regulation is rates, and the company was offering to return $22 million to consumers. The political reality is, as Morey Wolfson later said, "Utility commissions do not reject refunds." [43] The specter of Pacificorp put additional pressure on the commission to accept the settlement. Colorado business and political leaders were upset about the prospect that an outside utility might come into the state. There was little they could do, but their concern about Pacificorp helped to create a climate favoring a quick settlement that would clarify the service company's financial position.

The company increased the pressure on the commissioners even further by declaring that if the commission approved the proposed settlement, the company would finance a public-purpose nonprofit corporation to conduct research and provide technical assistance to energy users on conservation and renewable energy. During the special open meetings, Larry Flowers, of the National Renewable Energy Laboratory, had suggested creating a Partnership for Energy Efficient Colorado (PEEC), to be supported by the company and major energy users. Such partnerships had been established in New York, North Carolina, and other states, and were well regarded by many proponents of energy conservation. The commission had called a meeting to discuss the proposal for PEEC and had obtained favorable comments.

The LAW Fund and the Office of Energy Conservation were a counterweight to the pressure to accept the settlement. They were possibly in a position to block the settlement, since they had both intervened in the rate case. According to Ron Binz, the legal relevance of the concerns of the LAW Fund and OEC was unclear; they were interested in DSM and IRP, whereas the case had begun with a focus on rates and refunds and was now to be settled on those issues alone. But the presence of OEC and the LAW Fund provided political cover and a procedural reason not to accept the service company-OCC settlement as the last word.

So the utility commissioners stated firmly that they would not agree to the service company-OCC settlement unless adequate provisions were made to address DSM, IRP, and decoupling. A second settlement agreement was drafted. It put DSM, IRP, and decoupling on the agenda for decisions by the commission in September 1992, a short time before the end of Cook's and Nakarado's terms. Nakarado had made it clear that he was dissatisfied with the low salary that utility commissioners were earning—$48,000—and might not ask to be reappointed if the legislature did not raise salaries. The schedule would allow him to vote on IRP, DSM, and decoupling before leaving office.

The second settlement agreement was approved in July 1991. It accepted the service company-OCC settlement on the rate case and created four new dockets—on IRP, decoupling, DSM, and special issues for low-income consumers. As in New England and California, the DSM process was to be a formal collaborative process, which the utility would provide up to $400,000 to finance. Half would be available to OEC, the LAW Fund, and other intervenors so they might engage outside consultants to help design DSM programs. The commission would allow the service company to treat the $400,000 as an expenditure; in effect, it would be covered by the rate payers.[44] However, the OEC and the LAW Fund had a much weaker position in the DSM collaborative than Ralph Cavanagh and the Conservation Law Foundation (CLF) had enjoyed in California and New England. Cavanagh organized and chaired the collaborative process, and CLF had also been in charge. In Colorado, the collaborative process was run by a committee that included the service company and all of the intervenors. (There were several intervenors besides OEC and the LAW Fund, including the gas industry, the city of Denver, electrical contractors, and several renewable energy groups.) The LAW Fund had only one vote in the determination of how the intervenors' half of the $400,000 would be spent.

Even more important than the structure of the collaborative process was the fact that the commission was to consider IRP and decoupling as well as DSM. The settlement envisioned a negotiated rule-making process on IRP as well as discussions that would lead to agreements about decoupling service company sales and profits.

Collaborative efforts in most other states have received some policy guidance from state public utility commissions. For example, an IRP and a policy on decoupling would set targets for DSM collaborators, such as how much might be spent in total on DSM, how much demand might be replaced, and how much DSM should cost per unit of demand replaced. In such a situation, the task facing collaborators is to allocate known resources among various competing DSM strategies. The resulting package has to be technically sound, but it can also provide for DSM programs that would be operated by different providers and targeted to different groups of customers. Thus, the political task facing the collaborators was much like the task that legislators face in carving an appropriations bill to include a project in everyone's home district. In the Colorado collaboration, the lack of rules on IRP and decoupling meant the parameters of a DSM package were unknown, making it harder to come to agreement in the face of differences about the cost effectiveness of various DSM measures.

From this perspective, it would have made sense to schedule the hearings and the decision on IRP and decoupling before the DSM collaboration. But Nakarado thought that the political risk was too great. Before he could take a position on decoupling or IRP, he wanted to have evidence in the record, presented in a formal evidentiary process, to demonstrate that energy conservation was a sound idea and was supported by the service company. He expressed his concern quite openly at a hearing held to consider the draft work plan for the DSM collaborative:

> We in Colorado have been talking about decoupling and IRP for a long time. It was once more bitter. But if we are now to do something as counterintuitive as decoupling sales from profits, or paying a utility not to produce electricity, in a state that is not California but the old West, where there is a deep suspicion of government, I would like to be able to point to the record to say that this is not a wild idea from California but is a good hard dollar decision. . . . I am a Republican. . . . If I try to get reconfirmed in a year and go before the Republican senate, I need a record to point to, if someone asks where I am going. I want to be sure that the Office of Consumer Counsel and the major industrials [Amax and other large manufacturers] are on record with me.[45]

Things Fall Apart

The DSM collaborative began in the winter. The process went fairly slowly. Lawyers dominated the early meetings, and there were long debates about procedures and about the philosophy of DSM. These sessions were exhausting for all concerned and became quite bitter at times. As Bruce Driver recalls, "The process was brain damaging for a long time. We were in a trough for almost a year." There was little prospect for a large package of incentives—instead of hundreds of megawatts, the service company was willing to consider only a program on the scale of two 50-megawatt bids that the company had already offered, and no one seriously challenged this. Nakarado was restive about not participating in the collaborative process, which was confidential. But word of the acrimonious legal and rhetorical battles leaked out, because all of the stakeholders except the commissioners had representatives at the DSM table. Governor Romer is said to have called Del Hock at one point to ask if the service company was comfortable with the process, saying that it did not make sense to have a collaborative process if the company was not intent on reaching an agreement that would be mutually acceptable. Hock assured him that the company was committed to the process and to a good result.

The hearings on IRP and decoupling took place in this sour climate, in June 1992. There were dozens of witnesses and intensive cross-examination. At first, the OEC and the LAW Fund were pleased with how the hearings went. They thought that Nakarado and Cook were two likely supporters of their position, and hoped that Christine Alvarez might join them. Also, the service company supported decoupling in principle, saying it would give the utility incentives to do more DSM. There was opposition to decoupling; the Office of Consumer Counsel and industry intervenors opposed it in principle, and the commission staff favored postponing decoupling until an IRP process was completed. But if the service company was willing to go along with the concept, there seemed to be hope for an agreement on a specific mechanism. The LAW Fund and the OEC presented evidence that their approach to decoupling would be more effective than the company's proposal and were sure that their experts made a persuasive case.

As the hearings were drawing to a close, Augie Cook resigned from the commission under a cloud. In part, his departure was a consequence of a fundamental difference in perspective about the roles of the utility commissioners and the staff. A year earlier, the commissioners had asked that Suzanne Fasing, the executive secretary of the commission, be fired. The executive secretary manages the commission staff, which is required by law to provide advice to the commissioners; the staff reports to the director of the Department of Regulatory Agencies, who is a member of the governor's cabinet. Fasing felt that these arrangements indicated that the staff should be independent so that it could present a technically sound case to the commissioners for ruling on the merits. The commissioners, however, reasoned that if their job was to make policy—for example, to decide how to address energy conservation—they needed more people than Morey Wolfson working directly for them to develop policy ideas.

In addition, Fasing charged that Cook was engaging in unethical behavior. Specifically, Cook was said to have asked staff members to do personal favors for him, such as writing numerous letters that had nothing to do with commission business and checking out software for a firm that he had an interest in. When Fasing was fired, she appealed and hired a lawyer. The lawyer asked to see records about Cook and discovered that he had been in hot water before for ethical lapses. Most of these incidents were minor. For example, Cook allegedly asked USWest to get him a parking pass for Denver Bronco football games and spoke to a service company executive about hiring his son. It was not uncommon for contractors, which Cook had been, to ask such favors of a utility. But in the political climate of summer 1992, these lapses were unforgivable. Cook asked the governor if he still had the governor's confidence and some hope of reappointment. The governor temporized, and Cook quit.

This episode raised memories of the criticisms that had been leveled at Gary Nakarado for allegedly unethical contacts with utilities. There were comments in the press about the turmoil at the commission. And Cook's departure left the commission with two commissioners. Cook's comments and questions during the hearings had suggested that he would support the OEC-LAW Fund position firmly. By early July, Alvarez had asked enough questions and said enough during the hearings for most participants to assume that she would support much of the OEC-LAW Fund position.

But then Nakarado backed away from decoupling. This meant that the vote might be a 1-1 deadlock. Nakarado felt that the service company was resisting a significant commitment to DSM and that its proposal for IRP was very weak, amounting to little more than having to file the service company *Gold Book*, with minimal opportunity for comment and no way to assure that the IRP would constrain later decisions about rates and the construction of new plants. Nakarado expressed the view that perhaps giving the service company incentives would not be enough. Perhaps the commission should adopt an IRP process that would allow them to force the utility to engage in DSM. This approach has been taken in some other states; for example, in Iowa, the legislature passed a bill requiring utilities to spend 2 percent of their sales on DSM.

With Nakarado's vote seeming to waver, the service company changed its position. It had never agreed to the mechanism that the LAW Fund and OEC had proposed to implement decoupling. The company changed its position three times and eventually opposed any kind of decoupling. In a public hearing at the end of July, Nakarado and Alvarez discussed decoupling but were unable to reach an agreement. At this point, it seemed that this sixth effort to place the Colorado Public Utilities Commission on record with a firm policy of decoupling, IRP, and DSM might achieve nothing significant.

Moving Toward a Decision

From this low spot, the process moved slowly and fitfully toward decision. The governor appointed Robert Temmer as third commissioner. He was a career employee of the commission and had served temporarily as Fasing's replacement but had not been selected as the permanent executive secretary. He took a pay cut of over $14,000 to become the new chair of the commission and began reading the stacks of testimony and filings about decoupling, IRP, and DSM. Meanwhile, lawyers stopped attending the meetings of the DSM collaborative, except for a service company lawyer who chaired the meetings without raising legal questions. All sides gradually backed off their principled positions for or against DSM, as the shape of a compromise began to emerge. Technicians from the service company staff, OEC staff, weatherization contractors, and the consultants took over and began to spell out a modest package of measures. In the end, the collaborative produced a package for 37 megawatts of DSM, with measures directed toward each type of consumer.

At the same time, a separate group was working on measures to help low-income consumers. Originally, the discussion focused on billing and service issues, but then opportunities for DSM were raised. This group designed an innovative program that would use federal Low-Income Energy Assistance Program weatherization funds to leverage service company dollars to help weatherize homes and install electricity DSM measures, including compact fluorescent lighting. The final package proposed by this group doubled the size of low-income weatherization programs in Colorado to 7,000 homes and added several new services. The total came to an average of $1,500 of improvements per home, and the service company would get $60 per home for its efforts as well as being able to cover its costs in its rate base.

Over the summer, the commissioners moved slowly to a consensus on decoupling. Having been unable to reach agreement on the issue, Nakarado and Alvarez reopened the process to ask for more information. At subsequent meetings, with Bob Temmer joining the discussion, the three moved toward a solid agreement that the existing regulatory framework created incentives for utilities not to invest in DSM. But the three were unsatisfied with the specific mechanism that the LAW Fund and OEC proposed to deal with this issue. They pointed to testimony that this mechanism might lead to volatile fluctuations in rates or to other irrationalities. So the debate continued.

At a meeting in September when the commissioners were scheduled to discuss the issue, the service company, the OCC, the commission staff, and the industrial intervenors surprised the other parties by offering a settlement. Even though the commissioners clearly wanted to find a way to decouple profits from sales, the settlement rejected decoupling and stuck to traditional rate-setting practices. The commissioners were chagrined, but not particularly surprised, that their staff was in the opposite camp. They rejected the settlement, asked for yet more information and hearings, and in a meeting in mid-November made their positions clear. They would endorse decoupling in principle but postpone a decision about how to implement it until the next service company rate case. In the meantime, the DSM package that the collaborative had prepared would be handled as proposed by the company, with some incentives but no decoupling.

This was a victory, but only in principle, for the LAW Fund and the

OEC. The commission's decision was finalized in late December 1992. Ironically, Nakarado did not sign the decision. Any hope of legislative action to increase the salaries of utility commissioners had disappeared in the controversy surrounding Cook. Nakarado accepted a job as director of utility affairs at the National Renewable Energy Laboratory. Although he was serving out his final days on the commission when the decision was signed, Nakarado did not vote, wishing to avoid any questions about the propriety of his actions.

Meanwhile, the OEC and the LAW Fund were winning a more complete victory on IRP. Over the summer, Nakarado and Alvarez had accepted most of the proposal that the LAW Fund had made, and Temmer joined the consensus. In late August, the commissioners issued a draft IRP. As Bruce Driver later said, "the substantive policy backbone" for the rule was based on work done for the LAW Fund by Eric Hirst, a federal employee from the Department of Energy's Oak Ridge Laboratory who is a nationally recognized expert on IRP. The Department of Energy paid Hirst's salary while he worked full time for the LAW Fund on the Colorado litigation as well as on other cases. His presence was not an accident; it was the product in part of his long meeting one morning with Kelley Green, Bruce Driver, and a deputy assistant secretary from the Department of Energy who was interested in energy conservation. Hirst had been very effective during the hearings and was seen by many as the key to the OEC-LAW Fund victory on IRP. Nakarado said later, "Hirst was invaluable because he knew what the hell he was doing."

The commissioners' draft IRP rule rejected out of hand the service company's proposal that the commission accept a company's plan without ruling on its content. The commission could accept or reject a plan in part or in whole. The commissioners also accepted an idea that Ron Lehr brought to the debate, in his new role as attorney for the Colorado Solar Industry Association. Utilities would be asked to consider risk-adjusted discount rates. This might turn out to be an important innovation. Currently, the cost of all ways of meeting the demand for electricity are calculated using the same rate of return—perhaps 10 percent per year. Risk-adjusted rates would allow the use of different estimates for different sources of supply. Since some forms of DSM are permanent and have low risks, this could give an advantage to DSM.

Of the several points of disagreement in the process, one emerged as a hot political issue. It was the issue of "monetizing environmental externalities." In plain English, the issue was how an IRP would estimate the costs of various ways of generating electricity or reducing demand. Should an IRP take into account the environmental damage caused by mining and burning coal? The LAW Fund said it should. Or should the IRP look only at the costs to the utility and to the rate payer, assuming that once industry complied with environmental regulations, there were no further environmental costs to society? The service company said that this was the only fair option. OCC, the commission staff, and industrial intervenors took a middle position—that there were environmental costs and that the commission should take them into consideration, but that it was not feasible to quantify them. The LAW Fund position would have asked that IRPs estimate the environmental cost of contributing to the greenhouse effect; the service company's position would not.

In August, the commissioners announced a draft IRP rule with two options—the LAW Fund position and the middle position. This move galvanized the coal industry. Coal companies and the director of the council of governments in northwest Colorado, where the largest Colorado coal mines are located, led an effort to upset the IRP rule. Joined by the service company, the industrial intervenors, the Colorado Association of Counties, and the OCC, they filed a request for a review of the impact the proposed regulations would have on the utility and the coal industry. The coal industry also contacted the governor's office and key legislators, asking them to stop the commission from promulgating the IRP rule. The rail industry supported coal.

The LAW Fund tried to mobilize environmental groups to counteract this pressure. But they were only mildly successful. Some groups supported the OEC-LAW Fund position, but others did not. For example, the Western Colorado Congress (WCC) and the Colorado Public Interest Research Group (COPIRG) were initially reluctant to support the LAW Fund. COPIRG had criticized Nakarado's conduct, and the Western Colorado Congress (WCC) did not want to oppose Binz because it saw itself as a consumer group as well as an environmental group. Eventually WCC did write a letter opposing the coal companies' position. The LAW Fund had never invested much effort in mobilizing public support for its position; its strategy focused primarily on the commission and the DSM collaborative.

Although there was little support for or public understanding of what they were trying to do, the commissioners did not back down. To industry's request for the review, which was seventeen pages long, the commission responded with a seven-page statement that the impacts could not be quantified at this point in the process and would have to wait until IRPs submitted by the utilities provided the necessary data.

In late December, the commission promulgated the IRP rule. In the face of the assault by the coal industry, the commission decided not to support the LAW Fund position. The commissioners would not ignore environmental costs. They would make utilities submit information about environmental impacts. But the final IRP rule did not require that a utility estimate environmental costs. Intervenors could estimate the dollar cost of these impacts and introduce their estimate as evidence if they wished, but utilities need not try to quantify environmental costs.

The battle then moved to the state legislature. In February 1993, a legislator from the coal-producing region filed a bill that would prohibit the commission from considering environmental externalities at all. At this point, a new coalition emerged. The gas industry was not at all hostile to the concept of environmental externalities, as gas burns cleaner than coal. Gas interests joined the environmentalists, the OCC, and small firms in the DSM business (such as heating and electrical contractors and weatherization firms) to push for amendments to the legislation. As finally passed, the bill said that if the commission took account of environmental impacts, it must also estimate economic impacts, including the possibility of increased employment and income in the gas and DSM industries. A prominent lobbyist for the gas industry said that this was the first time that he had beaten an alliance of the coal industry and the rail industry in the Colorado legislature.

Next Steps in Colorado

Colorado has moved a long way since 1984, when Ron Lehr first suggested IRP and got nowhere. Policies have changed. The commission has adopted IRP regulations and seems committed (as of mid-1993) to adopting some kind of decoupling mechanism. DSM has been established as an acceptable way to meet consumers' demands. The service company's DSM programs represent only a tiny portion of the total company load. But the demand for electricity has been growing very slowly for several years, so there is not much room to fit DSM into the utility's strategy for meeting demand.

The substantive agreements and new spirit that emerged in 1992 will probably influence the decisions that remain. The commission scheduled a decision about a specific decoupling mechanism in 1993. This time, the decision about a mechanism may emerge not from debates in the commission's hearing room but from negotiations that began informally between the service company and the LAW Fund, and have now expanded to include other parties. In the spring of 1993, the company began meeting informally but regularly with the LAW Fund to try to craft a mutually acceptable formula.

The IRP process has also begun, and the commission planned to review IRPs in 1993. Perhaps the IRP process will work well. Will the service company and the other utilities welcome public participation? Will they seek involvement and try to make it easy for intervenors to use the company's computer models and tackle the complex technicalities of utility planning? And will the intervenors be ready to invest the time to make substantive contributions to utility plans, rather than just making rhetorical statements about the need to conserve or reduce monopolistic practices?

Meanwhile, at the commission, the relationship between the staff and the commissioners continues to change. The new executive secretary organized a series of staff meetings to develop a vision of the agency's goals and future, and under a new total quality management process, a staff task force is working on the question of how staff can provide commissioners with the advice and assistance they need.

If the decoupling negotiations, the IRP, and the implementation of DSM go well, the focus will turn to other issues. One issue is the future of the Fort St. Vrain nuclear plant. The service company would like to repower it as a gas-fired facility and to include the costs of repowering and operating it in the rate base. If this is not permitted, the company may have to write it off, which would cost $60 million and depress the value of company stock. Another issue that the service company and other utilities face is how to respond to independent generators of electricity. The federal Energy Policy Act of 1992 made major changes in the rights of independent producers to access the company's grids and to sell their power independently.

THE NEW POLICY AND POLITICS OF ELECTRIC POWER

Fifteen years after publication of Amory Lovins's article on the hard and soft paths, a cover story in *Business Week* announced that the idea of energy conservation had arrived in the mainstream of American corporate thinking. Utilities in particular are pursuing this idea [conservation], thanks mainly to regulatory changes.... Lovins's energy ideas don't sound so dim any more." [46]

Perhaps *Business Week* is right about wide *endorsement* of Lovins's ideas, but it would be inaccurate to say that *implementation* of conservation or DSM is far advanced. Only a handful of states have decoupled sales from profits, less than half have implemented IRP, and although utilities are spending as much as $2 billion on conservation and efficiency per year, this is a small sum compared to total sales of over $200 billion by the eighty-eight largest utilities. Furthermore, DSM is still a young discipline, whose potential has yet to be proven on a large scale. The demand for electricity is currently projected to grow at about 2 percent per year over the next decade, and some companies—notably Zach Willey's old adversaries, PG&E and Southern California Edison—plan to satisfy much of this demand with conservation and renewables. But other utility executives still foresee a need for large investments in traditional coal-fired plants, new gas-powered turbines, and even nuclear power.

Although there is room for debate about how heavily utilities can rely on DSM, it is already clear that advocates for energy conservation have had a great impact on utility policies and politics. The tools used to implement public policy are changing. Although states still deal with utilities in a regulatory context, DSM uses nonregulatory tools like subsidies, incentives, technical assistance, and public education. The politics associated with the use of these new tools has become less confrontational. Rate cases, which are legal confrontations, are still where final decisions are made, but a new array of collaborative processes have developed to feed into regulatory decisions. These changes have been accomplished without federal intervention. As in traditional utility regulation, most decisions have so far remained at the state level. However, federal agencies are important supporting players in state processes.

The New Tools

In the 1970s, the tools utility commissions used to shape public policy on electric utilities were regulatory orders that focused on costs and prices. Commissions established rates of return, devised accounting rules for utility expenditures, and set rate schedules for different classes of service on the basis of cost of service. The perspective of utilities was also quite narrow. As Rick Tempchin of the Edison Electric Institute explains, "Utilities used to think of their customers as meters. With DSM, they think of the customer as a refrigerator, or even better, as a person. With photovoltaics or other small-scale, decentralized technologies, they will think of them as power plants too." [47]

With new energy conservation policies, commissions are becoming cognizant of many other dimensions of utility operations and many other aspects of relationships between utilities and their customers. When they consider DSM proposals, commissions are framing policies about a wide variety of ways to influence behavior. DSM programs employ research, public education, subsidies, procurement, public services, goal setting, and example setting as devices to influence the demand for electricity.

The New Politics

New policies and new tools bring new politics. In the colorful words of Jay Brizie of the Colorado Office of Energy Conservation, traditional regulation of electric utilities pitted Ron Binz and his counterparts in other states in adversarial struggles "*mano a mano* [hand to hand] in the proverbial smoke-filled back room" with tough service company lawyers. IRP and DSM require the participation of a much broader range of stakeholders.

Designing a DSM program is even more complex than studying costs and setting rates. There are at least three reasons. First, DSM is a retail affair. To be effective, DSM program managers must understand a great deal about the specific energy needs of many different customers.

As Brizie explains: "Many experts feel that the behavioral side of energy conservation is more important than the hardware. This means that the engineers and companies that actually provide DSM services must know the territory. They must know the buildings, the institutions, and the markets." [48]

Michael Deland and James Watkins (former chair of the President's Council on Environmental Quality and secretary of energy, respectively) make a similar point in a recent article:

> Broad participation by electricity customers [in conservation programs] seems to depend on aggressive programs with direct customer contact and free installation services, even for many large industrial clients. In addition, flexibility and experimentation are essential because consumer needs vary widely. For example ... commercial lighting, heating and cooling offer vast opportunities for efficiency improvements, but programs must be tailored to local needs.[49]

Second, as well as requiring detailed information about a wide array of situations, DSM and IRP typically involve a much broader range of organizations and disciplines than traditional utility regulation. The models that are used in IRP, including ELFIN and many others, use data from all parts of a utility as well as from outside organizations. DSM also relies on information from diverse sources. Within the utility, DSM "requires coordinated decision making by so many functional groups within the utility: load forecasting, planning, distribution engineering, operations, rates, customer relations, marketing, communication, finance." [50] In addition, there are new players outside the utility, such as independent energy service companies, electrical contractors, public agencies involved in energy conservation, research laboratories, and applied research centers. All of these disciplines and organizations have something to offer when a DSM program is designed.

Third, because DSM is such a young field, the effectiveness of specific measures is hard to ascertain, so there must be efforts to monitor performance and make adjustments. In short, as suggested in Chapter 1, public policies to encourage energy conservation, a form of pollution prevention, are inherently more complex than classic regulation and often use nonregulatory tools.

In short, the participants in an IRP process or a DSM collaborative include not only service company lawyers and negotiators but also service company engineers and marketing experts as well as new participants outside the company, like electrical contractors who might help commercial and industrial firms use electricity more efficiently, DSM experts from other states, a new generation of energy service companies that are in business specifically to help firms and homes use energy more efficiently, community-based organizations and local government agencies that help the poor weatherize their homes (with funding provided by federal grant programs), managers of large office buildings and shopping centers, and many others.

As more participants crowd into the arena, the confrontation between "tribunes" of the people (using the phrase from "The Quest of the NARUC," p. 211) and utilities is muddied. As some parties propose to alter the basic rules for calculating utility rates (to remove disincentives for DSM and perhaps offer incentives to utilities to encourage energy conservation), the issues become muddier yet. The adversarial style of traditional regulation does not disappear, but the politics becomes one of wary cooperation. Jay Brizie expressed this mixture of attitudes as he explained the need to provide incentives to the service company: "Traditional utility regulators take the attitude of 'not a nickel too much.' Advocates for DSM want to give incentives, so that the utility has no choice but to cooperate. We make it sweet enough to choke on." [51]

The key policy decisions are still made in a regulatory context. The story of Colorado illustrates this dramatically. Lehr, Wolfson, Nakarado, and many others invested hundreds of hours in roundtables and informal discussions, but it took a rate case to put IRP and decoupling on the table. Even then, intervention by the OEC and the LAW Fund strengthened the commissioners' hand at a critical point and helped prevent a settlement that would have postponed a decision until new commissioners might be named. Moving away from a straightforward fight over dollars toward the complex, multifaceted pork barrel politics of DSM does not reduce the potential for conflict. It only makes the conflict more complex and increases the chance that today's adversary will be tomorrow's ally. Collaboration is not an absence of conflict, just a style of conflict that emphasizes opportunities for everyone to gain something from the process.

Although there are more participants in the process of making decisions, the politics of DSM and IRP is still an insiders' game. In New Mexico and Utah, Bruce Driver reports that he has obtained active support from a broad coalition of environmental groups and that he works closely with two volunteers from the Sierra Club. But in Colorado, the LAW Fund has focused its work on the commission and has had little success so far in building a vocal constituency for DSM and IRP. In the spring of 1993, it was turning to this task. However, DSM and IRP are highly technical issues and do not lend themselves easily to mass mobilization. It may be easier to mobilize broad citizen interest around the traditional issues of rates and profits or around opposition to a specific facility than around the OEC-LAW Fund agenda.

The Shifting Federal Role

When energy conservation first became a public issue following the energy crises of 1973 and 1979, federal policy and rising prices were the strongest spurs to conservation. However in the late 1980s, the most dramatic advances in energy conservation involved electricity, and the most important steps to encourage electrical utilities to embrace conservation were being taken by utility commissions. On the surface, the story seems to be a tale of a rash of state initiatives—one state copying another while the federal government sleeps. Critics of the Reagan and Bush administrations often drew this picture. For example, Rep. James H. Scheuer (D-N.Y.), vice chair of the House Energy and Commerce Committee, recently wrote: "The president's approach, a classic non-strategy, is a failure. . . . The lack of vision that characterizes White House thinking on energy policy stands in striking contrast to the leadership emerging in the states, in legislatures and in governors' offices, as well as in the private sector." [52]

There is some justification for this view. To the extent that the Bush and Reagan administrations had explicit energy policies, they emphasized fossil fuels and nuclear power rather than conservation. An explicit federal policy of strong support for conservation would encourage states to move more quickly. In addition, federal regulatory, tax, and trade policies, and foreign policy, can influence the price of energy—which in turn has a major impact on the use of energy. For example, a hefty federal tax on carbon or nuclear energy would greatly encourage conservation. The federal government can promote conservation directly through federally supported electrical utilities like rural electric cooperatives and federal power marketing authorities. As noted above, the Bonneville Power Administration was a pace setter in energy conservation in the early 1980s because Congress enacted legislation mandating conservation. Under the Clinton administration, federal agencies may speed up the pace of promulgating regulations that require certain products to be energy efficient. New standards for household appliances are expected to have a major influence on energy conservation in the next few years.

State public utility commissions have not pushed ahead with IRP and DSM entirely on their own. DOE energy conservation and weatherization programs have helped create a small industry of firms that are a moderately important force for expanding DSM. In addition, a few independent policy entrepreneurs in the federal government have encouraged states to act. The pattern is not so much one of independent action by states as a loosely coordinated effort by a number of people in a fragmented political system, including several federal officials as well as consulting firms, federal research laboratories, and national foundations, all focusing on decisions made at the state level.

The federal government could be doing more to support the states' movement toward IRP, decoupling, and DSM. The provision in the Energy Policy Act of 1992 requiring consideration of IRP had little influence on decisions in Colorado, although it did provide important symbolic support for decisions the commission was about to make. Also, Eric Hirst finished his year's residence at the LAW Fund, but the need for outside expertise did not vanish. The Department of Energy could be an important supporter to the future work of the OEC, the LAW Fund, and other groups working to increase the role of energy conservation in utilities' planning and activities.

At this point, public utilities are the obvious target for state energy conservation policy because they are large monopolies that have long been regulated. However, technological and economic changes may transform the industry in ways that make it a less accessible target for public policy. The Energy Policy Act of 1992 includes many provisions that will subject the utilities to new competition. For example, independent power producers are gaining access to electric grids and may be able to produce power more cheaply than the utilities. Also, technological and economic changes are moving in the direction of small-scale power production, for example, by making photovoltaics cost effective for more homes and small firms. In addition, the 1992 Energy Act contained tough new conservation standards for appliances, which may reduce the need for DSM programs that are targeted to this portion of the load.

In short, the model of the electric power that Samuel Insull created with large regional monopolies may be changing fundamentally. The current wave of state-led initiatives to promote energy conservation through DSM, IRP, and decoupling is built around large utilities that have strong monopoly positions. As these monopolies erode, the policies and politics of energy conservation will change again as well.

NOTES

1. U.S. Department of Energy, *National Energy Strategy: Powerful Ideas for America: One Year Later* (Washington, D.C.: Government Printing Office, 1992), 8.

2. David Moskovitz, Steven Nadel, and Howard Geller, *Increasing the Efficiency of Electricity Production and Use: Barriers and Strategies* (Washington, D.C.: American Council for an Energy-Efficient Economy, 1991), 9.

3. Ralph Cavanagh, Preface to *Energy Efficiency and the Environment: Forging the Link*, ed. Edward Vine, Drury Crawley, and Paul Centolella (Washington, D.C.: American Council for an Energy-Efficient Economy, 1991), xiii.

4. Robert H. Mnookin and Lewis Kornhauser, "Bargaining in the Shadow of the Law: The Case of Divorce," *Yale Law Journal* 88, No. 5 (1979): 950-977.

5. "The Top 1000 U.S. Companies Ranked by Industry," *Business Week*, April 10, 1992 (special bonus issue), 165-167, 204-208.

6. Public Service Company of Colorado, *Our Energy Force: Annual Report 1990* (Denver: Public Service Company of Colorado, 1991), 2.

7. Edward Kahn, *Electric Utility Planning and Regulation*, 2d ed. (Washington, D.C.: American Council for an Energy-Efficient Economy, 1992), 3-8.

8. "For Your Information: How Your Utility Rates Are Determined" (Denver: Colorado Public Utilities Commission, n.d.), 1.

9. Two additional states have appointed commissioners who regulate electric-

ity and elected commissioners for other industries. National Association of Regulatory Utility Commissioners, *NARUC Annual Report on Utilities and Communications Regulations* (Washington, D.C.: National Association of Regulatory Utility Commissioners, 1991).

10. "Opening the Door to Greater Competition," *National Journal,* April 6, 1991, 792.

11. "U.S. Electric Utility Statistics," *Public Power* 50, no. 1 (1992): 56.

12. National Association of Regulatory Utility Commissioners, "Members, Committees, Policy" (Washington, D.C., February 18, 1992), 89. The poem is by Paul Rodgers, NARUC administrative director and general counsel.

13. William T. Gormley, Jr., *The Politics of Public Utility Regulation* (Pittsburgh: University of Pittsburgh Press, 1983), 12; and Edison Electric Roundtable Discussion, Wye Island, Md., 1984.

14. Gormley, *The Politics of Public Utility Regulation,* 3, 211.

15. Amory Lovins, "Energy Strategy: The Road Not Taken?" *Foreign Affairs,* October 1976.

16. Gormley, *The Politics of Public Utility Regulation,* 128.

17. David Roe, *Dynamos and Virgins* (New York: Random House, 1984), 24, 28.

18. Ibid., 187-188.

19. Ibid., 74-75, 110-111.

20. Ibid., 199.

21. Morey Wolfson (Unpublished memorandum to the Colorado Public Utilities commissioners, Denver, n.d.).

22. Barakat and Chamberlin, Inc., *Least-Cost Planning in the United States: 1990,* Electric Power Research Institute, EPRI CU-6966, Project 2982-2 (Washington, D.C., September 1990), 5.

23. Moskovitz, Nadel, and Geller, *Increasing the Efficiency of Electricity Production and Use,* 26-27.

24. Clark W. Gellings and John H. Chamberlin, *Demand-Side Management: Concepts and Methods,* 2d ed. (Liliburn, Ga.: Fairmont Press, 1992), 169.

25. *An Energy Efficiency Blueprint for California: Report of the Statewide Collaborative Process* (ABC Enercom, Association of California Water Agencies, California Department of General Services, California Energy Coalition, California Energy Commission, California Large Energy Consumers Association, California/Nevada Community Action Association, California Public Utilities Commission Division of Ratepayer Advocates, Independent Energy Producers Association, Natural Resources Defense Council, Pacific Gas and Electric Company, San Diego Gas and Electric Company, South-

ern California Edison Company, Southern California Gas Company, and Toward Utility Rate Normalization, January 1990), 26.

26. Roe, *Dynamos and Virgins*, 200-202.

27. Eric Hirst, *Cooperation and Community Conservation, Final Report*, Hood River Conservation Project, DOE/BP-11287-18 (Washington, D.C.: U.S. Department of Energy, 1987), x-xv. In Hood River, 85 percent of eligible homes installed insulation, storm windows, or other improvements. Pacific Power and Light (PP&L) offered 100 percent grants and conducted an intensive marketing campaign to encourage participation. Moskovitz, Nadel, and Geller, *Increasing the Efficiency of Electricity Production and Use*, 38-39.

28. Bill LeBlanc, telephone interview with author, April 10, 1992.

29. Dick Russell, "The Power Brokers," *Amicus Journal* 11, no. 1 (Winter 1989): 31-35.

30. Ibid., 35.

31. *An Energy Efficiency Blueprint for California*, vi.

32. Ron Lehr, telephone interview with author, October 15, 1991.

33. John Rowe, foreword to *Profits and Progress Through Least-Cost Planning*, by David Moskovitz (Washington, D.C.: National Association of Regulatory Utility Commissioners, 1989), ii.

34. The rates set by commissions include enough revenue to cover all costs, including the large cost of amortizing billion dollar investments in electrical generating capacity, the somewhat smaller costs of actually generating and delivering electricity, and profit. Thus, if a utility can produce and sell an extra kilowatt hour of electricity beyond the amount used in the utility commission's calculations, without having to construct a new generating station, it incurs only a small additional operating cost but receives revenues that include the hefty cost of adding another unit of capacity.

Moskovitz adds that the problem lies in the formulas commissions use to set rates, especially in fuel adjustment clauses. The difficulty is as follows: the price of fossil fuel is volatile. To insulate utility stockholders from fluctuations in earnings, most commissions allow utilities to adjust their rates periodically to reflect changes in spending on fuel, without having to file new rate cases. The formulas that solve this problem do so by allowing rates to rise when spending on fuel increases, whether increased spending is the result of higher prices for fuel or of burning more fuel. Thus, the formula creates an incentive to burn more fuel to earn higher rates. Ibid., 6-7.

In 1979, California adopted a unique way of allowing for the volatility of fuel prices, which appears to remove the first disincentive. Its electricity rate adjustment mechanism sets rates on the basis of past costs and changes in the price of fuel, rather than on the basis of total spending on fuel.

35. Ron Lehr, telephone interview with author, October 15, 1991.

36. Generic inquiry concerning demand-side management issues, Docket 90I-227EG, *Draft Policy Statement*, Decision C90-1641 (Denver: Colorado Public Utilities Commission, December 5, 1990), 2.

37. Mike McGrath, "Whatever Happened to the Good Old PUC?" *Westword*, October 7-13, 1992, 12-17.

38. Ibid., 13.

39. Background summary, generic inquiry concerning demand-side management issues, interim decision of Commissioner Gary L. Nakarado, Docket no. 90I-227EG, Decision C90-1088-I (Denver: Colorado Public Utilities Commission), 5.

40. Gary Nakarado, interview with author, Washington, D.C., November 18, 1992.

41. Morey Wolfson, interview with author, Denver, October 29, 1991.

42. Energy Foundation, *Annual Report 1991* (San Francisco: Energy Foundation, 1992).

43. Morey Wolfson, interview with author, Denver, October 29, 1991.

44. Colorado Public Utilities Commission, Decision C91-918, Dockets 91S-091EG and 90F-226E, Clarification Order: (1) *Approving Settlement, Upon Clarification*; and (2) *Closing These Dockets* (Denver, July 17, 1991).

45. Gary Nakarado, statement at hearing of the Colorado Public Utilities Commission, October 29, 1991.

46. Emily T. Smith, "Amory Lovins's Energy Ideas Don't Sound So Dim Anymore," *Business Week*, September 16, 1991, 92.

47. Rick Tempchin, interview with author, Washington, D.C., March 17, 1992.

48. Jay Brizie, interview with author, Denver, October 29, 1992.

49. Michael R. Deland and James D. Watkins, "Efficient Is Beautiful," *Issues in Science and Technology* (Winter 1990-1991): 40.

50. Gellings and Chamberlin, *Demand-Side Management*, 448.

51. Jay Brizie, interview with author, Denver, October 29, 1992.

52. James H. Scheuer, "Leadership on Energy Policy Isn't Found in Washington," *Christian Science Monitor*, February 25, 1992, 19.

CHAPTER SEVEN

The Future
of Civic Environmentalism

The framers of most federal environmental statutes assumed that environmental protection is best ensured by tough, federally driven regulation. It would seem that when federal regulatory policies are clear and strong, states and localities must enforce them and polluters tend to obey. Thus, when federal policy is unclear or unstated, or when the executive branch fails to do its job and the courts, Congress, and environmental advocacy organizations cannot force the executive branch to act, we might predict that the quality of the environment will suffer.

However, over the past decade, a new kind of environmental politics has developed in states and localities: civic environmentalism. Civic environmentalism is no cure-all, no substitute for the Washington-focused approach to environmental policy and politics that burst forth in the early 1970s. But it is a useful complement to the traditional politics of command-and-control regulation and the federal "gorilla in the closet." Each approach has its strengths, weaknesses, and most suitable applications.

The first part of this chapter is a summary of the evidence about the extent, strengths, and limitations of civic environmentalism. The second part explores the possibility that civic environmentalism is an example of broader, long-term changes in how our society handles the public's business. It focuses on three features of civic environmentalism—its bottom-up nature, the importance of information both for public policy and for the political process, and the links between civic environmentalism and sustainable development. The third part presents an agenda for how the federal government and others can encourage the growth of civic environmentalism.

Part I: The Evidence for Civic Environmentalism

THE FIVE FEATURES

Chapter 1 suggested that there are five distinctive features of civic environmentalism:

1. A focus on the unfinished business of nonpoint problems, pollution prevention, and protecting ecosystems
2. Extensive use of nonregulatory tools
3. Interagency and intergovernmental cooperation
4. A search for alternatives to political confrontations
5. A new role for the federal government as a participant in decisions made at the state or local level

A Focus on Unfinished Business and on Nonregulatory Tools

As Chapter 3 showed, many states are still preoccupied with administering top-down, federally designed environmental programs. However, all states have taken independent initiatives as well. Often these initiatives address the issues of the unfinished business of the federal environmental regime, including nonpoint pollution, pollution prevention, and protection of endangered ecosystems, and often they use nonregulatory tools.

The three case studies provide additional information about how civic environmentalism works in the practical worlds of politics and agency management. (Three cases are too few to prove anything, but they do suggest how this style of politics and policy works.) Iowa's efforts to protect water from pollution by agricultural chemicals form the clearest example of civic environmentalism. The goal is to reduce nonpoint pollution. Iowa has emphasized nonregulatory tools.

In the Everglades, the debate about water policy is moving from the conventional, command-and-control model toward civic environmentalism. At the beginning of the story, when U.S. Attorney Dexter Lehtinen filed his suit, the central issue was the need for permits for four pumps—a point source, regulatory issue.* Broader proposals are now being discussed to change the flow of water from Lake Okeechobee through the Everglades and through canals to the sea. The focus is shifting from regulation to other tools of public policy, such as changes in how existing public works are operated, new public works construction, and perhaps higher fees for drinking water.

Like the Florida case, the Colorado case is a hybrid between civic environmentalism and old-style confrontational, command-and-control regulatory politics. Decisions are being made in a regulatory setting, that of adversarial rate-making and rule-making processes before a state public utility commission. The Colorado Public Utilities Commission has established rules that require electrical utilities to submit plans to set parameters for later rate cases. However, the issue is not forcing a utility to do something against its interests, but encouraging it to do something that proponents believe to be in the interest of both the utility and its customers. Also, the tools to be used by utilities to encourage conservation are wholly nonregulatory: education, technical assistance, and subsidies that may include free light bulbs or rebates on equipment that uses less electricity. No one is proposing to regulate users of electricity, and there would be no threat to scare users into conservation.

The issue in Colorado is one of energy conservation, which is a form of pollution prevention. One might also say that it is a nonpoint issue, in the sense that the goal is to encourage conservation by a large number of utility customers, including commercial establishments, ordinary citizens, low-income citizens, and some industrial customers. (Many of the biggest "point source" industrial customers have already engaged in extensive energy conservation.)

Interagency Cooperation

In each of the three states, a "shadow community" of employees in various agencies has provided much of the drive behind new initiatives. The term shadow community was suggested by Stephen Light, an offi-

---

*Technically, the pumps may not be a point source under the meaning of the Clean Water Act. This was the issue that environmentalists were about to litigate when Lehtinen filed his suit. However, the pumps clearly are points from which polluted water spreads into the Everglades.

cial of the South Florida Water Management District, in a paper that he cowrote about the evolution of public policy in the Everglades.[1] The shadow community in the Everglades includes career employees from the many public agencies that affect Everglades policy as well as academics and activists like Marjory Stoneman Douglas. Over the years these long-termers have gotten to know each other and have gradually developed into a community, divided internally but bound by common values, loyalties, and understandings. The members of the shadow community continue to work while the spotlight of public attention shines on itinerant politicians and executive directors.

There are two reasons why a shadow community might be especially influential. One reason is fragmentation. In the Everglades, as in Iowa and Colorado, numerous agencies have responsibilities for one or another aspect of the environmental issues discussed in the case studies. For example, in Iowa, the Extension Service, the Iowa Geological Survey, the state environmental agency, Iowa State University, and the state Department of Agriculture and Land Stewardship are all key players, and many other public agencies, nonprofit groups, and businesses also have played important roles in solving the problem of nonpoint pollution. If a shadow community exists and has some cohesiveness, it can function as a parallel system to unite fragmented authorities.

The second reason for the special influence of a shadow community is that it may be the source of new policy ideas. Politicians and executive directors may be interested in new policy ideas, but they do not have time to come up with them. Substantive changes in public policy can emerge when the shadow community comes to a rough consensus and hands its ideas over to the players who are in the spotlight.

In Iowa there does appear to be an influential shadow community. Key individuals have worked informally across agency lines for almost a decade to study how farm chemicals enter into ground and surface water and to develop strategies for reducing such pollution. These individuals have been united by shared values, professional commitments, personal friendships, and a vision of what can be done. Their agencies have legislative mandates to address problems that go beyond the capacity of any individual agency. In the face of fragmentation, the shadow community has built a network of informal and professional relationships to get the job done. From its earliest days, Iowa programs have been designed and operated as collaborative enterprises, uniting the agencies where members of the shadow community live through the Consortium on Agriculture and Groundwater Quality and its informal successors.

Interagency collaboration is also a key feature in Florida. The lawsuit disrupted interagency collaboration, but the path to settlement of the suit was opened when the governor asked state, district, and federal scientists to collaborate in designing artificial wetlands. Timer Powers, a longtime leader of the Water Management District, worked hard and effectively to keep the collaborative process going. Timer was a former politician who had made a commitment to the district and to bringing people together to solve problems. Interagency collaboration among researchers and operational staff will also be important in any further progress toward solving the problems of water quality and quantity. As in other ecosystems, the issues in the Everglades are characterized by a great deal of uncertainty, and thus by a need for pooling various sources of information and designing programs that can be modified as participants learn what works and what does not. Without a cohesive shadow community, the prospects for resolving the environmental problems facing the Everglades would be poor.

Collaboration is also the key to the events in Colorado, but the most influential shadow community does not seem to be confined to Coloradans. The long-termers who have come up with new policy ideas for Colorado so far seem to cluster around the Committee on Energy Conservation of the National Association of Regulatory Utility Commissioners. Some members of the shadow community are commissioners or staff members of commissions, while others are federal employees or former commissioners who are now consultants. Eventually a sizable Colorado-based shadow community may emerge. It may include energy conservation professionals and planners who work for utilities, environmentalists, staff of the state Office of Energy Conservation, commission staff, a few employees of the National Renewable Energy Research Laboratory, and employees of energy service companies and of nonprofit organizations engaged in energy conservation activities.

Alternatives to Confrontation

Although civic environmentalism involves collaboration, it usually has a stormy birth. In each of the three case studies, there was sharp conflict during the process. In Iowa the debate on the 1987 Groundwater Act legislation was confrontational and bitter. In Florida also, the political fights surrounding the lawsuit were bitter. There has been no comparable public drama in Colorado. However, the issues of integrated resource planning and demand-side management (DSM) were not put on the Colorado Public Utilities Commission agenda until they were raised in a contested rate case, and the initial meetings of the DSM collaborative were often hotly divisive.

In each of the three cases, the initial atmosphere of confrontation softened significantly once all parties accepted the central issue as legitimate. In Iowa, open opposition to the 1987 Groundwater Act backfired on the director of the Iowa Chemical and Fertilizer Association, and the political climate is now generally friendly and collaborative.

In Florida, there have been three negotiated settlements—the July 1991 settlement of the lawsuit, the May 1993 mediated technical plan, and the July 1993 agreement among the sugar industry, the federal government, the state of Florida, and the district. The mediation continues and might result in a fourth agreement: to spell out the details of the technical plan and to draft a statement of principles. The 1993 mediated agreement on a technical plan was a more open and a more amicable process than the 1991 negotiations. This is not to say that everyone agrees about restoration of the Everglades; at this writing, there is controversy surrounding the agreement with the sugar industry. But the politics are moving away from white hat-black hat confrontations about who is causing "cancer" in the Everglades to tough, multisided negotiations about multimillion dollar investments.

In Colorado as well as other states that have tried to implement demand-side management, shifting the focus from disciplining utilities to giving them incentives has transformed the regulatory process, adding new stakeholders and leading to a much more collaborative style of decision making.

To say that civic environmentalism often involves collaboration does not mean that there is no room in the process for advocacy. For example, environmental groups played an important role in the confrontational stage of getting the issue of water quality on the agenda in Florida, and they are still engaged in a more collaborative process. Webb, Parks, and others provided informal advice to Suzan Ponzoli and Dexter

Lehtinen as the federal lawsuit was being designed, and the Sierra Club Legal Defense Fund intervened in the litigation at a critical point, making it difficult for Washington officials to force Lehtinen to drop the suit. In the summer of 1993, nineteen environmental groups wrote the secretary of the interior to express their dismay about the agreement with the sugar industry, which they had not been asked to help write.

In Colorado, state officials in the Public Utility Commission and in the Office of Energy Conservation (OEC) pushed for years to place energy conservation on the agenda, with little success. The arrival of the Land and Water (LAW) Fund helped strengthen the OEC's hand, and more help from environmental groups would be of further assistance. Indeed, the difficulties that the LAW Fund experienced in getting other environmental groups in the state to speak out may have been a significant factor in weakening the eventual of decision of the utility commissioners.

The role of environmental groups was very different in Iowa. Environmental groups played a minimal role in the Iowa case. Iowa's groundwater protection programs were designed and created by state legislators and agency employees who were personally committed to environmental values. Environmentalists participated in legislative debates, but the leadership clearly lay with legislators and state officials. These insiders have achieved a great deal. However, there seems to be a limit to what they can achieve without obtaining broader public support. With Paul Johnson out of the legislature and with David Osterberg taking on new issues, some of the key members of the shadow community may be tiring. Perhaps it will take more vigorous action by local environmentalists or stimulus from the outside to push Iowa to the next step in addressing the problems created by application of farm chemicals.

One reason for the differences among the three states was the extent to which outside resources were available to support staffers of environmental organizations. In Florida, national environmental organizations contributed legal talent and supported local leaders like Jim Webb and the staff of the National Audubon Society's Everglades Campaign. The Pew Charitable Trusts of Philadelphia financed the LAW Fund in Colorado as part of its program of support for environmental advocacy.

Within the environmental movement, the large national environmental groups have sometimes been criticized for draining resources from the state and local levels. In a study of leadership in the environmental movement, Don Snow writes:

> State and local leaders ... often feel a lack of support from their counterparts on the national-international scene. The strongest critics see the large, national groups engaged in a heated competition for members, funding, and organizational growth—a competition that diverts them from successful involvement with state, local, and grass-roots groups in matters of importance to them all.... The existence of field programs among national organizations is not necessarily beneficial to local, grass-roots groups.[2]

However, in the last two or three years, several national environmental groups have given higher priority to activities at the state level. For example, in 1990 the Sierra Club established a training program for lobbyists at the state level and distributed grants to state chapters.[3] The same year, several national foundations helped establish the Environmental Support Center in Washington, D.C., which provides assistance and training to state-level groups that are not affiliated with national environmental organizations. Other environmental groups, such as the Environmental Defense Fund and the National Wildlife Federation, have long had regional offices or state affiliates that are actively involved in state environmental issues. The three case studies demonstrate that funding for state-level environmentalists and cooperation between state- and national-level activists can have a major impact on the course of state environmental politics.

When national environmental groups are not involved, "not-in-my-backyard" (NIMBY) groups may provide the stimulus to get civic environmentalism started, especially in the confrontational stages of getting issues on the table. As mentioned in Chapter 1, NIMBY groups that opposed the siting of landfills and incinerators in King County, Washington, have become important leaders in campaigns for recycling and waste minimization. And former grass-roots protesters have played an important role in pushing toxic use reduction legislation in Massachusetts, New Jersey, and other states. Such legislation includes both regulatory and nonregulatory elements; typically, it requires firms to disclose what toxins they use and dispose of, sets mandatory or voluntary targets for reduction, and provides technical or financial assistance in achieving these goals.[4]

The case studies also suggest the difficulties that environmental groups will face when they participate in civic environmentalism. As in other movements for social change, there have long been disagreements inside the environmental movement about whether environmentalists should be open to compromise. This is nothing new. However, the collaborative style of civic environmentalism may increase these conflicts. One reason is simply that some activists may be readier than others to accept the compromises that are inherent in a collaborative process. Another reason is that collaboration is inherently time consuming. Industry and governments usually have relatively deep pockets and can afford to spend more time in collaborative processes. In contrast, many environmentalists may not have enough resources to stay with the process. For example, Bob Dreher of the Sierra Club Legal Defense Fund had a budget of less than $10,000 for expenses on the complex Everglades case. Dreher works in Washington, D.C. Local grass-roots groups have even fewer resources.[5] In short, civic environmentalism is far from a perfect way of solving problems.

Federal-State Relationships

Chapter 1 included two figures that show how traditional policy making works. Environmental advocates, Congress, EPA, states, and polluters were shown in a hierarchical relationship, with requirements and orders flowing from regulators at the upper levels to polluters at the bottom. There are multiple hierarchies of enforcers for separate issues and statutes.

Civic environmentalism operates differently. It emphasizes incentives, education, and the provision of public services. Also, leadership comes from the state or local level—in each of the case studies, largely from state officials. In Iowa the leaders were state legislators, including Paul Johnson, David Osterberg, Ralph Rosenberg and several others, and the shadow community. In Florida, local federal officials like Dexter Lehtinen and Michael Finley acted independently in putting the issue of water quality in the Everglades on the agenda. Events moved beyond the deadlock of litigation and toward a solution when Gov. Lawton Chiles, Environment Secretary Carol Browner, and district officials like Timer Powers committed themselves to settle the suit. Later, the mediation process that the district organized and the efforts of the gov-

ernor and lieutenant governor laid the basis for the agreement that was
announced by the secretary of the interior. In Colorado, members and
staff of the state public utility commission and the Office of Energy
Conservation have carried the torch for energy conservation for years.

Because key leadership comes from states and the tools used are often nonregulatory, the relationships in civic environmentalism might
best be shown as horizontal, with information and resources flowing
across the system. However, as the case studies and Chapter 3 show,
civic environmentalism usually operates in the shadow of actual or potential command-and-control regulation. Rather than simply saying that
civic environmentalism is bottom-up, and thus implying that states and
localities go it alone, we might say that civic environmentalism is a new
kind of alliance between the national level and the state or local level.

To be successful, civic environmentalism relies on three kinds of top-
down intervention. The first kind is the use by states of federal regulations. Even when states do not regulate, there is often an implicit federal stick, or threat of a stick, behind the carrots that the state employs
to induce "green" (environmentally sensitive) behavior. Even in Iowa,
the purest case of civic environmentalism, the threat of federal regulatory action to force farmers to use fewer chemicals was a powerful be-
hind-the-scenes factor in influencing the Iowa legislature and farming
interests to support the 1987 Groundwater Act and the programs of the
Consortium on Agriculture and Groundwater Quality. In Florida the
possibility of a return to federal court no doubt encourages all participants to stick with the collaborative process, even when collaboration is
slow and cumbersome. The federal hand was perhaps lightest in the
Colorado case; the requirement in the 1992 federal Energy Policy Act
that states use an integrated resource planning process was too late and
too vague to have much influence on events.

Cash is a second kind of top-down support. The U.S. Department of
Energy supported state initiatives in Colorado by making key grants to
the National Association of Regulatory Utility Commissioners and en-
abling a skilled federal employee to work at the LAW Fund. In addition, as mentioned above, national foundations and environmental
groups fueled state advocacy with cash and skilled personnel.

The third kind of top-down support is information and expertise. In
the Everglades, years of federal investment in research helped build a

base of knowledge about environmental problems and about artificial wetlands. In Colorado the utility commission and the Office of Energy Conservation drew on a base of knowledge that had been developed during the 1980s. It may be inaccurate to call information top-down support because it does not always come from a higher level of government. For example, a great deal of the expertise and information used in Colorado came from independent initiatives in other states. It would be more accurate to refer to information as "outside-in" support.

The story of the aftermath of the Everglades lawsuit illustrates the nature of the federal role in civic environmentalism most clearly. During the litigation, federal officials played conventional roles, driving state and local policy. As of mid-1993 the Army Corps of Engineers is leading a federal study of how to reorient the federal system of canals and pumps to meet the new goals of environmental protection and water provision for the urban coastal regions. In addition, the corps, the Loxahatchee National Wildlife Refuge, the Everglades National Park, and other federal agencies are participating in state processes, such as the mediated agreement on the technical plan and perhaps the district's Water Supply Plan and a Florida Commission on Sustainable Development. Specifically, federal agencies are feeding state and local processes with information and expertise. In Colorado something similar is happening. Scientists and other experts from federal agencies are participating in state decision making, contributing their expertise and information to the design of state policy. This is a far cry from the conventional vision of Washington, D.C., as the center of the federal system and of federal agencies as forcing states to act responsibly. Even in the process of forcing issues onto the state agenda in Florida and Colorado, the federal role was not entirely hierarchical. The federal officials who forced the state and local hand were acting as policy entrepreneurs, not simply doing what congressional statutes told them to do.

Could the federal government have played a much stronger role in each of the case studies? If power in Washington were in the hands of committed environmentalists like Carol Browner and Al Gore, and if they were backed by a new spate of environmental laws, might not the federal government take over leadership of civic environmentalism?

For example, could the federal government pass and enforce legislation that would force farmers in Iowa to submit plans for reducing their use of farm chemicals? Or suppose that Congress were to amend the statute that created the Central and South Florida Water Project, which established the purposes for which the South Florida Water Management District operates the web of canals and pumps in Florida. Could this legislation overcome the fragmentation of authority in South Florida and mandate a process of research and experimentation to reduce the scientific uncertainties and move decisively to restore the Everglades? Might the Energy Policy Act of 1992 and regulations promulgated by a "green" U.S. Department of Energy force the Public Service Company of Colorado and the Colorado Public Utilities Commission to agree on an integrated resource plan that would include a hefty dose of energy conservation?

Perhaps. Congress and "green" officials in federal agencies could take these steps. But with respect to the unfinished business of environmental policy, including the problems in Iowa, Florida, and Colorado, there are limits to how much the federal government can achieve on its own initiative. The diversity of local conditions makes it impossible to draft solutions in Washington to many local nonpoint or ecosystem problems or to institute prevention. Furthermore, the power to implement decisions is fragmented beyond the ability of federal laws or persuasive federal officials alone to put it back together. Fragmentation is a problem beyond the public sector as well; for Colorado to craft effective demand-side management or for Iowa to design low-chemical methods of farming, private interests like hundreds of electrical contractors and local weatherization program operators and the many members of the Iowa Fertilizer and Chemical Association must bring to the table both information and the willingness to collaborate in taking action. Unless state, local, and private leaders willingly join in collaboration, the benefits of a "green" takeover in Washington will be limited.

Part II: The Larger Meaning of Civic Environmentalism

Civic environmentalism is an example of three larger changes in how the public's business is being done. First, civic environmentalism illustrates the distinctive contribution that states can make to solving public problems—which we call the comparative advantage of states. Second, civic environmentalism is an example of the increased importance of information in how governments operate in an information-based society. Third, civic environmentalism supplies the political dimension that has been lacking in discussions of sustainable development.

CIVIC ENVIRONMENTALISM AND
THE COMPARATIVE ADVANTAGE OF STATES

What are the best ways to sort out the respective roles of federal, state, and local governments in environmental policy? The usual approach is to focus on the scope of the environmental problem. For example, if the problem involves transboundary issues or harms lands of national interest, such as a national park, then federal intervention would seem to be justified. If an environmental problem is local and involves things that are traded in local markets, like land, states may have adequate reach.

This approach leads to the conclusion that the federal government should have a central role in many environmental issues, because so many problems involve transboundary problems, lands of national interest, or markets that are national in scope. Even the pollution caused by cars driving around town is arguably an environmental problem of national scope, because cars are sold in national markets. Most states could not expect automobile manufacturers to comply with a local requirement to install special equipment. Only California is large enough to force firms to adopt its requirements. If other individual states were to adopt their own standards, the manufacturers might write off the market or charge excessive prices, and customers would purchase cars elsewhere.

However, there is another way to approach the issue, which has less to do with the scope of a problem than with the tools that government might use to address it. This approach rests on the assertion that states have a comparative advantage in using nonregulatory tools.

That states have a comparative advantage is not a new idea. Many federal programs are designed for close partnership with states and localities. For example, federal investment in education, transportation, and community development is often made through intergovernmental grant programs giving state or local governments significant freedom in deciding how to operate the program. Furthermore, recently some political scientists have suggested that using different tools of public policy may lead to a different pattern of federal-state-local relations (Appendix B). The connection between tools and federalism is worth describing in some detail.

The starting point is the observation that states are not just smaller versions of the nation. They differ in two obvious ways: scale and diversity. States are smaller, with correspondingly smaller populations and geographic areas. Each state is also less diverse than the nation as a whole in terms of problems, values, institutions, and other circumstances that governments face. (Similarly, most localities are smaller and less diverse than states. To keep the argument simple, we will focus on the federal-state comparison and refer to state-local comparisons only when necessary for completeness.)*

Because states are smaller and less diverse than the country as a whole, state governments have the capacity to customize their policies to local circumstances, to engage citizens and organizations, and to span interagency and professional boundaries. However, there are other things states cannot do easily, such as taking advantage of economies of scale. This does not make state governments better or worse than the federal government, just different.

States' Ability to Customize

Dealing with the diversity of local institutions, objective conditions, and values is a challenge for the federal government. There is always

---

*Local governments' capacities are different from those of states or the federal government. In general, the principles that distinguish states from the federal government also distinguish local governments from states. For example, local governments can mobilize and customize even more effectively than states. However, the application of these general principles is much more complex for state-local relations than for federal-state relations, for two reasons. One is that local governments vary widely in size, much more so than states. Over three-quarters of local governments are actually zero-employee governments. Second, the authority and capacity of local governments varies widely from state to state, both in terms of the relative strength of local governments vis-à-vis states and in the type of local government that has the greatest authority. Furthermore, local governments may not have enough diversity of expertise and opinion to organize a process that is truly open.

pressure within the federal government to standardize activities or pro-grams. Federal regulations and grant programs are typically designed for the average state or locality, and thus never fit well anywhere. States, in contrast, can customize initiatives to distinctive state-level conditions, institutions, and values if they have the technical ability to assess conditions and to make the necessary adjustments (and if the federal government allows them to do so).

States' Advantage in Engaging Citizens

Federal leaders can reach out to the populace through national media and, increasingly—although with additional effort—through satellite feeds to regional and local media. Yet national politics is usually passive. We become informed, develop opinions, vote in national elections, serve in the military or send our children off to serve in the armed forces, and perhaps once or twice in our lifetime are asked to respond to a national opinion survey. However, in a smaller political unit, there are many more opportunities for active, personal involvement in making political decisions. There are more opportunities to serve on commit-tees, attend hearings, run for office, or know top officials personally.

Furthermore, in smaller units of government the number of problems and options open for public action are somewhat reduced. It is less work to bone up on a local issue than a national or international problem. Local issues can involve fundamental clashes of values, and information can be hard to come by, but the facts are likely to be fewer and the range of opinions is likely to be narrower than those at the national level. For this reason, individuals may find it easier to accept respon-sibility for state or local problems and harder to opt out of community decisions.

States' Flexibility to Work Across Boundaries

Both citizens and officials tend to take a different approach to public questions when they are posed within the context of a smaller political unit. Because state governments are smaller organizations than the fed-eral government, and most state capitals are smaller towns than Wash-ington, D.C., state officials are more likely to know their counterparts in other agencies on a personal basis. This means that it is often easier for state officials to develop informal understandings and ties that will make it easier to work across professional and agency lines.

Similarly, citizens of a state may know people who support another side of an issue; they may know people and sensitive lands that would be harmed by an action of state government that would benefit themselves. As a consequence, citizens may feel more able and more inclined to take personal responsibility for developing ideas about policy and for taking action to implement them. Also, citizens and officials may perceive multiple sides of an issue more easily. And in the relatively less diverse setting it may be easier for citizens and officials to understand multiple aspects of an issue and to frame comprehensive answers.

In particular, in a smaller governmental unit, it may be more difficult for officials or advocates to separate economic and environmental values. Even the most ardent environmentalist may know people who depend on polluting industries for their income, and even the most rapacious business owner will not be able to avoid seeing environmental degradation and will probably hear about it over the dinner table.

States' Capacity to Act Effectively

Governments must have a basic modicum of administrative capacity. If states or localities lack the technical expertise to address environmental issues, their comparative advantage means nothing. As many observers have commented, the institutional capacity of state governments, although difficult to measure, is much greater today than ever before. And although bigger state governments are not necessarily stronger or more effective, most experts would agree that virtually all state governments are much stronger institutions in the 1990s than in the past. The capacity of a government to take coherent and meaningful action depends on many factors: availability of funds, existence of skilled staff and established institutions, tradition of past activity, and the presumptions created by traditions. By many measures (such as number of employees, professionalism of employees, and the openness and representativeness of the legislative process), state governments of the 1990s are quite different from those of the 1950s. In the 1960s, states were called the "fallen arches" of the federal system. Larry Sabato called the governors of those days "goodtime Charlies." But with a few exceptions, those governors are gone and that institutional weakness is much reduced.[6]

Even if states have built their capacity significantly, their relatively small size means that they have less capacity than the federal government in some respects and a greater capacity in others. For example, the federal government can more easily capture any economies of scale that exist in governmental activities. Sometimes scale is critical. It makes no sense to have multiple systems for measuring and collecting demographic, economic, or environmental data or for setting safety standards. There are obvious economies of scale in supporting many kinds of research, especially basic research and expensive projects. There are economies gained by having a relatively consistent national system of taxation, especially for personal and corporate income, which may be earned in one state and spent in another. Larger governments can hire more specialized staff, and some services, such as defense, are inherently more effective if they are larger enterprises, provided that they are well managed.

There are also diseconomies of scale. Most notably, many big organizations may find it difficult to act quickly and with precision. This idea is an everyday consideration to many people who work in state government. When asked why they have chosen to work at the state or local level, they often say that it is easier to get things done in states and localities than in the federal government. They say that the federal government is so big and complex that it is difficult for one individual to have an impact. On the other hand, many federal employees take pride in the fact that their level of government can hire more specialists with technical expertise or knowledge.

The distinctive capacity of state governments is not only a matter of size but also a matter of history. States have traditionally been responsible for the financing and standards of education, road construction, and serving institutionalized populations. Perhaps these functions could be transferred to another level of government, but there would be costs and inefficiencies involved in making the change.

If our interest were in state-local relationships, this discussion could be repeated for differences between state and local governments. In this context, states would enjoy greater economies of scale and face fewer external diseconomies. States are at the middle level in the social and political organization, and their comparative advantage lies in activities that require some scale but not too much.

Limits of States' Advantage

The discussion of the comparative advantage of states so far is idealized. The small size of a governmental unit has other negative consequences besides those listed. Although it is generally easier for citizens to become involved in public policy decisions in smaller governmental units, there is no guarantee that people will take advantage of the opportunity. Political scientists have documented, and mobile suburbanites know instinctively, that many Americans know little and care less about state and local politics. For example, more people know who represents them in Congress than who represents them in the state legislature. Furthermore, divisions of opinion about public policy or differences of interest in the outcome of a political debate can become bitter personal or social cleavages. Small town politics can be nasty.

In addition, small-scale polities are not necessarily freer. *Federalist No. 10* pointed out that small polities can be captured by small factions that might be repressive.[7] Small communities can be repressive. Opportunities for individual self-expression and the range of acceptable roles are often limited. These limits may weigh particularly heavily on minorities or others without power.

However, for the average citizen—provided the polity is not so deeply divided that no average exists—opportunities to become involved, and thus government's capacity to mobilize citizen action, are greater in a smaller political unit. To the extent that people care about the values involved in public policy—in this case, to the extent that two decades of environmental consciousness-raising have succeeded—the potential for greater popular engagement in decision making and for fuller integration of environmental values with other values can be achieved.

The logic that smaller units of government can mobilize citizens more effectively, for good or for ill, applies to state-local differences as well as to federal-state differences. Local governments can mobilize more effectively than states. Indeed, assertions about how smaller political units can mobilize a vital participatory democracy, with more citizen engagement and a broader perspective on community problems, are usually made with local governments in mind. Montesquieu wrote eloquently of how democracies could function in communities of a few thousand. Jefferson felt that the liberty and soundness of the nation depended on vibrant local communities of yeoman farmers.

It is a big step from Jefferson's vision to the contemporary reality of state government. Perhaps states that are smaller, more homogeneous, and have media markets of their own are more likely to see community behaviors, both positive and negative. If the notion of California as a community is too difficult to swallow, perhaps it makes more sense for Rhode Island, Wyoming, or even Michigan. But even in large states, politicians invoke the idea of the state as a community. Consider Gov. Mario Cuomo's theme, in his first inaugural address, of the "family of New York," or President Clinton's statement that when he was governor of Arkansas, he usually knew someone personally at a factory that laid off workers.

States' Comparative Advantage and the Tools of Governance

Although we must be careful not to idealize the comparative advantage of states, the idea is robust enough to suggest some important implications for how governance in states is different from governance at the federal level.

In short, the link between civic environmentalism and the comparative advantage of states is the concept of the tools that governments use. Civic environmentalism involves using nonregulatory tools, such as grants and subsidies; efforts to catalyze changes in private behavior by example, exhortation, or information; and provision of public services. These tools are best used by governments able to customize programs to fit local situations, engage active participation by citizens, and work across agency and professional boundaries—it is in these activities that states have a comparative advantage. However, in regulatory activities, which require uniform application of guidelines and insulation of the regulator from outside pressures and concerns, the federal government has a comparative advantage. The federal government also has a comparative advantage in redistributing resources from one large segment of the population (for example, the rich) to a weaker one. (See Appendix B for a discussion of how political scientists have used the concept of tools in discussing intergovernmental relations.) States' comparative advantage in engaging citizens in government is a disadvantage when it comes to using regulatory tools. It is usually neither necessary nor desirable to engage a wide range of people in the process of applying regulatory tools. This is not to say that regulators should be shielded from public involvement or scrutiny. Participation by a limited number of people, for example, on an advisory or policy-making board, is often useful for oversight and for suggesting when the application of generalized rules must be bent to accommodate special circumstances. If the enterprises or individuals being regulated gain control of regulatory agencies, it is useful to have advocates for other perspectives on advisory boards. However, the essence of regulation is consistency and predictability, features that are inconsistent with the active involvement of large numbers of people. Judges wear robes and sit on benches for a reason. They are meant to be removed from private influences. Regulators also seek to be insulated from external pressures, so they can focus on protecting the values they are mandated to safeguard.

Thus, regulators are often reluctant to engage in collaborative activities with other agencies, even with other regulators. Their mandate is to protect certain specific values. Consistency is important, and law gives them little room for balancing the values they are supposed to protect with competing values. This does not mean that regulators cannot engage in any interagency collaboration or in public-private partnerships. However, there are strict limits. It is relatively easy for regulators to join in efforts that inform others about their requirements, and sometimes to synchronize decision processes. But sharing in a decision, or bargaining about outcomes, is harder to do. So states' superior ability to cross interagency boundaries with informal agreements and understandings is of no particular use when it comes to regulation.

States' ability to customize is also of limited utility in regulation. There are limits on how much regulations can be customized to local conditions, institutions, and values without undermining the legitimacy of the regulations. Flexibility may be needed, but there are advantages to having clear, centrally established standards, guidelines, and accountability. If these are missing, there may be confusion, public misunderstanding, and even charges of corruption.

Redistributive tools also do not lend themselves to citizen engagement or customizing. Redistribution involves taking from some, often from the majority, and giving to others, often the disadvantaged or powerless. Redistribution is more defensible if it is consistent. Therefore, it is not particularly useful to customize redistributive tools to local institutions, values, or conditions. Nor is it necessary to mobilize the citizenry to become directly involved in using redistributive tools. If redistribution extracts resources quietly, it is more likely to be accepted.

Subsidies, public services, and catalytic tools operate quite differently from regulation and redistribution. Because public funds are almost always limited, it is usually advantageous to attract private resources to complement investments of public funds. Mobilizing broad participation by citizens may be a useful avenue. It also may make sense to reach across program and agency lines, to try to leverage other resources. Collaboration makes sense when all parties gain something, even though their objectives and values may be different or even conflicting. The uniformity inherent in regulation can make collaborative bargaining difficult, but subsidies and public services involve discrete investments, so it is easier to customize them to fit local conditions and to leverage other resources.

The purpose of catalytic tools is to encourage independent, voluntary action. Thus it is almost always useful to mobilize broad public involvement in the design and use of such tools. Also, it is almost always desirable to customize a tool to local circumstances, unless the purpose of using the tool is contrary to local values or interests.

When the federal government uses subsidies and catalytic tools or provides public services, bureaucratic and political forces create a tendency toward standardization and ineffectiveness. Often federal programs rely heavily on states and localities to manage federal subsidies and catalytic efforts. Such federal-state partnerships operate quite differently from federal-state regulatory and redistributive programs.

Some subsidies and public services do require a capacity to act that is beyond the scope of decentralized collaborative efforts. Subsidies for building transcontinental railroads, other programs to open the West, and the construction of the interstate highway system fall into this category. These activities are interstate in character and were clearly beyond the reach of state and local government, so federal involvement was essential. However, such programs can often be effectively implemented by involving state and local governments as partners, sharing the costs of management and construction.

States' Comparative Advantage and Unfinished Business

As explained in Chapter 2, tackling the unfinished business of environmental policy—nonpoint pollution, pollution prevention, and protection of endangered ecosystems—often requires the extensive use of nonregulatory tools. If this is true, and if states (and localities) have a comparative advantage in the use of these tools, then we should not be surprised to see states and localities assume a larger role in addressing unfinished business.

Furthermore, we should expect a less confrontational style of environmental politics at the state level, as long as the focus is on the use of nonregulatory tools. As Theodore Lowi explained twenty-five years ago, the selection of tools shapes the politics surrounding an issue. Regulation tends to involve ideological and confrontational politics. Developmental politics is less confrontational. It tends to involve assembling changing coalitions of diverse interests into a consensus that permits action.[8] So as states play a larger role in a policy area and focus on problems that they can handle most effectively with the tools they use best, they are likely to encounter a style of politics that is different from the struggles of private interests against crusaders.

These propositions are stated as tendencies instead of iron laws. One reason is that, obviously, federal-state-local relationships do not sort out neatly in terms of tools. As Joe Browder says, politicians and activists do not worry particularly about which level of government is best suited for using which tool, so the specific arrangements in a policy area at a particular time often contradict the broad patterns that we have sketched here. Many government programs use several tools simultaneously, and all levels of government use tools from each category. So it takes care to discern how the tools are really working. States do redistribute and sometimes attempt to regulate matters that are clearly interstate in character. The federal government invests billions of dollars in subsidies and public services that are clearly local in scope, and it also tries to catalyze private action. However, when states take independent initiatives, as happened in many policy areas in the 1980s, the differences between state and federal capacity become more apparent.

A second reason for describing the above-mentioned propositions as tendencies, not laws, is that the division of labor between federal and state governments is muddied by fragmentation. Because power is fragmented in most areas of public policy, very little gets done that does not involve some activity at all levels of government. States get drawn into areas that are dominated by the federal government, and the federal government is pulled into state and local issues. The comparative advantage of states emerges more clearly when states take a leadership role in framing policy and initiating action. Thus the comparative advantage of states is a question not of who is involved but of who leads.

The third reason for stating these hypotheses as general tendencies is that things change slowly. It is only in recent years that large numbers of states have begun to develop independent environmental initiatives. Meanwhile, the regulatory regime established in the 1970s for environmental governance is still firmly entrenched. We should expect that it will take time for states to understand their comparative advantage in environmental policy making and to embark on new initiatives. Also, the picture of independent state initiatives will be complicated by federal efforts to maintain a tough regulatory regime for point source pollution.

It may be useful to summarize these ideas into four formal propositions about the role of states and the federal government in civic environmentalism:

- Whenever they act independently, outside the framework established by federal environmental laws, states will tend toward civic environmentalism; that is, they will use catalyzing tools, subsidies, and public services rather more often than regulation, or at least they will use nonregulatory tools extensively in concert with regulation.
- Whenever they act independently, outside the framework established by federal environmental laws, states will tend to focus on nonpoint pollution, protection of ecosystems, and pollution prevention. Also, public policies about these three kinds of environmental problems tend to involve states.
- When states address these problems and use nonregulatory tools, the politics will tend to involve bargaining and consensual behavior, rather than public confrontations and bitter divisions between polluters and representatives of environmental values.

• The federal government can play an important role in state and local civic environmentalism, by supporting state and local initiatives through information, resources, standards, and threats of regulation.

INFORMATION AS THE KEY TO CIVIC ENVIRONMENTALISM

There is another way that civic environmentalism fits into broader trends in how our society governs itself. The development and use of information are the key to civic environmentalism. Its policies often use information as a tool to reduce pollution, and its politics often involves the sharing of information.

It is a cliché to say that we are entering a knowledge-based economy. This statement means several things. Most of us have received more formal education than our grandparents, and once we enter the labor market, we must continue to learn in order to stay employed. We have accumulated a vast amount of technical and scientific knowledge, and the pace of technological change seems to be quickening. Computers and modern telecommunications make it possible for us to tap into this knowledge and transfer it from place to place quickly. We also have access to extensive information about markets, products, tastes, and ideas, far more rapidly than ever before. The world is being joined into a single economic unit, where goods, money, technologies, and ideas can be quickly moved from place to place. These changes are so fundamental that we must depart from the old-fashioned view of economics, which sees production as a process of combining land, labor, machinery, and finance. Knowledge is also a critical ingredient of production, and perhaps more important than all the other factors.

If one accepts this description of the modern economy, a logical next question is whether we are also entering a knowledge-based political system and, if so, what this might imply.[9] Our discussion of environmental policy and politics suggests some possibilities. The themes of knowledge, risk, and uncertainty have run through our discussion like red threads in a green tapestry. Managing information may even emerge some day as the heart and soul of environmental policy.

Why should governments take notice of pollution? The answer that was generally accepted in the 1970s was the one offered by Garrett

Hardin and many others—the tragedy of the commons. That is, self-interest often encourages businesses and people to pollute. It costs money to remove pollution from smokestacks; farmers can raise more corn by using chemical fertilizers; it takes time to separate the paper, plastic, aluminum, and glass for recycling instead of dumping them all in the trash. So the answer that we accepted in the 1970s was that someone else must *make* us do right—must give us incentives, give us orders, or teach us new values so that we internalize the social costs of pollution.

But now suppose that the process of changing values and incentives is successful. Suppose Iowa farmers decide they want to avoid polluting the water and that they could grow as much corn with less fertilizer, that Colorado firms and homes want to use less electricity and could do so while still enjoying cold beer and hot showers, that the sugar industry in Florida really has decided that it must reduce the phosphorus in the water draining off its fields, for better public relations if for no other reason. Would that be enough?

When pollution is visible, traceable, and clearly obnoxious, a change in values, incentives, or social discipline is enough to change behavior. However, the three case studies suggest that something else is needed, beyond these changes, to protect ecosystems, prevent nonpoint pollution, and promote conservation. In addition to changed values and incentives, information is needed.

For example, today there is not enough information available to design the ultimate restoration plan for the Everglades. For the foreseeable future, a restoration plan must include extensive research, experimentation, and fine tuning. Agencies in Florida need more information about the effects of changes in the flow of water through the Everglades. Also, no one yet knows how the artificial wetlands will work, because they will be on a larger scale and will deal with smaller concentrations of pollutants than any artificial wetlands built so far.

Information is also the key to demand-side management (conservation of electrical energy) and to preventing pollution by farm chemicals. As explained in Chapter 4, farmers can use fewer chemicals if they can obtain information about the level of nitrogen in the soil or the number of pests in the fields. For example, a spring nitrogen test could reduce the use of fertilizer; but to make this test work, a data base must be

assembled and maintained to track the effects of winter rains and snows
on the amount of nitrogen in fields with different soils, surface cover,
and exposure. As explained in Chapter 6, demand-side management
requires a more extensive sharing of information among the departments of a public utility than traditional rate setting. Exchanging information with outside organizations, including electrical contractors,
energy service companies, and publicly supported programs to
weatherize homes of low- and moderate-income people, can also be
helpful, because these organizations have experience that utilities lack.
Also, providing information to customers is a central feature of many
demand-side programs.

When the key to protecting the environment is gathering and exchanging information, rather than changing values, providing incentives,
or disciplining polluters, the nature of the political process changes in
fundamental ways. If you adopt different values, you leave old values
behind; if you receive an incentive, someone else pays; if you are pun-
ished, the process is adversarial. But the exchange of information is different. If you and I have information and we exchange it, both of us are
more fully informed. Also, since new information may open new perspectives to us, the exchange may increase the total of knowledge beyond what each of us knew before. With information, two plus two may
equal five.*

For information to be pooled successfully, three things must be in
place. First, participants must share a common language, so they can
communicate effectively. Second, there must be a venue where they
can interact comfortably. And third, the venue must be one where multiple perspectives are welcomed and sought.

The American governmental system is not structured to encourage
the pooling of resources or information. It is a fragmented system, designed to attain "liberty and justice for all" and to reduce the opportunity for centralized, autocratic rule. However, within this fragmented

---

*In a situation of competition, information can be used as a weapon. Also, se-
crets can create monopoly profits. Knowledge is power, and patents can be cash
cows. However, to the extent that two parties share values, as we are assuming
in the case here, the effects of sharing information are very different from the
effects of exchanging other resources, such as money, labor, or raw materials.

system, some settings are more favorable than others for pooling information. For example, it may be easier to pool information—across agency and professional lines and between the public and private sector—at the level of state governments than at the federal level.

The reason is the comparative advantage of states. It is easier to mobilize citizens to act as a community—that is, to become personally involved and to recognize multiple aspects of a problem—in a smaller polity. Also, the facts of a public issue are often fewer in a smaller setting, so it is easier for citizens to understand them all. For example, if it is difficult to get a group to come to a joint understanding about the problems facing the Everglades, consider how much more complex it would be to come to an equally detailed understanding of water quality issues in the entire nation. Also, it is easier to customize policies and programs in smaller polities; so if an issue demands ongoing assessment and fine tuning, these also can be accomplished more easily at the state than at the federal level.

On the other hand, there are economies of scale in some aspects of the production and exchange of information. It is more economical for the federal government to develop expertise in highly specialized fields. So the best strategy for bringing specialized expertise to bear on an environmental problem may be for federal experts to participate in state- or local-level decision processes. This is exactly what is emerging in Florida and how the collaborative process is working in Colorado. Also, even for nonpoint pollution, some uniform national standards may be appropriate, for example, to address the health risks that a chemical poses for humans. So one way of configuring a decision-making process would be to have the federal government set standards and the states decide how best to meet these standards. This is how groundwater policy is being handled in Iowa, and in Wisconsin as well.

When the approach is to pool information, the optimal federal role is thus much different from when the strategy is to change values, create incentives, or impose social discipline. In a system built to encourage the pooling of information, the federal role would not be authoritative, not to serve as a source of power and money, but as a contributor of specialized technical information and of universally applicable standards. The state or local level would be the nexus, where information is pooled and decisions are made, and the federal role would be to feed state-level processes with information, including information developed by federal experts as well as information developed around the country about initiatives, best practices, and research findings. The federal government would thus be both a source of specialized information and also a gatherer, sifter, and distributor of information produced elsewhere. In a phrase, the state would decide, and the federal government would lead through the management of information.

Perhaps, as social values change so that more individuals and businesses live by environmental values and come to see their self-interest as including stewardship of natural resources—just as most people see their self-interest as including the well-being of their children, family members, and friends—we should expect to see fewer point source problems, because individuals will clean up after themselves. However, many environmental problems will still require the social management of information. These problems would demand not so much the imposition of federal authority but the pooling of information about environmental problems in decentralized communities that share a common language, have institutions that can function as venues for the exchange of information and for learning, and are open to diverse perspectives and kinds of expertise. The fragmentation of the American system of government will make it difficult for these kinds of communities to form, but we should expect that they will occur more often at the state level than at the level of the federal government.

CIVIC ENVIRONMENTALISM AND SUSTAINABLE DEVELOPMENT

As explained in Chapter 2, sustainable development means reconciling environmental protection with economic prosperity. The evidence from the case studies suggests that civic environmentalism may include a search for win-win solutions. The day of easy solutions, when it will be in the self-interest of polluters to be clean, has not yet arrived in any of the three states, and there is still a need for a strong voice for environmental values. However, in the Everglades, Joe Browder and Jim Webb hope that the coastal cities and developers of real estate property along the coasts will eventually find it in their self-interest to support restoration of the Everglades. In Iowa, it may be that agricultural co-ops that sell fertilizers could instead profit from selling information about how to get along with fewer chemicals. And in Colorado, the goal of new state policies is to make it profitable for utilities to sell *less* electricity.

As explained in Chapter 2, advocates for sustainable development want to push environmental values into the circles where decisions are made about economic goals, rather than seeing environmental values treated after the fact, as a constraint. Where are these decision-making centers? For the Third World, the obvious places are the World Bank and similar institutions. For some global issues, like the greenhouse effect and the deterioration of the ozone layer, any agreement about how to reconcile economic prosperity with these issues will involve agreements between nations. But in advanced market economies like that of the United States, decisions about development are decentralized. Most investments are made in the private sector. Some decisions about development policy are made at the state and local levels. State and local decision makers design many of society's investments in infrastructure, including highways, airports, water systems, and waste facilities. In addition, many state and local governments have spent heavily on grants, tax breaks, and technical assistance to businesses.

Fifteen years ago, the prospects for state or local participation in framing a sustainable development strategy would have been minimal, because state and local investment decisions were cast in narrow terms. Until the early 1980s, state and local efforts to promote development consisted simply of "smokestack chasing," that is, offering incentives to firms that would locate a plant in the area or expand an existing facility.

During the 1980s, state spending on economic and community development quintupled. Some of the new spending was for the old purpose of smokestack chasing, but states and localities also invested heavily in applied research, transfer of technology to industry (especially to small business), work force training, public education, and other elements of what is sometimes called industrial policy. As Peter Eisinger wrote, "In the economic policy domain, in the 1980s, it has been the states, not Washington, that seem to deliver the goods." [10]

In the early 1990s, many states have faced budget shortfalls and some have cut back development programs. But economic forces may be making smaller economies more important and may force states and localities to continue to expand their role in development policy.

Ten years ago, Jane Jacobs wrote in *Cities and the Wealth of Nations* that large metropolitan areas are the driving force behind economic growth. Only there are the markets large enough to handle new products and only there can a full combination of expertise, initiative, and resources be mobilized easily to meet new market opportunities. More recently, others have argued that global competition has reduced the importance of national boundaries and hence of national policies. For example, in *The Competitive Advantage of Nations*, Michael Porter marshals evidence that metropolitan areas with clusters of world-class firms in related industries may emerge as the most important economic units in the global economy. Usually, he says, these clusters flourish because the home region has a concentration of skilled workers, technical expertise, specialized finance, and public and private institutions that allows the rapid deployment of these resources. Porter argues that the most important contributions that city governments can make to international competitiveness lie in areas that have traditionally been funded or governed primarily by state and local governments, including university education, infrastructure, local regulations, local research initiatives, and information.[11]

The three case studies in this book all provide clues about how a sustainable development agenda might emerge at the state, local, or city-state level. The agenda would have two parts—assisting firms that are in the business of conserving energy or reducing pollution, and designing public works projects that would both protect the environment and provide benefits to developers and urban interests. In Colorado, programs emerging from decisions by the public utility commission are financing a rising number of energy conservation businesses. In Iowa, agricultural co-ops may profit by selling information about how to use fewer chemical pesticides and fertilizers, and independent consultants are already earning their living this way. In Florida, the choices are still cast as a tradeoff between the profitability of the sugar industry and the health of the Everglades. But environmentalists are trying to make an alliance with coastal developers and other urban interests with the argument that providing adequate clean water to the Everglades will also ensure the availability of water for urban growth. In other states, the emerging alliances might link environmentalists with low-impact tourism or environmental cleanup firms.

Federal legislation might also provide a way for states to enter into a serious dialogue on sustainable development. The 1991 Intermodal Surface Transportation Efficiency Act could be a model. This act provides that metropolitan planning organizations, which include local governments in metropolitan areas, allocate federal dollars only after considering environmental values as well as the traditional goals of spurring and accommodating economic growth. Similar legislation for mandating regional planning for investments in water management, including both quality and quantity concerns, and for conditioning federal investments on compliance with the plan, could be another vehicle for the dialogue. However, many regional planning bodies and some states may still lack the capacity to meaningful.

Part III: An Agenda for Civic Environmentalism

This book has described the changing role of states and localities in environmental policymaking and has argued that a new style of environmental policy and politics is emerging. The book has been essentially descriptive and analytical. However, if one starts with the premise that someone ought to work on the unfinished business of environmental policy, then the description of civic environmentalism in this book can be phrased as an agenda for action.

For states, the central theme of this agenda is that they can be more than implementers of federal regulations and more than laboratories for testing ideas that are transferred to the federal level if they work out well. Specifically, states can design their own ongoing initiatives, focusing their efforts on nonregulatory tools like education, technical assistance, grants and other economic incentives, and improved service delivery to address the unfinished agenda of protecting endangered ecosystems, preventing pollution, and reducing nonpoint pollution.

The traditional reasons for addressing environmental problems are to protect health and to improve the local quality of life. In addition, states can often link their environmental protection efforts directly to their economic development agendas. One way to make this link is to build environmental values into decisions about investments in public infrastructure, especially in places like South Florida where there are major environmental problems that suggest the region is living beyond its carrying capacity. For example, the state and the South Florida Water Management District could explore alternative ways of meeting the need of the urban coasts of South Florida for water and could work with federal agencies to integrate these plans into the design of a restoration program for the Everglades.

Another way to link environmental protection to economic development is to build environmental considerations into economic development programs. For example, Colorado and Iowa are finding that energy conservation and low-chemical agriculture are creating business opportunities for new and existing businesses. State-supported organizations that provide technical and financial assistance to small and medium-size businesses and farms, with the goal of making these firms and the economy more competitive and helping speed the adoption of new technologies, can also help firms prevent pollution and conserve energy. Indeed, the most important reasons businesses conserve energy and prevent pollution are to cut costs, to capture new markets, and to increase profits. State economic development agencies can also organize sector-specific programs that will achieve environmental goals; examples would include building a stronger recycling industry and offering better environmental engineering services.[12]

As states become leaders in environmental policy, they can work in partnership with federal agencies, nonprofit organizations, and local governments. States can convene forums where the fragmented array of federal, state, and local agencies comes together, along with leaders from the private sector, local communities, and the nonprofit community, to address local problems (like the preservation of valuable lands and waters), to explore opportunities for "greener" manufacturing processes, or to discuss broad issues, like the formulation of state and regional strategies for sustainable development. State leadership can also involve mobilizing resources outside the public sector. For example, as explained in Chapter 3, many states have become important sources of funding and technical support for nonprofit organizations that are researching specific problems or trying to protect valuable lands and waters.

Local governments can also become leaders in environmental policy. The underlying theme here is that local governments must go beyond their traditional role of regulating land use and providing such environmental services as collecting trash, managing parks, providing drinking water, and disposing of waste water. The emerging local agenda includes policymaking, planning, environmentally sound economic development, and environmentally sound investments in public infrastructure. As in King County, Washington, local governments can promote recycling and help create markets for recycled products. Localities can help design public investments in transportation that will reduce air quality problems and help clean up hazardous waste sites to make these sites good locations for industrial development.

Will states and localities act on this agenda for implementing civic environmentalism? This book has presented evidence that civic environmentalism is emerging as an inherently persuasive and powerful way of addressing many environmental problems. But it has also shown that civic environmentalism faces limits. Other stakeholders in environmental policy, especially the federal government, can help state and local governments to pursue an agenda of civic environmentalism. Their assistance may be needed if the full promise of civic environmentalism is to be achieved.

In mid-1993, we may be at a critical juncture in environmental policymaking. As described in this book, states and many local governments assumed new responsibilities and became creative innovators in environmental policy in the 1980s. In the early 1990s, states and local governments have faced tight budgets, which have made it difficult to organize new initiatives for any purpose, including protection of the environment. In Iowa, the state has not picked up the slack left by exhaustion of the federal funds that supported research on and demonstrations of low-chemical farming. In Florida, the willingness of taxpayers to invest hundreds of millions of dollars in restoring the Everglades will be challenged by tight state budgets and anti-tax fervor.

For the most part, states have not shrunk from their commitment to environmental programs. Indeed, the most recent data available indicate that states provide most of the funds for their environmental programs, relying on federal grants for only 14.8 percent of program budgets.[13] And most states have not cut their environmental budgets significantly.

However, as mentioned in Chapter 2, local governments have begun to complain about the total cost of environmental regulation. The city of

Columbus, Ohio, was one of the earlier sparks in this prairie fire of protest about "unfunded environmental mandates." It prepared a widely publicized study of the total costs it faces to comply with existing federal regulations, estimating costs at over \$1 billion in 1992-2001, or about \$470 per household per year.[14] Several other cities performed comparable studies and claimed that their taxpayers would revolt if city officials tried to raise fees or taxes by enough to cover costs. Other studies have shown that small towns will face major costs in complying with drinking water regulations. Especially controversial are new regulations requiring small towns to monitor their water supplies quarterly for dozens of chemicals, whether or not these chemicals are used locally. A few states have joined in by declaring their unwillingness to force municipalities to comply with federal drinking water regulations, which are said to be particularly costly while providing little reduction in risk.

These studies have used various methodologies for estimating cumulative costs, and some studies have no doubt overestimated the costs. Furthermore, some of the studies have been accompanied by blasts of strong anti-environmental, anti-regulation rhetoric, which seems to suggest the real concern is not so much cumulative cost as regulation itself.

Whether or not the studies are sound, they do seem to have struck a nerve. Of course, concern about unfunded mandates is not confined to local governments or to environmental issues. For example, Congress has expanded Medicaid coverage, requiring states to pay half of the additional costs, and federal courts have made states and local governments build or renovate jails and institutions. These unfunded mandates have provoked outraged protests by state and local officials.

Continued rancor about the cumulative costs of unfunded environmental mandates could erode the willingness of state and local officials to continue to invest in *any* kind of environmental policy. And of course civic environmentalism is not a stand-alone policy but one that is complementary to regulation. So a federal agenda to promote civic environmentalism might have two parts. First, the federal government could take practical steps to support bottom-up state and local environmental initiatives. Second, federal policymakers could maintain a tough federal regulatory regime and strict enforcement while also building a better knowledge base about which regulations are most effective in reducing risks to human health and to the environment. Federal policy might also allow state officials' greater flexibility in developing compliance schedules, so that local governments can address the greatest risks first rather than spending their energies in protests about high-cost, low-payoff mandates.

A FEDERAL COMMITMENT TO BOTTOM-UP INITIATIVES

The EPA already provides a great deal of assistance to states—and a small amount of assistance to local governments—in building capacity for effective environmental management. EPA grants provide significant financial support for state regulatory programs. In addition, smaller EPA grants support state initiatives in areas like pollution prevention, management of estuaries, and wetlands protection. EPA also operates several data bases and publishes information about state and local initiatives. Through grants to associations of state and local officials, EPA has provided opportunities for state and local officials to travel to meetings, where they can exchange ideas about "best practices" at the state and local levels, as well as about federal-state relations.

In early 1993, a joint EPA-state task force recommended several additional steps that could be taken to build state capacity for effective environmental management. The task force called for amending federal environmental statutes to say that EPA's mission includes building such capacity. Other recommendations included:

- Joint setting of goals and priorities by EPA and the states;
- Legal changes to allow state environmental officials to participate throughout the process of developing EPA regulations;
- State participation in the EPA budget process;
- Joint training by EPA and the states;
- Efforts to build state capacity for managing environmental data;
- More flexible EPA grants to the states.[15]

These are all useful ideas. They might gain broader support if they were linked to a clear vision of the comparative advantage of states and localities in environmental policy—not only as implementers of federal programs, but also as independent forces in addressing certain kinds of environmental problems. For example, if federal legislation is amended

to endorse building state and local capacities for environmental management, perhaps as part of a bill to create a cabinet-level Department of
the Environment, the legislation might authorize EPA and other federal
agencies both to strengthen states as managers of federal regulatory programs and to participate in independent state and local efforts to address the issues that civic environmentalism can address most effectively—the unfinished business of managing ecosystems, preventing
pollution, and addressing nonpoint pollution.

The analysis in this book suggests five other ways in which the federal government could support civic environmentalism: (1) by providing financial assistance; (2) by contributing knowledge and skills;
(3) by forming partnerships; (4) by helping evaluate environmental
initiatives; and (5) by setting an example. Each of these activities might
be authorized by new legislation, but many could be started immediately on the basis of current authority. Indeed, some of these activities
are already happening, on a scattered, ad hoc basis.

First, federal agencies could provide financial assistance for collaborative cross-media activities at the state or local level. This assistance
would not take the form of a new formula grant or a categorical grant
program, but rather would consist of pools of financial resources whose
use would be directed by joint teams of state, local, federal, and perhaps
even nonprofit and private sector experts. States and localities should
provide their own funds to match federal dollars contributed to these
pools. The pools might support competitive grants, awards to consortia
of agencies, and nonprofit organizations working to achieve jointly-
agreed-upon performance objectives.

Most of the federal funds that currently go to states are earmarked
for specific regulatory programs. The goal of the new pools would be to
build state and local capacities to engage in initiatives where they have a
comparative advantage—in using nonregulatory tools, often in partnership with nonprofit organizations and private businesses, to prevent pollution, protect ecosystems, and address nonpoint pollution. There already are grant programs to states for pollution prevention, comparative
risk studies, and other specific topics, but few to local governments or
for general environmental planning and management.

The grants should build capacity not only within state regulatory
agencies but also in other agencies and in nonprofit partnerships. For

example, such a grant might provide initial support for a state-level organization to promote energy conservation, like the proposed Partnership for an Energy-Efficient Colorado that was mentioned in Chapter 6. Grants might also be used as seed funds for state sustainable development initiatives, or for writing city or county environmental plans.

Second, the federal government could contribute its knowledge and skills to state and local initiatives. This could take the form of conducting special studies for states on a cost-sharing basis, sharing data and building links between state and federal data systems, posting federal officials to work at the state or local level—either in public agencies or in nonprofit organizations—or simply encouraging federal experts to participate actively in state-led roundtables and collaborative activities. As described in Chapter 6, a Department of Energy scientist played a key role in spurring energy conservation in Colorado while serving as an expert witness in state regulatory proceedings; this example could be repeated many times over. For example, the staff from the Department of the Interior or the Forest Service could work in county and state governments to contribute expertise to sustainable development initiatives or to studies of management strategies for critical areas with mixed federal, state, and private lands.

Third, the federal government may be able to form partnerships to address broad environmental issues at the state, local, or ecosystem level. There are several models. Some models join states and federal agencies in planning for large ecosystems; examples are the Northwest Power Planning Council, which unites the Bonneville Power Administration and five states, and the Chesapeake Bay agreement, which involves EPA, the states of Maryland, Virginia, and Pennsylvania, and the District of Columbia. EPA's National Estuary Program, which is modeled on the Chesapeake Bay agreement and on activities in the Great Lakes, provides funding for five years of research, data gathering, and planning, directed by a "management conference" of agencies responsible for environmental protection, land use planning, agricultural management, and fish and wildlife conservation. The federal Intermodal Surface Transportation Efficiency Act of 1991 gives metropolitan planning authorities a central role in ensuring consistency between state plans for transportation and those for clean air.

Each of these models is built around policy objectives that are clearly specified by the federal government. The federal government has also occasionally supported large-scale partnerships driven not by specific federal policies but by work plans that are developed cooperatively at the state or local level by a wide mix of officials. The state rural development councils that were organized in 1991-1993 by U.S. Department of Agriculture staff are a possible model. Several federal agencies pooled funds to pay the salaries of state executive directors and of a small core staff in Washington, and the work of the councils was driven by collaborative processes in Washington and in the states.[16]

Fourth, the federal government could play a central role in helping states and localities evaluate their independent initiatives. It would be unusual for a federal agency to organize program assessments that were unconnected to federal regulations or grants, but this could be a useful federal role. Currently, there is rarely a strong incentive for states and localities to evaluate their own initiatives, and little opportunity for anyone else to gather systematic information about "best practices." Membership associations of state and local officials document innovative practices, but they have little incentive to investigate failures or to look beneath the surface and publish candid reports about the institutional and political factors that often determine success or failure.

As with the third recommendation of partnerships for action, it would be worth looking at unconventional strategies for organizing evaluation. One federal agency could take responsibility for a series of grants to evaluate specific programs. But a better approach might be to convene peer groups of federal, state, and local officials, as well as representatives of environmental organizations and private business, to develop a research and evaluation agenda and to guide the process of working on this agenda. A neutral organization might accept the role of organizer of this "learning community," receiving support for its activities from federal agencies, private foundations, and industry.

Finally, the federal government can build state and local capacities by setting an example. For example, the president recently named a Commission on Sustainable Development, which includes leaders of three environmental organizations and six CEOs or other top officials of major businesses, as well a state official, a tribal official, and a philanthropist.

As of this writing, it is not clear whether the commission will focus its attention mostly on international issues, including several arising from the 1992 Rio conference on sustainable development, or whether it will also address domestic issues. A clear statement that the agenda for domestic sustainable development is important and that there are opportunities for leaders at the state and local levels to participate in the meetings of the president's commission, could encourage the formation of state and local commissions.

TOUGH, TARGETED FEDERAL REGULATION

As we said earlier, civic environmentalism is not a stand-alone approach; it complements regulation. The federal government has a comparative advantage in writing uniform rules for goods that are traded in national markets. So the federal government must support bottom-up initiatives by maintaining a strong regime of top-down regulation.

Since states implement most federal regulatory programs, EPA must carefully monitor state performance. There is room for more effective oversight. States have long complained that EPA regulations are often in flux and that EPA staff spend far too much time second-guessing decisions state regulators make about individual permits.

More fundamentally, the federal government might target its regulatory activities more understandably and more effectively. As we have learned more about threats to the environment, the standard practice for the past two decades has been to add new programs and new regulations. Each time a new regulatory program is added, there are protests about the cost of compliance. Often the grumbling quiets down as polluters find ways to achieve the new standards. However, as the mountain of regulations piles up, complaints begin to surface about the total cost of compliance.

In the late 1970s, business interests argued that environmental regulations were putting American industry at a disadvantage in competing with other countries. As other countries adopted tougher regulations, these complaints tapered off somewhat. Perhaps the recent complaints of local governments about cumulative compliance costs are also a temporary phenomenon. However, it certainly would be prudent to build a stronger knowledge base to support effective regulation.

Ideally, a regulatory system would be based on an understanding of current environmental conditions, of the relative importance of different threats to human health and to ecosystems, and of the cost and effectiveness of different regulatory and nonregulatory options. If such information existed, there would be a basis for debate about the values to be applied to different risks, and for negotiating adjustments to the regulatory system. But by and large, such a knowledge base is lacking.

EPA and the state regulatory agencies annually spend vast sums of money on gathering and managing information about the environment and about environmental management activities. Most attention is given to information about regulatory activities, such as the number of permits issued, violations cited, and fines levied. Congressional committees often ask for such data, probing for evidence that a small number of violations means lax enforcement. These data are clearly inadequate and are widely scorned as being useful only for "bean counting." They are only indirect measures of how vigorously states are enforcing the law. Few violations and small fines might mean that states are overlooking serious problems, or they might mean that permittees are in full compliance except for occasional lapses. Even if they were in full compliance, this would not necessarily mean that industry and regulators were focusing on the most important threats to human health and the environment, or that environmental threats were decreasing.

EPA and other federal agencies are trying to expand the knowledge base about environmental threats and about the current status of environmental quality. Recently, the Interior Department announced it would organize its research expertise on ecosystems into a National Biological Survey, which would develop a national information data base about the current status of ecosystems as well as collect information about threats and management strategies. Many blue-ribbon committees and experts have suggested that EPA must move its research activities to the Office of Research and Development, away from short-term investigations that support decisions about new regulations and toward longer-term research about environmental conditions and trends. But federal environmental research and information are highly fragmented. EPA has a smaller budget for environmental research than four other federal agencies, and many key data systems are managed by the Departments of the Interior, Commerce, Agriculture, or Energy, or by the

National Aeronautics and Space Administration. Even within EPA, it is difficult to compare data about different forms of pollution; for example, an enforcement action is defined differently in air and water programs. The few cross-cutting standards for information systems are just now being applied systematically to state and EPA agencies. Power and financial resources still lie with the narrow regulatory programs, and funds for cross-media projects are limited. In July 1993, EPA Director Carol Browner took an important step by centralizing authority for enforcement. And there have been proposals to strengthen federal environmental research and information gathering by organizing a National Institute on the Environment, consolidating the Geological Survey and the National Oceanic and Atmospheric Administration, or encouraging more aggressive leadership on environmental issues by the White House Office of Science, Engineering, and Technology.[17]

In short, the federal government and the states are building a stronger base for responding to complaints about burdensome regulation, but there is still a long way to go. If EPA were to relax its enforcement selectively, as local officials are asking, without clear reasons and solid data to support targeting, the result would be a weakening of the regulatory system.

In the short run, it would be wise to arrange for an authoritative study of the cumulative costs of environmental regulation, in small towns and other local communities. Also, a small number of local governments might be asked to use this information to tailor regulations to local circumstances. EPA has begun to work with states and localities on balancing different environmental risks. Following up on the *Unfinished Business* study mentioned in Chapter 2, EPA has supported studies in almost half of the states and in several local governments to assess the comparative risks of different threats to the environment.

These studies can be criticized on several grounds. They have rarely addressed the incidence of risk to different parts of the population. There is evidence that some kinds of environmental risks, like toxic and solid waste dumps and emissions from major industrial facilities, cluster in poor neighborhoods and minority communities. So the comparative risk studies that have been completed so far are open to the charge of being insensitive to environmental justice. The studies have also been criticized for relying on inadequate data, for postponing decision making, and for being so technical as to exclude citizens from decisions. This last criticism is particularly telling, because one's estimate of risk depends on one's values, so an assessment of comparative risks is inevitably a political decision.[18]

By themselves, studies of comparative risks do not give enough guidance to support good decisions about targeting regulation at the most pressing problems. As well as the risks involved, decision makers need to know about the costs and effectiveness of various kinds of regulatory and nonregulatory strategies in different settings. EPA has invested little in this kind of program evaluation. Most program evaluations gather data about program activities and focus on "bean-counting."

Even without substantive program evaluations, EPA can make some progress by participating in a joint federal-state strategic planning process. The EPA-state task force mentioned earlier recommended that the states join with EPA regional offices to set goals that would cut across the various regulatory programs and set up a system of peer review to evaluate progress toward these goals. In addition, the task force endorsed experiments in Colorado and Vermont to allow states to shift funds from one program to another based on findings of comparative risk studies. The report also endorsed investing more EPA dollars in cross-media programs. Most of the funds that EPA grants to states are earmarked by Congress for specific purposes, so these experiments will be small. But they may be incremental steps toward a more targeted approach to environmental regulation.

BUILDING A BROAD CONSTITUENCY FOR CIVIC ENVIRONMENTALISM

Others besides the federal government can help state and local governments to pursue an agenda of civic environmentalism. Several steps can be taken to provide a more friendly climate for the spread of civic environmentalism. Environmental groups, foundations, private businesses, and even researchers can help build capacity at the state and local levels for civic environmentalism. All of these groups can help build civic environmentalism simply by paying more attention to environmental policy and politics at the state and local levels. In particular, they can pay more attention to independent initiatives that go beyond management of federal regulations.

For example, environmental organizations can use the *Green Index* and the Renew America *Environmental Success Index* to insist that states and localities do a better job of protecting environmental values. Sustainable development, the protection of endangered ecosystems, pollution prevention, and nonpoint pollution prevention all can provide good rallying cries for environmental activism at the state and local levels. Foundations that support environmental groups can focus their initiatives on sustainable development, ecosystem management, and other elements of unfinished business, following the example of organizations like the Joyce Foundation, which has invested in cleaning up the Great Lakes.

New constituencies for sustainable development may emerge in the private sector at the state and local levels, drawing their support from businesses that sell environmental control technologies or provide information and expertise about production processes that minimize environmental problems.

Researchers can also contribute by testing the ideas suggested in this book. Specifically, researchers might revisit the assumption that localities and states systematically relax environmental policies to attract industry; might investigate barriers to collaboration between economic development forces and environmental agencies; and might evaluate state and local efforts to solve environmental problems with unconventional means.

CONCLUSION

Civic environmentalism is a new phenomenon, just emerging in our politics and policies. The focus of environmental policy is still on command-and-control regulation. However, as we seek to tackle new environmental problems, use information in new ways, and put environmental values on an equal footing with economic values, our policies and politics are changing. The future does not hold a return to the pre-1970 days, when few states and localities paid attention to environmental problems. The forest of federal regulations, the army of environmental professionals, and new public attitudes have ended those days. The future does hold elements of the past; the scope for independent state and local initiatives will be widened. But future policies can build on a much stronger civic base, as individuals, communities, and many businesses come to understand and believe that they can prosper while protecting environmental values.

NOTES

1. S. S. Light, L. H. Gunderson, and C. S. Holling, "The Everglades: Evolution of Water Management in a Turbulent Ecosystem" (Unpublished paper, Arthur R. Marshall Laboratory, University of Florida, Gainesville, 1993).
2. Donald Snow, *Inside the Environmental Movement: Meeting the Leadership Challenge* (Washington, D.C.: Island Press, 1992), 28.
3. Tom Arrandale, "The Mid-Life Crisis of the Environmental Lobby," *Governing*, April 1992, 36.
4. Jeff Tryens, Center for Policy Alternatives, Washington, D.C., personal communication with author.
5. For a thorough discussion of how national, state, and local environmental groups deal with these problems, see Snow, *Inside the Environmental Movement*.
6. Larry Sabato, *Goodbye to Goodtime Charlie: The American Governorship Transformed*, 2d ed. (Washington, D.C.: CQ Press, 1983). See also Anne O'M. Bowman and Richard Kearney, *The Resurgence of the States* (Englewood Cliffs, N.J.: Prentice Hall, 1986).
7. Garry Wills, ed., "The Federalist No. 10: Hamilton," in *The Federalist Papers by Alexander Hamilton, James Madison and John Jay* (New York: Bantam Books, 1982).
8. Theodore J. Lowi, "Four Systems of Policy, Politics, and Choice," *Public Administration Review* 32, no. 4 (1972): 298-310. Following in Lowi's footsteps, several writers have described in more detail how specific tools tend to be associated with different expectations or results and different patterns of alliance and conflict. See Lester Salamon, ed., *Beyond Privatization* (Washington, D.C.: Urban Institute Press, 1989); and Ann Schneider and Helen Ingram, "Behavioral Assumptions of Policy Tools," *Journal of Politics* 52, no. 2 (1990): 510-529.
9. For a provocative treatment of this question, see Steven A. Rosell et al., *Governing in an Information Society* (Ottawa: Renouf, 1992).
10. Peter Eisinger, *The Rise of the Entrepreneurial State: State and Local Economic Development Policy in the United States* (Racine: University of Wisconsin Press, 1988), 5, 127.

11. Jane Jacobs, *Cities and the Wealth of Nations: Principles of Economic Life* (New York: Random House, 1984); Michael E. Porter, *The Competitive Advantage of Nations* (New York: Free Press, 1990), 622.

12. For a list of such efforts in the western states, see *The Environmental Industry in the West: A State-by-State Survey of Private and Public Development Initiatives,* (Denver, Colo.: Western Governors' Association, 1993).

13. Personal communication with author, August 13, 1993. Brown offers the following figures, based on data to be published in *State Environmental and Natural Resources Expenditures* (Lexington, Ky.: Council of State Governments, 1993), 126, 127, and 134. Percentage of state spending from federal funds: Hazardous waste programs, 10%; mining reclamation, 19%; fish and wildlife, 20%; pesticides control, 26%; drinking water, 28%; air quality, 33%; marine and coastal programs, 33%.

14. *Ohio Metropolitan Area Cost Report for Environmental Compliance,* prepared by representatives of the cities of Columbus, Akron, Cincinnati, Lima, Mansfield, Toledo, and Zanesville, the Ohio Municipal League, and the Northeast Ohio Regional Sewer District, September 15, 1992, 64.

15. Environmental Protection Agency, Office of Regional Operations, State and Local Relations, *Draft Implementation Plan Outline for State Capacity,* April 21, 1993.

16. See Beryl Radin, "Rural Development Councils: An Intergovernmental Coordination Experiment," in *Publius: The Journal of Federalism* 22 (Summer 1992): 111-127; and DeWitt John and Eric Walcott, "Reinventing Government for Rural Development: Principles, Examples, and Action" (Washington, D.C.: National Academy of Public Administration, 1993).

17. For example, see *Environmental Research and Development: Strengthening the Federal Infrastructure,* a report of the Carnegie Commission on Science, Technology, and Government, New York, 1992; and publications of the Committee for the National Institute for the Environment, Washington, D.C., including *A Proposal for a National Institute for the Environment: Need, Rationale, and Structure,* 1993.

18. See "Setting National Environmental Priorities: The EPA Risk-Based Paradigm and Its Alternatives: A Conference Synopsis" (Washington, D.C.: Center for Risk Management, Resources for the Future, 1993).

Selection of the Case Studies

A short note on the selection of case studies may be helpful. There were several criteria. First, we selected cases that represented important efforts to address the three major elements of unfinished business: prevention, ecosystems, and nonpoint pollution. The Iowa case illustrates a nonpoint pollution problem for which the federal government has repeatedly tried, but failed, to design a coherent statutory framework. In addition, Iowa's initiatives focus on preventing pollution rather than regulating it or cleaning it up. The conflict in South Florida is a dramatic example of an ecosystem whose future is imperiled. The Colorado case involves energy conservation, which is a form of pollution prevention.

Second, we sought cases that involved major questions about environmental values and about the economic future of the state. In Iowa, agriculture is a major industry, and groundwater is widely used for drinking. The Florida case is the story of a struggle between the powerful sugar industry and advocates for protecting water for the Everglades National Park—an ecosystem of global significance. The cost of electricity is an important element of the local business climate in Colorado, as in other states, and utilities are powerful economic and political forces. As utilities account for a third of carbon dioxide emissions in the United States, this case also addresses a significant part of the global greenhouse effect.

Third, we sought to balance cases in which nonregulatory tools were used with those in which regulatory tools were used. In Iowa, the focus was clearly on nonregulatory tools. The Florida case was the opposite; it concerned litigation over whether the state was bound to regulate discharges from cane fields. The Colorado case involved proposals for inserting energy conservation objectives into regulatory policy, which has traditionally been focused on questions of economic equity.

Fourth, we sought cases in states that are in the middle range of environmental policy—not among the most pro-environment or innovative, but not among the laggards, either. There are no cases from such states that are well-known leaders in environmental policy, such as California, Oregon, Minnesota, Wisconsin, New York, or Massachusetts, because an analysis of civic environmentalism would not be convincing if examples were taken only from such states. Often case studies of state policy focus on examples of especially creative innovation, and are therefore perhaps of limited usefulness.

Fifth, the case studies represent a range with respect to three key variables that are said to influence state environmental policies: economic structure, political structure and climate, and the strengths and achievements of pro-environmental forces.[1] Colorado and Florida have economic bases dominated by service industries, including tourism and retirement. Iowa's economy is based on agribusiness (including farm equipment and food processing as well as farming) and on manufacturing.

The states also represent different political structures and climates. These can be measured by institutional factors and an index of political culture. Colorado and Florida have relatively weak governors, and Iowa is a middle case. Colorado and Iowa have governors of one party (Democratic and Republican, respectively) and legislatures dominated by the opposite party. Florida had a Republican governor and a Democratic legislature at the start of our story, but Democratic control of both branches later. The states also differ in terms of political culture, the label many political scientists give to the various kinds of political action and orientation.

With respect to the power and achievements of the environmental movement, the states are quite diverse. According to a recent comprehensive ranking of states on environmental policies and problems, Colorado is an underperformer, with a high number of members of environmental groups per capita but with very low spending on environmental programs and a weak policy performance. Its environmental problems

TABLE A-1

ENVIRONMENTALISM IN THE CASE STUDY STATES

	Number of Conservation Association Members per Capita	Severity of Environmental Problems	Environmental Spending per Capita	Index of State Pro-environmental Policy
Colorado	5	40	34	26
Florida	31	20	13	11
Iowa	26	21	22	17

Source: Bob Hall and Mary Lee Kerr, *1991-1992 Green Index: A State-by-State Guide to the Nation's Environmental Health* (Washington, D.C.: Island Press, 1991), 5, 11.

Note: Rankings are among the fifty states.

are ranked as less serious than those of most other states. In contrast, Florida is an overachiever, with few conservationists but a high level of spending and performance. Its problems rank as moderately serious (thirtieth of fifty states, with fiftieth being most severe). Iowa is about average on all scores. The rankings of the three states are shown in Table A-1.

Finally, the cases selected for study also represent a range with respect to two key factors: success and leadership. Iowa is a success story of a sort; its groundwater act of 1987 was widely viewed as a model for other states, but key funds have run out, and the state now faces a decision about how, and whether, to continue. Leadership on the act came directly from the state legislature. In Florida, a federal attorney, a governor, and the U.S. secretary of the interior all have played highly visible public roles at important stages of the Everglades controversy. They have made substantial progress toward an agreement to restore the Everglades. However, as of this writing, a final agreement among the key parties about how the settlements are to be implemented is still at least a few months away. The Colorado case study is more clearly a success. After years of incremental movement, the major electrical utility in the state and the public utility commission have made a strong commitment to energy conservation while agreeing to changes in the way decisions about future investments in energy conservation are arrived at. The key decisions in Colorado have been made by the state public utility commission.

Each of the case studies could be the subject of several long books. Indeed, there are volumes on water quality in the Everglades, the Florida sugar industry, and growth management in Florida alone. The case studies are much less than comprehensive examinations of the full range of technical, economic, and political aspects of each case. They focus on three things: describing enough about the environmental problems and economic factors to reveal whether states are indeed addressing the kinds of issues that would be expected; exploring the nature of the state policy initiatives and determining whether they employ the tools of civic environmentalism; and telling enough about the initiatives to explain whether hypotheses about state environmental politics are borne out by the cases. Each case focuses on a few critical events—the passage of legislation or a legal settlement. The case studies are snapshots of the issues, the tools, and the players at turning points in policy and politics.

NOTE

1. See James P. Lester and Emmett N. Lombard, "The Comparative Analysis of State Environmental Policy," *Natural Resources Journal* 30 (1990): 301-319.

Tools for Accomplishing Public Goals

T he analysis in this book distinguishes among five types of governmental tools. Governments can define and enforce rules of behavior; they can exhort; and they can transfer wealth and resources. This
last category is very broad, and it is useful to further divide it into three
subcategories, depending on how many people receive the wealth, resources, or assistance. Thus the five categories are regulatory tools, catalytic tools, public services, redistributive tools, and subsidies.

Regulatory tools are those that involve framing rules of behavior that
are applied to specific individuals or organizations through an enforcement process. Usually these rules are framed as applying to all people
equally, because all in the nation are equal under the law, and rules that
exclude some people are discriminatory. As a practical matter, some
regulations apply to all people (traffic regulations apply to all drivers),
but many rules actually affect only a few. For example, most environmental regulations are framed as if they apply to everyone, but in practice they apply only to companies that emit the pollutants in question.
Our analytical framework bundles these categories together. Whether a
rule affects few or many, it is still a rule.

There are many types of regulatory tools beyond simple prohibitions
and constraints. Governments can require specific actions, create liability, and establish procedures that will have important effects on private
behavior. In current discussions of environmental policy, analysts usually draw distinctions between command-and-control and market mechanisms. Under command and control, analysts include written rules; under market mechanisms, they usually include devices like tradable

emissions rights, which operate as supplements to a regulatory system. There are many other market mechanisms that can be used independently of regulation. However, as discussed in Chapter 2, some market mechanisms, including tradable emissions rights, are closely associated with regulation.

The second type of governmental tool involves exhortation. This category applies to those public actions that are not backed up with enforcement power and whose stated objectives are not supported with governmental resources. Examples include speeches by public officials, setting goals for a community, or organizing volunteer programs.

Usually governmental efforts to exhort are called symbolic politics. This word suggests that government is doing nothing significant and that policy makers would be avoiding responsibility by favoring policies that use symbolic tools. In fact, one of the major functions of government is to lead by articulating the public interest and widely held values and concerns. I prefer the term *catalytic*, which suggests that such tools are plainly incapable of achieving any action themselves but might have an impact if they were to motivate private and individual action.

The last three categories include governmental activities that involve the transfer of resources, such as information, services, facilities, or dollars. Sometimes governments provide resources to everyone. These are "public services" such as public education, ownership and management of public lands, or operation of public works projects. At other times, resources are provided to large groups or classes, often to the disadvantaged but sometimes to groups that are defined by geography or by occupation. These are redistributive tools. Examples would include progressive taxation, welfare payments, tax credits, Social Security, and targeted aid to disadvantaged areas. The final group of tools consists of subsidies, which include resources provided to a small number of communities, individuals, or corporations. For example, governments build public facilities, make grants and loans to private businesses, provide technical assistance to individuals, ensure specific transactions, and finance research projects.

These five categories are a modification of the well-known distinction that Theodore Lowi makes between redistributive, regulatory, and distributive or developmental tools. Lowi defined redistributive policies as those that involve transferring wealth from one class to another. Regulatory policies involve restricting the activities of powerful interests to protect the public. And distributive policies include subsidies and "pork barrel" spending.[1] (Paul Peterson and his colleagues call distributive policies developmental. I prefer the term *subsidies* because they involve the use of public resources by a relatively small segment of the population. The word *distributive* is too close to *redistributive* and could be confusing, and the term *developmental* suggests that these tools are investments in "developing" something by increasing the productivity of the recipients or improving their quality of life. Sometimes this is the case, but often it is not.)

Other writers have used different terms to distinguish between governmental activities. The label *tools* is taken from work by Lester Salamon and others, which parallels descriptions by G. Bruce Doern and Peter Au Coin about different "instruments" of governmental policy.[2]

This book makes the case, especially in the second part of Chapter 7, that different tools involve different kinds of federal-state-local relationships. Specifically, civic environmentalism, which uses nonregulatory tools, is state- and locally centered. In making this case we follow Joseph Zimmerman, Paul Peterson, and Deil Wright, who have also tried to link different tools with the different roles of federal, state, and local governments. Zimmerman distinguishes among different "functions." His study of federal preemption identifies nine types of federal mandates. The differences among the nine types involve policy objectives like civil rights, public safety, and uniform service levels for public goods that every citizen has a right to enjoy, such as drinking water.[3]

Peterson and his colleagues use Lowi's categories in *When Federalism Works*. They present evidence that federal-state-local relations concerning redistributive policies are systematically different from those concerning developmental policies. Specifically, intergovernmental relations are more harmonious when developmental issues with similar federal and local objectives are on the table. Both seek to promote local economic growth. However, local governments may not share the objectives of federal redistributive policies. Therefore, intergovernmental relations are often marked by conflict when a redistributive program is being established.[4]

Local officials may protest that federal requirements in redistributive programs are difficult to administer, and federal officials may tighten requirements to prevent local subversion of federal purposes. However, Peterson and his coauthors found that in the programs they studied during the early 1980s, these conflicts simmered down over time as local and federal officials accepted a common view of the purposes of programs, and as an understanding developed of "an appropriate balance between what is desirable [from the federal perspective] and what is possible [from the local perspective]." [5] In short, they found that federalism does "work" in the sense of settling eventually into a relatively smooth administrative pattern. But the course of events is much different with developmental policies than with redistributive policies.

There will be several interesting sequels to the story that Peterson and his colleagues tell. Their field work was conducted in the early 1980s, before the era of shrinking federal grants, reduction of federal responsibilities, and state activism began in earnest. After they wrote, states began to turn away from the traditional goals of redistributive policies (for example, by incorporating in welfare programs economic development objectives and by including in economic development programs redistributive efforts to raise the skills of the work force).

This shift raises an important point about the difficulties of using Lowi's categories in a context of changing policies and politics. Often programs and policies that start out in one category evolve into another. The evolution of the Economic Development Administration (EDA) is a classic example. Originally, the plan involved subsidies to geographic areas that were experiencing long-term unemployment and economic distress. Over time, eligibility requirements were loosened by Congress to the point that 85 percent of the nation is now eligible for EDA assistance.[6] So is EDA redistributive or developmental? Is it both? Or is it first one, then the other?

A related problem is that many programs incorporate both regulatory and developmental policies, and perhaps redistributive elements as well. The difficulty lies in knowing how to apply Lowi's appealing and persuasive concepts to specific public activities when policies and politics are changing.

Wright defines the three categories in terms of who benefits from governmental action and who bears the costs.[7] Developmental policies are those for which the benefits or results are concentrated or clearly focused; their costs are widely dispersed and small. Regulatory policies involve concentrated costs and small, widely dispersed benefits. Redistributive policies involve costs for many and benefits for many (such as large groups of disadvantaged people or social classes). This definition closely follows Lowi's conceptualization.

Peterson and his colleagues define the triad in a slightly different way—in terms both of the intentions of the law and of who benefits and who loses. Developmental policies are those "intended to improve the economic position of a community in competition with other areas," and redistributive policies "are those that primarily benefit low-income or needy groups." [8]

Regardless of which definition is used, it is difficult to determine whether a specific policy is intended to, or actually does, redistribute wealth or promote economic growth. The answers are not always straightforward and often change over time. Thus, if we are to use Lowi's categories in our discussion of changing patterns of federal-state-local relations, we must find a new way to define them. We must define the categories in terms of what government actually does (in other words, the tools it uses), rather than in terms of intentions or results. But then the categories themselves would have to be changed slightly, as in our discussion.

NOTES

1. Theodore J. Lowi, "Four Systems of Policy, Politics, and Choice," *Public Administration Review* 32, no. 4 (1972): 298-310, and Theodore J. Lowi, "Europeanization of America? From United States to United State," *Nationalizing Government: Public Policies in America,* ed. Theodore J. Lowi and Alan Stone (Beverly Hills, Calif.: Sage, 1978), 15-29.
2. Lester Salamon, ed., *Beyond Privatization: The Tools of Government Action* (Washington, D.C.: Urban Institute Press, 1989); G. Bruce Doern and Peter Au Coin, eds., *Public Policy in Canada* (Toronto: Macmillan, 1979). See also Ann Schneider and Helen Ingram, "Behavioral Assumptions of Policy Tools," *Journal of Politics* 52, no. 2 (1990): 510-529.
3. Joseph F. Zimmerman, *Federal Preemption: The Silent Revolution* (Ames: Iowa State University Press, 1991), 146-157.

4. Paul Peterson et al., *When Federalism Works* (Washington, D.C.: Brookings Institution, 1986), 105-106.
5. Ibid., 20.
6. DeWitt John, *Shifting Responsibilities: Federalism in Economic Development* (Washington, D.C.: National Governors' Association, 1987), 51-55.
7. Deil S. Wright, *Understanding Intergovernmental Relations*, 3d ed. (Pacific Grove, Calif.: Brooks/Cole, 1988), 291-438.
8. Peterson et al., *When Federalism Works*, 12, 15.

Advisory Commission on Intergovernmental Relations. *The Condition of Contemporary Federalism: Conflicting Theories and Collapsing Constraints.* Washington, D.C.: Advisory Commission on Intergovernmental Relations, 1981.

_____. *Protecting the Environment: Politics, Pollution, and Federal Policy.* Washington, D.C.: Advisory Commission on Intergovernmental Relations, 1981.

Arrandale, Tom. "The Mid-Life Crisis of the Environmental Lobby." *Governing,* April 1992, 36.

Batie, Sandra. "Sustainable Development: Challenges to the Profession of Agricultural Economics." Presidential address to the American Agricultural Economics Association, Baton Rouge, La., July 30, 1989.

Bauer, Blair T., and Betsy A. Lyons. *Keeping Florida Afloat: A Case Study of Governmental Responses to Increasing Demands on a Finite Resource.* Washington, D.C.: Conservation Foundation, 1989.

Bauer-Stamper, Judith. *Save the Everglades.* Austin, Texas: Steck-Vaughn, 1993.

Beck, Susan, and Michael Orey. "Skaddenomics: The Ludicrous World of Law Firm Billing." *American Lawyer,* September 1991, 92-97.

Berger, John J., ed. *Environmental Restoration: Science and Strategies for Restoring the Earth.* Washington, D.C.: Island Press, 1990.

Bowman, Anne O., and Richard Kearney. *The Resurgence of the States.* Englewood Cliffs, N.J.: Prentice Hall, 1986.

Bryce, James. *The American Commonwealth.* 2d ed. Vol. 1. London: Macmillan, 1891.

Buck, Susan J. *Understanding Environmental Administration and Law.* Washington, D.C.: Island Press, 1991.

Budget of the United States Government, FY 1990. Washington, D.C.: Government Printing Office, 1989.

Cahn, Robert, and Patricia Cahn. "Florida's Threatened Sanctuaries: Will Agricultural Pollution Ruin a Famous National Park and a Major Wildlife Refuge?" *Defenders,* May-June 1990, 12.

Canadian Council of Resource and Environment Ministries. *Report of the National Task Force on Environment and the Economy.* September 1987.

Carter, Luther J. *The Florida Experience: Land and Water Policy in a Growth State.* Baltimore: Johns Hopkins University Press, 1974.

Cavanagh, Ralph. Preface. In *Energy Efficiency and the Environment: Forging the Link.* Edited by Edward Vine, Drury Crawley, and Paul Centolella. Washington, D.C.: American Council for an Energy-Efficient Economy, 1991.

Colborn, Theodora E., Alex Davidson, Sharon N. Green, Tony (R. A.) Hodge, C. Ian Jackson, and Richard A. Liroff. *Great Lakes: Great Legacy?* Washington, D.C.: Conservation Foundation; and Ottawa, Ontario, Canada: Institute for Research on Public Policy, 1990.

Colby, Michael. "Environmental Management in Development: The Evolution of Paradigms." *Ecological Economics* (1991): 193-213.

Combs, James, Don Koch, Richard Kelley, Lisa Smith, Monica Wnuk, and J. Edward Brown. *The Role of Standards in Iowa's Groundwater Protection Program: A Report to the Iowa General Assembly.* Des Moines: Iowa Department of Natural Resources, 1989.

Commoner, Barry. "The Failure of the Environmental Effort." Paper presented at the seminar series of the Air and Radiation Program and Office of Toxic Substances, EPA, Center for the Biology of Natural Systems, Queens College, City University of New York, January 12, 1988.

Conservation Foundation. *State of the Environment: A View Toward the Nineties.* Washington, D.C.: Conservation Foundation, 1987.

Corwin, Edwin S. "A Constitution of Powers and Modern Federalism." *Essays in Constitutional Law.* Edited by Robert G. McCloskey. New York: Alfred A. Knopf, 1962.

Council of State Governments. *Resource Guide to State Environmental Management.* Louisville, Ky.: Council of State Governments, 1990.

Crenson, Matthew A. *The Un-Politics of Air Pollution: A Study of Non-Decisionmaking in the Cities.* Baltimore: Johns Hopkins University Press, 1971.

Davies, J. Clarence, and Barbara Davies. *The Politics of Pollution.* Indianapolis: Pegasus, 1975.

Deland, Michael R., and James D. Watkins. "Efficient Is Beautiful." *Issues in Science and Technology*, Winter 1990-1991, 40.

Devall, B., and G. Sessions. *Deep Ecology: Living as if Nature Mattered.* Salt Lake City: Peregrine Smith Books, 1985.

Diamond, Craig. *An Analysis of Public Subsidies and Externalities Affecting Water Use in South Florida.* Submitted to the Wilderness Society. Fort Lauderdale: Florida Atlantic University and Florida International University, Joint Center for Environmental and Urban Problems, 1990.

Doern, G. Bruce, and Peter Au Coin, eds. *Public Policy in Canada.* Toronto: Macmillan, 1979.

Doherty, Steven Joseph. "The Politics of the 1987 Iowa Groundwater Protection Act." Master's thesis, Iowa State University, 1990.

Douglas, Marjory. *The Everglades: River of Grass*, rev. ed. Sarasota, Fla.: Pineapple Press, 1988.

Dubnick, Mel, and Alan Gitelson. "Nationalizing State Policies." *The Nationalization of State Government.* Edited by Jerome J. Hanus. Lexington, Mass.: Lexington Books, 1981.

Dye, Thomas, and Dorothy Davidson. "State Energy Policies: Federal Funds for Paper Programs." *Policy Studies Review* 1, no. 62 (1981): 255.

Eisinger, Peter. *The Rise of the Entrepreneurial State: State and Local Economic Development Policy in the United States.* Racine: University of Wisconsin Press, 1988.

Energy Foundation. *Annual Report 1991.* San Francisco: Energy Foundation, 1992.

Environment 2010: The State of the Environment Report. Olympia: Washington Department of Ecology, 1989.

Environmental Opinion Survey. Washington, D.C.: Environment Opinion Study, June 1991.

Everglades Coalition. *Everglades in the 21st Century: The Water Management Future.* Washington, D.C.: Everglades Coalition, 1992.

Fallows, James. *The Water Lords: Ralph Nader's Study Group Report on Industry and Environmental Crisis in Savannah, Georgia.* New York: Bantam Books, 1971.

Fosler, R. Scott, ed. *The New Economic Role of American States: Strategies in a Competitive World Economy.* New York: Oxford University Press, 1988.

Freeman, A. Myrick III. "Water Pollution Policy." In *Public Policies for Environmental Protection*. Edited by Paul R. Portney, Washington, D.C.: Resources for the Future, 1990.

Gellings, Clark W., and John H. Chamberlin. *Demand-Side Management: Concepts and Methods*. 2d ed. Liliburn, Ga.: Fairmont Press, 1992.

Getches, David. "Groundwater Quality Protection: Setting a National Goal for State and Federal Programs." *Chicago-Kent Law Review* 65, no. 2 (1989): 392.

Gluckman, David. "The Marjory Stoneman Douglas Everglades Protection Act." *Environmental and Urban Issues* (Fall 1991): 17-27.

Gormley, William T., Jr. *The Politics of Public Utility Regulation*. Pittsburgh: University of Pittsburgh Press, 1983.

Gottlieb, Robert. *A Life of Its Own: The Politics and Power of Water*. San Diego: Harcourt Brace Jovanovich, 1988.

Hall, Bob, and Mary Lee Kerr. *1991-1992 Green Index: A State-by-State Guide to the Nation's Environmental Health*. Washington, D.C.: Island Press, 1991.

Hallberg, G. R., C. K. Contart, C. A. Chase, G. A. Miller, M. D. Duffy, R. J. Killorn, R. D. Voss, A. M. Blackmer, S. C. Padgitt, J. R. DeWitt, J. B. Gulliford, D. A. Lindquist, L. W. Asell, D. R. Kenney, R. D. Libra, and K. D. Rex. *A Process of Iowa's Agricultural-Energy-Environmental Initiatives: Nitrogen Management in Iowa*. Technical Information Series 22. Des Moines: Iowa Department of Natural Resources, 1991.

Hayes, Denis. Speech to the Washington Natural Resources Council. Washington, D.C., December 1989.

Hirst, Eric. *Cooperation and Community Conservation, Final Report*. Hood River Conservation Project, DOE/BP-11287-18. Washington, D.C.: Department of Energy, 1987.

Hoffman, Steven M., and Kristin Sigford. *State Air Quality Control Programs: A Comparative Assessment*. St. Paul, Minn.: Project Environment Foundation and the University of St. Thomas, 1991.

Horton, Tom, and William Eichbaum. "Four Key Battles." *Turning the Tide: Saving the Chesapeake Bay*. Washington, D.C.: Island Press, 1991.

Hoyer, Bernard E. "Policy Perspectives on Groundwater Protection from Agricultural Contamination in Iowa." Unpublished paper, Iowa Geological Survey, Iowa City, n.d.

Hoyer, Bernard E., James E. Combs, Richard D. Kelley, Constance Cousins-Letherman, and John H. Seyb. *Iowa Groundwater Protection Strategy: 1987*. Des Moines: Iowa Department of Natural Resources, 1987.

Ingram, Helen. *Water Politics: Continuity and Change.* Rev. ed. Albuquerque: University of New Mexico Press, 1990.

Iowa State University Extension Service. *A Survey of Pesticides Used in Iowa Crop Production in 1990.* No. PM1441. Ames: Iowa State University Extension Service, 1991.

John, DeWitt. *A Brighter Future for Rural America? Strategies for Communities and States.* Washington, D.C.: National Governors' Association, 1988.

_____. *Shifting Responsibilities: Federalism in Economic Development.* Washington, D.C.: National Governors' Association, 1989.

Kahn, Edward. *Electric Utility Planning and Regulation.* 2d ed. Washington, D.C.: American Council for an Energy-Efficient Economy, 1992.

Kamieniecki, Sheldon, and Michael R. Ferrall. "Intergovernmental Relations and Clean-Air Policy in Southern California." *Publius: The Journal of Federalism* (Summer 1991): 143-154.

Kneese, Allan V., and Charles L. Schultze. *Pollution, Prices and Public Policy.* Washington, D.C.: Brookings Institution, 1974.

Landy, Marc K., Marc J. Roberts, and Stephen R. Thomas. *The Environmental Protection Agency: Asking the Wrong Questions.* New York: Oxford University Press, 1991.

Lester, James P. *Environmental Politics and Policy: Theories and Evidence.* Durham, N.C.: Duke University Press, 1989.

Lester, James P., and Emmett N. Lombard. "The Comparative Analysis of State Environmental Policy." *Natural Resources Journal* 30 (1990): 301-319.

Light, Stephen S., John R. Wodraska, and Joe Sabrina. "The Southern Everglades: The Evolution of Water Management." *National Forum: Phi Kappa Phi Journal* 69, no. 1 (1989): 11-14.

Lovins, Amory. "Energy Strategy: The Road Not Taken?" *Foreign Affairs*, October 1976, 65-96.

Lowi, Theodore J. "Europeanization of America? From United States to United State." In *Nationalizing Government: Public Policies in America.* Edited by Theodore J. Lowi and Alan Stone. Beverly Hills, Calif.: Sage, 1978.

_____. "Four Systems of Policy, Politics, and Choice." *Public Administration Review* 32, no. 4 (1972): 298-310.

Lowry, William. *The Dimensions of Federalism: State Governments and Pollution Control Policies.* Durham, N.C.: Duke University Press, 1992.

Meadows, D. H., D. L. Meadows, J. Randers, and W. W. Behrens. *The Limits to Growth*. New York: Potomac Associates/Universe Books, 1972.

Melamed, Dennis. "As the Feds Bow Out, Communities Seek New Ways to Pay for Clean Water." *Governing*, July 1990, 19.

Moe, Terry M. "The Politics of Bureaucracy." *Can Government Govern?* Edited by John E. Chubb and Paul E. Peterson. Washington, D.C.: Brookings Institution, 1989.

Morone, James A. *The Democratic Wish: Popular Participation and the Limits of American Government*. New York: Basic Books, 1990.

Moskovitz, David, Steven Nadel, and Howard Geller. *Increasing the Efficiency of Electricity Production and Use: Barriers and Strategies*. Washington, D.C.: American Council for an Energy-Efficient Economy, 1991.

Mussen, Irwin. "Toward a New Federalism for Environmental Restoration: The Case of Air Quality Through Intergovernmental Action—From Community to Global." *Environmental Restoration: Science and Strategies for Restoring the Earth*. Washington, D.C.: Island Press, 1990.

Nathan, Richard P., Fred C. Doolittle, and Associates. *Reagan and the States*. Princeton: Princeton University Press, 1987.

National Association of Regulatory Utility Commissioners. *NARUC Annual Report on Utilities and Communications Regulations*. Washington, D.C.: National Association of Regulatory Utility Commissioners, 1991.

National Research Council, Board on Agriculture, Committee on the Role of Alternative Farming Methods in Modern Production Agriculture. *Alternative Agriculture*. Washington, D.C.: National Academy Press, 1989.

"Nitrates in the Des Moines River: Not a New Problem." *Leopold Letter*, Spring 1992, 10-11.

"Opening the Door to Greater Competition." *National Journal*, April 6, 1991, 792.

Paehlke, Robert C. *Environmentalism and the Future of Progressive Politics*. New Haven: Yale University Press, 1989.

Peterson, Paul E., Barry G. Rabe, and Kenneth K. Wong. *When Federalism Works*. Washington, D.C.: Brookings Institution, 1986.

Piore, Michael J., and Charles F. Sabel. *The New Industrial Divide: Possibilities for Prosperity*. New York: Basic Books, 1984.

Porter, Michael E. *The Competitive Advantage of Nations*. New York: Free Press, 1990.

Public Service Company of Colorado. *Our Energy Force: Annual Report 1990*. Denver: Public Service Company of Colorado, 1991.

Rabe, Barry G. *Fragmentation and Integration in State Environmental Management.* Washington, D.C.: Conservation Foundation, 1986.

Renew America. "Environmental Success Index." Unpublished data, Washington, D.C., 1990.

Rivlin, Alice. *Reviving the American Dream: The Economy, the State, and the Federal Government.* Washington, D.C.: Brookings Institution, 1992.

Roe, David. *Dynamos and Virgins.* New York: Random House, 1984.

Rowe, John. Foreword. In *Profits and Progress Through Least-Cost Planning,* by David Moskovitz. Washington, D.C.: National Association of Regulatory Utility Commissioners, 1989.

Russell, Dick. "The Power Brokers." *Amicus Journal* 11, no. 1 (1989): 31-35.

Sabato, Larry. *Goodbye to Goodtime Charlie: The American Governorship Transformed.* 2d ed. Washington, D.C.: CQ Press, 1983.

Salamon, Lester, ed. *Beyond Privatization: The Tools of Government Action.* Washington, D.C.: Urban Institute Press, 1989.

Sanjour, William. "In Name Only." *Sierra,* September-October 1992, 75-77, 95-103.

Scheuer, James H. "Leadership on Energy Policy Isn't Found in Washington." *Christian Science Monitor,* February 25, 1992, 19.

Schneider, Ann, and Helen Ingram. "Behavioral Assumptions of Policy Tools." *Journal of Politics* 52, no. 2 (1990): 510-529.

Scott, Bruce R., and George C. Lodge, eds. *U.S. Competitiveness in the World Economy.* Boston: Harvard Business School Press, 1985.

Smith, Emily T. "Amory Lovins' Energy Ideas Don't Sound So Dim Anymore." *Business Week,* September 16, 1991, 92.

Snow, Donald. *Inside the Environmental Movement: Meeting the Leadership Challenge.* Washington, D.C.: Island Press, 1992.

South Florida Water Management District. "Surface Water Improvement and Management Plan for the Everglades: Draft." West Palm Beach, January 2, 1992.

Stanfield, Rochelle. "Ruckelshaus Casts EPA as 'Gorilla' in States' Enforcement Closet." *National Journal,* May 25, 1984, 1034-1038.

Stewart, William H. *Concepts of Federalism.* Lanham, Md.: University Press of America, 1984.

"The Top 1000 U.S. Companies Ranked by Industry." *Business Week,* April 10, 1992 (special bonus issue), 165-167, 204-208.

"The Tragedy of the Commons." *Science* 162 (1968): 1243-1248. Reprinted in Hardin, Garrett, and John Baden, eds. *Managing the Commons.* New York: Freeman, 1977.

Underwood, Joanna. "Groping Our Way Toward an Environmental Ethic." In *Voices from the Environmental Movement: Perspectives for a New Era.* Edited by Donald Snow. Washington, D.C.: Island Press, 1992.

U.S. Department of Energy. *National Energy Strategy: Powerful Ideas for America: One Year Later.* Washington, D.C.: Government Printing Office, February 1992.

"U.S. Electric Utility Statistics." *Public Power* 50, no. 1 (1992): 56.

U.S. Environmental Protection Agency, Office of Policy Analysis, Office of Policy, Planning, and Evaluation. *Unfinished Business: A Comparative Assessment of Environmental Problems: Overview Report.* Washington, D.C.: EPA, 1987.

U.S. Environmental Protection Agency, Science Advisory Board. *Reducing Risk: Setting Priorities and Strategies for Environmental Protection: Relative Risk Reduction Project,* pt. 1, pt. 4, app. C. Washington, D.C.: EPA, 1990.

U.S. Soil Conservation Service, Iowa Association of Soil and Water Conservation District Commissioners, and Iowa Department of Agriculture and Land Stewardship, Division of Soil Conservation. *Lines on the Land.* Washington, D.C.: Government Printing Office, 1991.

Vig, Norman J., and Michael E. Kraft, eds. *Environmental Policy in the 1990s.* Washington, D.C.: CQ Press, 1990.

Walker, David B. *Toward a Functioning Federalism.* New York: Little, Brown, 1981.

Webb, James. "Managing Nature in the Everglades." *EPA Journal,* November-December 1990, 50.

Wilkinson, Alex. *Big Sugar: Seasons in the Cane Fields of Florida.* New York: Vintage Books, 1989.

Williams, Eileen Gannon. "Evaluating Future Strategies for Iowa Farmer-owned Cooperatives in Supplying Agricultural Products and Services: An Assessment of Integrated Crop Management Services." MBA thesis, Iowa State University, 1991.

Williamson, Richard S. "1980: The Reagan Campaign—Harbinger of a Revitalized Federalism." *Publius* 11, no. 3-4 (1981): 151.

Wills, Garry, ed. "The Federalist No. 10: Hamilton." *The Federalist Papers by Alexander Hamilton, James Madison, and John Jay.* New York: Bantam Books, 1982.

World Commission on Environment and Development. *Our Common Future.* New York: Oxford University Press, 1987.

Wright, Deil S. *Understanding Intergovernmental Relations.* 3d ed. Pacific Grove, Calif.: Brooks/Cole, 1988.

Zimmerman, Joseph F. *Contemporary American Federalism: The Growth of National Power.* New York: Praeger, 1992.

———. *Federal Preemption: The Silent Revolution.* Ames: Iowa State University Press, 1991.

D eWitt John is the director of the Center for Competitive, Sustainable Economies at the National Academy of Public Administration. The author of *A Brighter Future for Rural America? Strategies for Communities and States* (1988), *Shifting Responsibilities: Federalism in Economic Development* (1987), and *Indian Workers Associations in Britain* (1969), he received his Ph.D. from the University of Chicago in 1992. He has worked for the states of Colorado and Massachusetts, the National Governors' Association, and the Aspen Institute, where he began work on this book. He lives with his wife and children in McLean, Virginia.

E stablished in 1985, the Aspen Institute's Rural Economic Policy Program (REPP) fosters collaborative learning, leadership, and innovation to advance rural economic development in the United States. REPP aims to create a shared agenda for future policy learning and experimentation, to help rural decisionmakers better understand how local choices fit into the larger economic context, and to speed the adoption and application of a comprehensive set of public and private initiatives that will sustain rural progress. Headquartered at the Aspen Institute in Washington, D.C., REPP is funded by the Ford and W. K. Kellogg Foundations. The Aspen Institute is an independent, nonprofit educational organization, founded in 1949, whose broad purpose is to seek consideration of human values in the areas of leadership development and public policy formulation.

The Center for Competitive, Sustainable Economies at the National Academy of Public Administration (NAPA) helps improve governance by exploring ways to mobilize private and public resources to protect the environment and to build competitive regional economies. NAPA is a nonprofit, nonpartisan organization chartered by Congress to improve governance at all levels—federal, state, and local. The four hundred fellows of the academy include current and former cabinet officers, elected officials from all levels of government, public managers, jurists, business executives, and scholars who have been elected because of their distinguished contributions to the nation's public life. Since its establishment in 1967, NAPA has responded to many requests for assistance from various agencies and Congress, as well as working with private foundations and corporations. This book is the work of the author and does not represent the official policies or views of NAPA or of its fellows.